Wardle

Rochdale

Heywood

Bury

Milnrow

Rochdale

Crompton

Saddleworth

ury

Royton

Middleton

Oldham

Chadderton

Oldham

Lees

itefield

Prestwich

Mossley

endlebury

Salford

Failsworth

Ashton under Lyne

d

Droylsden

Stalybridge

Manchester

Dukinfield

Audenshaw

Tameside

atford

Manchester

Denton

Longdendale

Hyde

Stockport

Bredbury & Romiley

Stockport

Marple

Cheadle & Gatley

Hazel Grove & Bramhall

Ringway

KEY

County boundary

Bury District boundary

Altrincham Former authority boundary

© Cartographic Services Manchester

Miles
0   1   2   3

TRADITION
IN ACTION

To Margaret, with love and gratitude

'I am thoroughly convinced of the value of tradition in our modern lives.'
(*HRH Princess Anne, on receiving the Freedom of the City of London on 27 February 1976.*)

COAT OF ARMS OF THE GREATER MANCHESTER COUNTY

Shield: The Shield bears ten turrets in gold, representing the ten Districts of the County, on a red ground.

Supporters: The Shield is supported on each side by a lion rampant in gold. Each lion bears on its shoulder a badge in red, the lion on the right of the shield bearing a badge with a French horn, representing music and culture, and the lion on the left of the shield bearing a badge with an open book, representing learning and the academic life of the County.

Crest: The helm is surmounted by a demi-lion carrying a banner bearing ten small turrets in gold on a red ground.

Motto: Ever Vigilant.

TRADITION
IN ACTION

The Historical Evolution of
the Greater Manchester County

N. J. FRANGOPULO

This edition first published 1977 by
EP Publishing Limited
East Ardsley, Wakefield,
West Yorkshire, England

Text set in Monophoto Baskerville
Printed in Great Britain by
Fletcher & Son Ltd, Norwich

Contents

Illustrations

*Note: The letters MPL signify Manchester Public Libraries, Local History
Library*

viii

FOREWORD

This book traces the development of the area now represented by the metropolitan county of Greater Manchester. Its history and traditions are revealed in all their strengths and richness and the inescapable conclusion is that the event which took place on 26 October 1972 (when the Local Government Act received the Royal Assent) was, so far as Greater Manchester is concerned, more than the statutory grouping for local administrative purposes of a series of townships. It was also the official recognition of the bonds which have been forged between them down the centuries.

How did this sense of community arise in an area of 500 square miles reaching from Saddleworth in the Pennines to Wigan and the fringe of the West Lancashire plain, and from Littleborough and Ramsbottom in the north to Ringway and Bramhall in the Cheshire plain? The author takes as his starting-point the development of the Domestic System in which not only the merchant of Manchester, but the dealer in wool and linen of the neighbouring towns of Rochdale, Bolton, Bury, Oldham, Ashton and Stockport co-operated with the farmer-weaver families of the surrounding villages and hamlets in the production of cloth. Then came the Industrial Revolution with the growth of a new style of society, bringing with it new triumphs but also new tribulations. It is in this soil that the traditions took root, but as society developed they spread beyond the confines of industry and commerce. Thus the music-making in the choirs and brass bands of the chapels and mills of the towns and villages, the cricket clubs of the Central Lancashire League with their local pride and healthy rivalry and the corresponding regional pride in the Hallé Orchestra and the County Cricket Club at Old Trafford – all contributed their distinctive traditions.

Similarly, in the fields of education and culture, institutions arose, many of which have woven themselves into the fabric of the region and are contributing in their several ways to the new

County. Important too is the traditional hospitality of the region which has always been extended to 'strangers of every description' and has been applied again in post-war years to the reception of New Commonwealth immigrants who have found homes for themselves in all districts of the County.

Finally, the book outlines the hopes and aspirations of the County and of its ten Districts – eleven local authorities working together for the greater good of the whole. The author believes that after the stresses and strains of the new birth have been worked out, the traditions which are analysed here will be found to be the mainspring of the strength of the new County as much as they have been the source of inspiration for this book.

W. A. Downward

Lord Lieutenant of Greater Manchester

County Hall, Manchester

July 1976

Introduction

What has created the Greater Manchester Metropolitan County? Officially it is the Local Government Act (October 1972) by which the structure of local government in England and Wales was reformed so as to reconstitute the existing pattern of forty-five counties and seventy-nine county boroughs into a new pattern of six metropolitan counties and forty-seven unitary counties. Greater Manchester is one of the six metropolitan counties in company with Merseyside, West Midlands, West Yorkshire, South Yorkshire and Tyne and Wear.

What is a metropolitan county? The Government responsible for this Act took the view that the area of a local authority should be large enough in size, population and resources to meet the needs of its citizens and, in particular, the maintenance and development of a trained and expert local government service. To fulfil these requirements the Government adopted the criterion of an area containing at least 250,000 population, bound together by common interest and living as a recognisable community. As there are only twelve cities and towns in England, outside London, with at least this size of population, it was clear that the greater part of the country would have to be divided into comparatively large areas of counties unitary in character in the sense of having one authority responsible throughout its area for all services, both environmental and personal. On the other hand, it was recognised that there were six densely populated areas, in themselves totalling one-fifth of the national population, which were divisible into Districts, each of which was populous and compact, having a population of at least 250,000. Moreover, while the personal services such as education, libraries and welfare could effectively be undertaken by authority within such a District, there were certain larger-scale or environmental services such as planning, transport, police, fire-service and major development which by their nature required the control of an authority responsible for the whole area. It was for these reasons that the Government decided to accept the concept of the Metropolitan County.

Was this metropolitan concept merely an administrative convenience? There is precedence for such a structure. When the Local Government Act of 1888 ended the historic predominance of the country gentlemen by setting up popularly-elected councils for counties and county boroughs, a parallel Act was passed which created the London County Council to govern all London except the old 'City' area. Eleven years later, a London Government Act provided for twenty-eight elected borough councils, while more recently a major reform of London Government was undertaken and completed in 1965. But what was achieved by the Local Government Act of 1972 in creating the Greater Manchester Metropolitan County was infinitely more than the statutory acknowledgement of a densely populated area. What it achieved, wittingly or not, was the official unifying of a region which, through history and tradition, had forged for itself over many centuries bonds as slender as silk but strong as steel between the communities of town and village, each of which was the embodiment of the character of this region.

On what grounds may one claim an historical evolution for this new County? Dr L. P. Green, whose notable prognosis in the mid-1950s of the future of local government in South-East Lancashire led him to formulate his concept of a *Provincial Metropolis*, based his views upon the vibrant reality of this region as observed in its own resilient characteristics. He was convinced also of its metropolitan nature in that it contained a great political and government centre which was also a commercial and industrial giant and by tradition the cultural capital of the region. This is indeed the meaning of the word 'metropolis'—the 'mother-city'—such as Manchester is, provincial though it may be, in relation to its region. But this is not to say that what follows is an adulatory dedication to the greater glory of Manchester. With all his admiration for 'the most wonderful city of modern times', Disraeli wisely set the balance of judgements when he arranged for his impressionable Coningsby to be confronted by a stalwart of a neighbouring town in the coffee-room of his Manchester hotel. 'We have all of us a very great respect for Manchester, in course; look upon her as a sort of mother, and all that sort of thing', said his companion, certainly with affection but also with a discernible condescension, which he reinforced by adding, 'If you want to see life, go to Stalybridge or Bolton. There's high pressure.' Those who know their South-East Lancashire are well aware that one could produce dozens of stalwarts of this calibre from many towns of this great region. Indeed, such is the nature of this civic pride that one wonders whether it is not within the Districts themselves rather than in their relationship to the metropolis that this distinctive quality is most clearly evident. This is not surprising, for its roots lie deep in the history and traditions of the region.

Here, then, is the historical approach to a many-sided subject. It is not intended to be the sole approach. Indeed, in this respect the author is conscious of an affinity with Isaac Newton, who once pictured himself as a boy playing on the sea-shore, 'finding a smoother pebble or a prettier shell than ordinary, whilst the great ocean of truth lay all undiscovered' before him. Doubtless the sociologist would concern himself with the rationale of the interrelationships, interactions and interdependence of the parts (now Districts) of the Metropolitan County; the economist would ponder the statistics of industry, commerce and finance in a region rich and vital in these spheres; the geographer would glory in the cartographical features of the region in relation to its natural and human wealth; and the administrator would delve at once into the problems inherent in the very creation of a metropolitan county made up of many towns which formerly administered themselves.

It is for this reason that a detailed Bibliography has been compiled of the histories of some twenty-seven towns and villages which have, among others, gone to the making of the Greater Manchester County. It is hoped that it will encourage local historians to find out for themselves and to demonstrate the contribution of their own homestead to the reality of this new County, of which they constitute an indispensable part. It is a region eminently rich not only in its natural resources and in its native talents but also in its great traditions, which are the mainspring of this new County and the source of inspiration for this book.

N.J.F.
Didsbury, Manchester
May 1976

Acknowledgements

While the services of many friends and of local government and other officers have been individually acknowledged in the references at the end of the book, I must thank corporately the Chief and Senior Officers of the Greater Manchester Council and of all the District Councils for their indispensable help and advice. I should like to thank, also, those who serve in the public libraries and archives departments of the Districts, who seem almost to take it for granted that one's need of the moment is their immediate concern. Their personal help has been invaluable.

One remembers with gratitude those old friends who embarked with the author on this venture and encouraged and supported him throughout the long journey: Dr Peter Lowe of the Department of History, Manchester University; Dr Norman Burkhardt of the same University; and Mr J. J. Bagley, formerly Reader in History at the Institute of Extension Studies, Liverpool University. Similarly I am indebted to other old friends and new who have made their valuable contribution to particular aspects of the book: my former colleague, Mr L. Wharfe, for his professional advice generously given on the function and design of all the maps; Mr C. W. Heaps, Cartographic Services, Manchester, for his immaculate execution of the same and for his timely support in the compiling of the Index; Mr H. Milligan, whose innate wisdom and rare knowledge of the photographic art I have unashamedly drawn upon; and Mr John Wood, Photographic Technician of the North Western Museum of Science and Industry, for the products of his professional skill.

I am further indebted to Mr W. H. Shercliff, with whom I have worked and collaborated for nearly twenty years in our happy hunting-ground of local history. He has applied his customary skill and thoroughness to the revision of all the proofs and given me wise advice and help throughout the production of this book. I count myself fortunate to have had regular access to the records of the Lancashire Bibliography, housed in the Central Library, Manchester, for which privilege I am indeed grateful to Mrs P. Turner, B.A., Editor of the Lancashire Bibliography. It was also a pleasure to be allowed to use some of the resources of *The Guardian* Library, Deansgate, where I was courteously assisted by Mr Brian Whiteley.

Finally, I should like to thank the secretaries throughout the County who, in their several ways, so often made 'the rough places plain' and showed me the way I should go. Their contribution is incalculable.

Chapter 1

'. . . our ends by our beginnings know'

When, in the middle years of the first century A.D., the Romans first cast their eyes upon the region which is now the Greater Manchester County, what was its position and to whom did it belong? Strategically it was important to the Romans as it lay between the mountainous North Wales, occupied by the Ordovices, and the Yorkshire Pennines, occupied by the Brigantes. Separately these two tribes were formidable enough; if they had acted in concert they might have caused serious trouble to the Romans. The Brigantes, numerically the largest tribe in Britain, had for some centuries inhabited not only Lancashire but also Yorkshire, Westmorland, Cumberland, Northumberland and Durham, thereby 'stretching from sea to sea', as the geographer, Claudius Ptolemaeus of Alexandria, described their territory in the second century A.D. More recently it has been said of ancient Brigantia: 'This great area, sundered by the Pennines and their spurs into numerous divisions, each large enough to maintain powerful warbands, must always have owed its cohesion to mutual advantage and to local balances rather than to inflexible domination from a single centre.'[1] It is not surprising, then, to find that at this time the Brigantian realm under its Queen, Cartimandua, was a client-kingdom in alliance with Rome, thus retaining a measure of independence and freedom from invasion. This temporising policy, however, was not to last for, opposed to Cartimandua, there was within her realm a clamorous anti-Roman party. Their opportunity came when, in A.D. 69, the Roman world was torn asunder by civil war. Cartimandua was overthrown and the anti-Roman party converted the Brigantes from a friendly buffer-state into a hostile tribe.

It was the arrival in A.D. 78 of Julius Agricola as Governor of Britain which changed the scene. He had already served in Britain as commander of the Twentieth Legion under the governor, Cerealis, and his predecessor, Frontinus, and had begun the erection of the legionary fortress at Chester as a base for the conquest of North Wales. Fully conversant, therefore, with the military situation in the north-west, this great Governor laid his plans for the consolidation of northern Britain. After completely defeating the Ordovices, he seized Anglesey, secured his hold upon North Wales by placing forts at the river mouths, established an inner line of penetration based upon the upper Dee valley, and consolidated the great legionary fortress at Chester in order to block the escape route into Brigantian territory. Agricola was now ready to enter Lancashire. For his major objective of conquering northern Britain and the further prospect of reconnoitring the possibilities of bringing at least the Scottish Lowlands under his control Agricola may well have regarded the shallow bowl of the north-east Cheshire Plain and the equally accessible moor and woodland territory of South-East Lancashire (the future SELNEC proposal of the Maud Commission) as 'the soft under-belly' for his invasion of Brigantia, in much the same way as the Allied Command in the Second World War regarded Mussolini's Italy for its invasion in 1943 of Nazi-occupied Europe. Unlike its Cheshire neighbour, South-East Lancashire in general exhibited a lack of Iron Age hill-forts, which would seem to indicate that its sparsely-spread population, probably living at a low subsistence level, had no obviously recognisable political structure. It was through this territory and beyond that Agricola resolved to build a military cross-country road linking the two legionary fortresses of Chester and York. To protect this base-line for his advances into northern Britain he established auxiliary forts at intervals. Thus came into being the military stations at Manchester, Castleshaw and Slack—the first two named being within the region of the Greater Manchester County and the third (near Huddersfield) some seven miles beyond its eastern boundary. Of the three, the Manchester fort was by far the largest, being some five acres in extent and accommodating about 1,000 infantrymen. It lay in the angle of land formed by the confluence of the rivers Irwell and Medlock.[2] The smaller fort at Castleshaw was built by Agricola in A.D. 80 and its position on a well-defined spur of the Pennines with a clear view of the surrounding heights provides an example of this governor's skill in his choice of sites. Intended to cover the western approaches to the Pennines, the fort consisted of an area of just over two acres. It was for some reason abandoned after a brief occupation and lay neglected until, early in the second century, it was replaced by a fortlet about half an acre in size, which evidently acted as a small police-post. Although the site of the fort at Castleshaw, where one may still admire the firm and stately outlines of the surrounding hills, is now partly covered with grass, the lines of the fort are still discernible to those who seek them out carefully with the aid of F.

H. Thompson's description and detailed plan of the trenches and other features.[3]

The only other Roman fort likely to have been established within the region of the Greater Manchester County is that of *Coccium*, said to have been sited in the area of Wigan. No structural remains of Roman occupation have been found here but evidence from finds made in and around Wigan, such as cinerary urns, a cemetery, a headless statue and various hoards of coins, give some credence to a military origin for the Roman establishment at Wigan. While this 'elusive site of Coccium'[4] is usually placed at or near Wigan, the general indication would appear to be that there was a small fortified post situated upon the summit of the elevation in the centre of Wigan on which the Parish Church stands today. What is more to the point is that three Roman roads from Manchester, Wilderspool and Walton-le-Dale converged on this site,[5] wherever its exact position may have been.

More germane to the historical relationship between the region of the Greater Manchester County and its Roman occupation for over three centuries is the manner in which Manchester became the greatest centre of communications for the whole area of Lancashire. Indeed, a study of the Ordnance Survey Map of Roman Britain reveals that more roads radiated from Manchester (*Mamucium*) than from any other town in the Roman Province. From this military station of *Mamucium* as many as six, if not seven, roads issued.[6] Reference has already been made to two: that to Chester via Northwich and that to York via Castleshaw and Slack. A third road proceeded southwards to Buxton via Stockport and a fourth was the military road northwards which linked *Mamucium* with the important fort at Ribchester, where the complementary force of 1,000 cavalry men was stationed. A fifth proceeded south-eastwards to a fort at Melandra, near Glossop, and on to Brough, while a sixth road, now completely obliterated by continuous urban and industrial development, linked *Mamucium* with Wigan. A seventh road, the initial course of which is shrouded in conjecture, is in some way linked with the fine, pavemented section of the road over Blackstone Edge, a few miles north-east of Rochdale. What is more certainly known is that this section of the road eventually superseded the original section of the Manchester-to-York road, passing through Castleshaw and Slack via Standedge. It rejoined the original cross-country road at a point beyond Slack.[7]

It must not be thought that the presence of these roads gave a

3

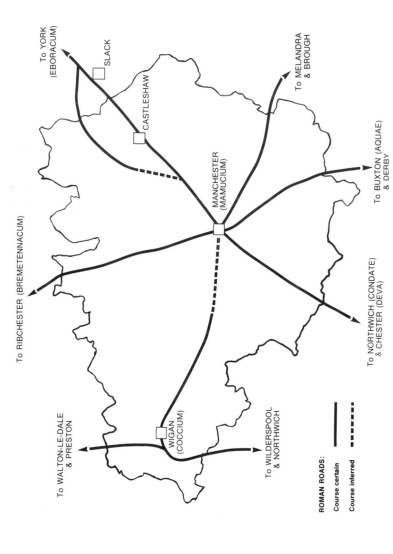

ROMAN ROADS:

Course certain

Course inferred

The strategic site of Greater Manchester during the Roman occupation

SLACK

CASTLESHAW

MANCHESTER
(MAMUCIUM)

WIGAN
(COCCIUM)

To YORK
(EBORACUM)

To MELANDRA
& BROUGH

To BUXTON (AQUAE)
& DERBY

To NORTHWICH (CONDATE)
& CHESTER (DEVA)

To WILDERSPOOL
& NORTHWICH

To WALTON-LE-DALE
& PRESTON

To RIBCHESTER (BREMETENNACUM)

prominent place to the region of the Greater Manchester County in the pattern of communications with which the Romans endowed the province of Britain. The purpose of these roads and others beyond this region was to enable Agricola, in his campaign against the Brigantians, to move up the west side of the Pennines through Lancashire, which seems to have been somewhat peripheral to the more hostile region of Brigantian domination beyond the Pennines. It has been said that 'Roman Cheshire led to Deva and North Wales; Roman Lancashire led to nowhere in particular —except to Lancashire.'[8] This implies that the region around Manchester lay off the main axis of the province inasmuch as the routes to the south from the Hadrian's Wall country, from both the west and east ends of the Wall, proceeded east of the Pennines, eventually joining near Catterick. Even the important military road from Manchester to Ribchester continued north only to drop down into the valley of the Lune and complete its course at Ravenglass on the Cumberland coast, a port of some value to the Romans. It has even been suggested that 'it is possible that no roads at all went through the fort at *Mamucium*, that the fort lay off the main line of the road and had access to it by a side branch.'[9]

However this may be, it is clear that the Romans, in their zeal for establishing efficient military communications and for making their power speedily felt, evidently decided upon their *Mamucium* as a strategic centre from which roads could radiate to other military strongholds. One may doubt whether they contemplated embarking upon a complicated network of cart and wagon ways comparable to what may now be seen in the modern motorways at Spaghetti Junction in the vicinity of Worsley, but they evidently saw the possibilities of a Greater Mamucium, within the limits of the environment, at least in communication by roads. One may imagine these roads in their construction being added section by section as the military needs arose and forts and camps were established. They were built primarily for marching men and pack animals for whom there would be abundant man-power at hand, either troops or slaves, to assist in manipulating the vehicles over difficult places. These roads were looked upon, also, as the pioneers of Roman civilisation, the communicative instrument of *Pax Romana*. Yet the nature of the countryside which now constitutes the Greater Manchester County and the disposition of the native inhabitants were such at that time as to discourage the establishment of the kind of towns and villas characteristic of the more

5

southerly areas of Roman Britain. To the Romans, Lancashire was hardly attractive, mainly because of its climate and its distance from the continent of Europe. It is possible that some Roman traders lived for short periods in the neighbourhood of *Mamucium* and that some ex-soldiers, who had served their term of years in the Roman army, married local girls and stayed on here, 'rather like the Polish settlement in Lancashire eighteen centuries later'.[10] This is why 'there is in Lancashire, as in the surrounding counties (except Yorkshire), a remarkable absence of the remains of Roman villas.'[11]

On the other hand, there seems to be increasing evidence of the presence of a civil settlement adjoining the Roman fort at *Mamucium*. Such a 'vicus', as it was called, was by no means unknown during the Roman occupation of Britain. In the course of time, many settlements of this nature outstripped their parent military sites and from them sprang, especially on the Continent, some of the great towns of the Middle Ages. Probably the nearest example of a civil settlement in Roman Britain was at Chester, where, for some distance from the Eastgate, the main settlement extended on either side of Foregate Street, in which a large quantity of Roman pottery has been recovered from various sites, suggesting an occupation which began at about the time the great fortress was founded and reached its maximum intensity during the second century. Yet it is significant that a former Curator for many years of the Grosvenor Museum in Chester, while acknowledging that 'civil settlements at other fortresses . . . are known to have achieved the eventual dignity of a town', advises caution in regard to Chester as 'much more evidence is needed to confirm the theory.'[12]

In regard to Manchester, a remarkable opportunity arose early in 1972 for the obtaining of more evidence in the vicinity of the Roman site itself. It became known that the Corporation was proposing to establish a temporary car-park just outside the known position of the North Gate of the fort in preparation for the building of an inner relief road on the north-western side of Deansgate. The tantalising factor in all this was that hints given by finds and in the reports of excavators who worked on the site during the nineteenth and early twentieth centuries seemed to indicate that the *vicus*, or native civilian quarter, lay outside and beyond the northern defences of the Roman fort—precisely where the Corporation's proposed temporary car-park was sited.

6

For Professor Barri Jones, of the Department of Archaeology at Manchester University, this was an opportunity not to be missed. A preliminary investigation of the site during an all-too-brief weekend in February 1972 revealed that 'a completely unsuspected wealth of stratified material survived', which undoubtedly whetted the appetite for a more prolonged investigation during the summer, which was sanctioned by the now fully co-operative Corporation. 'The Deansgate Dig', as it came to be called, attracted many volunteers, who undertook the manual tasks during the seven weeks of the operation, while the trained archaeologists sifted the gold from the dross in the form of Roman pottery, small finds and coins. The most exciting revelation was the locating of thirty-three smelting furnaces, some perforated hearths and a group of plain bowl hearths. The discovery of these indicated different aspects of the smelting process (possibly of iron), and of the use of coal. The late Sir Ian Richmond has attested that coal was mined in Roman Britain and specifically refers to its use in the fort at Manchester and for smelting iron and glass at Wilderspool,[13] which probably obtained its supplies from the Wigan area.[14]

Was this civil settlement, adjacent to the Roman fort, the beginning of Manchester? On that intriguing question the prime promoter of 'The Deansgate Dig' has this to say:

'The speedy development of Manchester in the Industrial Revolution threw up a series of random finds from Knott Mill to Deansgate . . . (which) suggested that Manchester's fort was surrounded by a very substantial civil settlement that developed partly along the present Chester Road and partly along the line of the present Deansgate. Indeed the sheer size of the area in which remains were recorded in the last century, however unsatisfactorily, suggested that the civil settlement may have overshadowed the fort in size.'[15]

The presence of this settlement in Roman Manchester, whatever form it took, has long been accepted by many local historians.[16] One of them, however, carries the subject a significant stage further:

'Whatever the character and origin of the first English immigrants in the area, their settlements were really consolidated during the period of Mercian supremacy in the eighth century

7

... By this time the area of the Roman *vicus* was probably overgrown with scrub, but along the adjacent length of Deansgate some kind of trading or market centre seems to have persisted, in Anglo-Saxon terms as *port*, which eventually became *Aldport*, the "old market" (presumably when a new market area was established nearer the manor).'[17]

A find in 1820 of Mercian coins in the vicinity of Aldport persuaded Dr Bu'lock to regard this hoard as 'tangible evidence (now most unfortunately lost) of the beginnings of Manchester's commercial history'. But it is his reference to 'a new market area at the northern end of the Deansgate axis' which postulates the presence of an English settlement in this naturally constructed site of Hunt's Bank. This 'bluff of red sandstone', formed by the confluence of the Irwell and Irk rivers and its southern boundary by Hanging Ditch, was the fifteen-acre site which eventually became the centre of medieval Manchester. Although the only direct archaeological evidence is a fragment of Saxon sculpture called the Angel Stone (c. A.D. 900) which may be seen in the Cathedral, it was this site which upheld the Saxon church to which, in company with the daughter church of St Michael in Ashton-under-Lyne, the Domesday account of the area in 1086 makes reference. It was on this site that the lord's manor-house and church, his mill on the river Irk where his tenants by custom ground their corn, and his oven near the manor-house at which the same tenants baked their bread, found their place.

Thus, in its origin, Manchester was a typical early medieval manor over which the Grelleys, a family of Norman descent, ruled through eight of its members for two centuries. Territorially it was included in the 'Royal Manor or Hundred of Salford' which, at the time of the Domesday Survey, was very poor and sparsely populated, containing only, it has been estimated, about 3,000 people. While the lord of the manor of Salford was either the monarch or a great lord, Manchester was ruled by humbler lords and in size was no more than a tiny village. So, also, were its neighbours of Wigan, Bolton, Bury, Rochdale, Oldham, Ashton-under-Lyne and Stockport which, in the main, constituted the major part of the Salford Hundred and together, 900 years later, became the Greater Manchester County.

In attempting to traverse these centuries so as to reveal the natural, organic growth of this great region into a modern metropolitan county, one is conscious of 'turning the accomplishment of many years into an hour-glass'. In so doing, it may well be pertinent to recall the wise words of a minor poet who also held the post of Surveyor of Works to Charles II: 'We may our ends by our beginnings know.'[18]

Chapter 2

'To all my burgesses . . .'

How towns began is an absorbing subject, whether they owe their
origin to a royal charter or to the grant of a Norman lord. That the
town of Manchester belonged to the latter group may be taken as
virtually certain, as may be said also of its neighbouring towns in
the Greater Manchester County, apart from Wigan which
received its borough charter from the Crown when, in 1246, Henry
III granted Wigan an extension of the trading rights he had
conceded the previous year.

In the early manor of Manchester, which was a purely agricultural local unit, most of the tenants were tied to the land and
bound to help in the cultivation of the lord's demesne. By the
thirteenth century, however, an urban element had already begun
to show itself. In 1227 Henry III granted Robert Grelley a licence
by charter, 'that he and his heirs may have forever one fair at his
manor of Mamecestre, yearly during three days, viz: on the eve
and on the day and on the morrow of St Matthew the Apostle.'
(The days were 20 to 22 September.) This fair was held on a piece
of arable land, adjoining the town, called *Acresfield* or *Four Acres* (so
called because it contained four large Lancashire acres). It was
then common ploughland and pasture, bounded on all sides by a
close hedge and a ditch filled with water from some rills in the
vicinity. As this extensive area was the common property of the
inhabitants of the manor, they claimed access to it by prescriptive
right. It has been recorded that 'A very ancient custom prevailed
for the inhabitants to assemble long before daybreak upon the first
day of the fair, armed with whips and acorns, in protest against the
intrusion of the lord, cracking their whips and pelting with acorns
the first sheep, cow, pig or horse which entered the arena of the
fair.'[1] When the corn had been cut and the harvest gathered in,
access to the fair was by Toll Lane (renamed St Ann Street in
1832), where the lord's officials collected the tolls on everything
brought for sale. In 1708, when Lady Ann Bland, daughter of
Edward Mosley of Hulme Hall, was authorised by Parliament to
enclose the Acresfield for the building of St Ann's Church, it was
on condition that the open space in front of the church should be
thirty yards wide so as to accommodate the fair, which continued
to be held annually until 1876, when it was finally abolished.

The medieval market, which seems to have been prescribed by custom and not by charter, was the centre of the town's life. The traders who inhabited the nearby streets, Hanging Ditch, Mill Gate, Market Stead Lane and Deansgate, conducted their business here. At times they were so numerous that they overflowed into the surrounding streets. Pigs wandered about the place, and even into the churchyard, to such an extent that the Court Leet appointed a public swineherd who 'assembled his charges with a horn in the morning and led them to the lord's waste at Collyhurst', where he kept them 'until evening that they come into their houses again.' For this service the townsmen paid the swineherd a penny quarterly for every pig. Close by the market cross were the stocks, pillory and whipping-post, and round the ornamental conduit, which drew its water from fresh springs in the region of Fountain Street and Spring Gardens, swarmed the women, with buckets on their arms to draw water, and the latest scandals on their tongues to delight their neighbours. Early in the eighteenth century the first Exchange was built here and the first Post Office was lodged at Bull's Head Inn, at which the mail coach from London arrived three times a week, having taken four-and-a-half days to do the journey.

The market and fair were the property of the lord of the manor who, through his Court Leet, enforced what was called the assize of bread and ale, which was based upon statutory regulations fixing the weight of the penny loaf and the price at which ale might be sold. He safeguarded the quality of the local food supply by appointing special ale-testers and 'officers for wholesome bread', the two most important kinds of food at that time. Dr G. H. Tupling, to whom students of Lancashire's history are forever indebted, has demonstrated the necessity of a market to an early community. Seeing it as a 'recognised meeting place for the purchase and sale of goods' and as 'one of the principal factors which encouraged the settlement of a non-agricultural community' in which 'the artisan and trader found his best chance of obtaining a livelihood', he concluded that 'the market thus distinguished an agricultural community from its neighbours, and transformed it into a town, which subsequently grew more or less rapidly according to the convenience of its situation for industry and trade.'[2] It is not surprising, then, that the Norman baron in England, far from looking askance at all forms of town life, positively encouraged the traders under his manorial jurisdiction. He was well aware not only of the income which could be drawn from a developing town under his control but also of the development of his estates which such trading activities promoted. Thus Thomas, the last of the Grelleys, who drew from the weekly market and annual fair a yearly income of £5 13s. 4d. (at least £500 now), naturally lent a willing ear to the appeal of his Manchester burgesses, who by the end of the thirteenth century numbered at least 150, for a re-affirmation of burgess rights and privileges by charter in perpetuity, the more especially as their neighbours across the river in Salford had already secured their charter earlier that century from Randle de Blundeville, Earl of Chester.

On 14 May 1301, Thomas Grelley gave and granted his charter 'to all my burgesses of Manchester'. A burgess was a free man who held a burgage, that is a house on a town-plot with a street frontage and with a large garden or 'backside' away from the street. He was free, within certain limits, to sell, transfer or bequeath his holding and, if he died, his widow was permitted to continue to live in his house 'so long as she is willing to remain without a husband'. The burgesses were authorised 'to elect anyone they please from their own number to be reeve and to remove the reeve'. He was, in effect, the mayor of the borough, subject to acceptance by the lord's steward who was responsible for the conducting of the business of the Court Leet. Matters of dispute, in which the burgesses were concerned, were to be settled at their own Court which is named in the charter as the Lawmoot or Portmoot according to the time of meeting. The reeve was authorised by the charter 'to assign to every burgess and the tensers [those engaged in trade and enjoying some privileges but who were not burgesses] their stalls in the market place and receive from them one penny for the lord'. They were also bound to grind their corn at his mill, for which service they paid to the lord a certain proportion of the grain, and to bake their bread at his oven, payment for which was also taken in kind. A heavy fine of 'twelve pence' was placed upon 'whoever breaks the assize of bread or of beer', indicating the seriousness with which the lord viewed his duty of enforcing the statutory regulations concerned with the nation's staple diet and beverage.

There are two interesting clauses governing the conduct of one burgess towards another: 'That if any burgess shall fall out with another and in anger strike him without shedding blood, and be able to regain his house without being challenged by the reeve or his servants he shall not be impleaded by the reeve'; and 'That if any burgess shall wound another burgess within the borough on Sunday or from noon on Saturday to Monday he shall forfeit twenty shillings; and if he shall wound anyone on Monday or any other day of the week he shall forfeit twelve pence to the lord.'[3]

That Manchester, even with the granting of the Grelley Charter, was not a 'free borough' but merely a humble 'market town' was judicially decided just over fifty years later when Roger la Warr, lord of Manchester, in a dispute with his overlord, the Duke of Lancaster, was denied this claim. Perhaps this may explain why Daniel Defoe saw fit to describe the Manchester he visited in 1725 as 'one of the greatest, if not really the greatest mere village in England'.[4] Even as late as 1786 Yates' map of Lancashire, in its explanation of the status of towns, exemplifies Manchester in italic capitals as one of the 'Market Towns which are not Boroughs'. Manchester, like its neighbouring towns of the Greater Manchester County, had still to wait for its grant of incorporation.

It may be appropriate at this point, when contemplating the nature of Manchester as a market town, to visit the present site of the old market place to see what is going on within the confines of the great hoardings which at present encircle it. What is going on is important and evocative, arising as it does from deliberations which the Manchester Corporation began in the early 1960s. At least two paramount conclusions evolved out of these deliberations: first, that the need for care and attention to the quality of environment was vital to the character of civilised city life; and second, as a corollary, that intending developers and their professional advisers should recognise the need for a co-ordinated and comprehensive approach based upon a longer-term view of their own and the City's interest. As the medieval Market Place is at the very heart of the Central Area of Manchester today, it was imperative that its modern counterpart be not only convenient and efficient but also inviting and attractive.[5] Fortunately, two factors, one of modern and the other of medieval origin, have felicitously influenced the architects in the planning of the total design of this crucial area. In the first place, the removal in the early 1960s of Marks and Spencers to a new building in the Market Place area tended to close up the gap left by war damage. In the second place, although war damage was also responsible for the virtual destruction of the old Market Place area, the Old Wellington Inn, scheduled as an Ancient Monument and officially recognised as a building of special architectural and historical interest, survived the devastation of war and stands still as a reminder of Manchester's medieval past. So, too, adjoining it, stands the eighteenth-century Sinclair's Oyster Bar, also a 'listed' building. In an extraordinary way, the survival of these two historic buildings inspired the enlightened and historically-minded Manchester City Council (for such it must have been) to undertake an ingenious plan for raising the two buildings six feet on their existing sites in order to facilitate pedestrian movement by means of walkways linking the modern Market Place with two neighbouring developments now in the course of construction, the Arndale Centre and the Market Cross Centre.[6] It did more than that, however. The decision to retain the two historic buildings, thus elevated in 1971 on concrete pillars, served to influence the whole design of the modern Market Place.

The thoughtful and sensitive approach of the architects responsible for this important scheme reveals a rejection of the erecting of buildings of normal commercial scale in a preference for the creating of a human scale to accord with the domestic style of the Old Wellington Inn and Sinclair's Oyster Bar. Thus the new building behind them, instead of towering over the comparatively low historic buildings, has windows of a horizontal and comely design and contains four storeys only. It is this building, with its frontage on Market Street, which forms the Marks and Spencers extension both in stores and office accommodation. Opposite the two historic buildings is an attractively designed edifice for shops, offices and a walkway, with each floor stepped back so as to avoid dwarfing the Old Wellington Inn and Sinclair's Oyster Bar. The shopping centre itself is approached by four unpretentious entrances designed so as to enable the pedestrian to assimilate the impression of the Square gradually, in much the same atmosphere of friendly intimacy as one experiences on entering St Ann's Square today through St Ann's Passage. In these ways, the architects have followed the English tradition of preserving what is desirable in the old combined with what is deemed necessary in the new era, conjoined in one harmonious whole. Edmund Burke, in reference to the British Constitution, once said: 'By all means, let us have reform, but let the reform be as near as possible to the architecture of the original.' It is in this sense that the new Market Place enters 'The Shape of Things to Come', with the continuing of its historic

Raising the Wellington Inn and Sinclair's Oyster Bar in the early 1970s

15

New Market Place, Manchester (south-east prospect)

16

function as the heart of a great regional shopping centre and as an attractive and worthwhile place to visit.

Manchester was not the only town within the region of the new County where markets and fairs were held. In medieval times itinerant merchants were to be seen in Bolton, Rochdale, Salford, Wigan and Stockport, when the annual fair was held. This was an event of sufficient importance to bring people from the surrounding hamlets to share in the merrymaking and the more serious business of buying and selling. It was an occasion for social gathering and a centre for entertainment as well as for trade. It may be that the post-war shopping precinct, which each of these towns now proudly proclaims as the desirable rendezvous for its neighbouring shoppers, is the modern equivalent of the medieval fair, though diurnal and not annual.

It may well seem that this early growth of the town of Manchester at the centre of a manor and barony, governed by a manorial court whose lord was a frequent absentee, was greatly to its disadvantage. Historically it is correct to say that Manchester did not free itself completely from the grasp of manorialism until the middle of the nineteenth century. Yet by that time it had already become the centre of a region which was known all over the world as the classic example of modern industrialisation. 'The shock city of the industrial revolution' is the way one historian has described it in this period.[7] Disraeli wrote of it as 'the most wonderful city of modern times', and he considered that 'it is the philosopher alone who can conceive the grandeur of Manchester and the immensity of its future.'[8] Why was this, in view of its early handicap? The answer lies in the extraordinary paradox that its apparent disadvantages came to be its real advantages, at least until the late eighteenth century. One reason was the very nature at that time of its manorial system of government. Whatever the disadvantages for a rapidly growing community, at least it gave Mancunians freedom from an oligarchical municipal corporation, with its vested priorities which might well have constricted, in its own narrow interest, the economic development of the town. James Ogden, as late as 1783, saw this: 'Nothing could be more fatal to its trading interest if it should be incorporated and have representatives in Parliament.'[9] This view was supported by John Aikin twelve years later when he declared the position of Manchester as 'an open town destitute of a corporation and unrepresented in Parliament' as 'probably to its advantage'.[10] Further, what came to be the greatest advantage of all to the trading interests of the town, and indeed to the very ethos of the place, as will be shown in a later chapter, was the open-door policy of its somewhat archaic system of government, however inadvertent it may have been at that time. 'Nothing has more contributed to the improvements in trade here,' proudly proclaimed Ogden, 'than the free admission of workmen in every branch, whereby the trade has been kept open to strangers of every description, who contribute to its improvement by their ingenuity.'[11] One wonders whether Daniel Defoe, in describing Manchester in 1724 as 'neither a wall'd town, city nor incorporation' whose inhabitants 'send no members to Parliament, and the highest magistrate they have is a constable or head borough',[12] realised the implications of what he evidently regarded as the town's inferior status.

Such a status, however, could not continue indefinitely to the town's advantage. By the beginning of the nineteenth century, its population had increased rapidly. When Bonnie Prince Charlie withdrew from Manchester in December 1745, he left a busy country town of some 17,000 inhabitants, who depended for street-lighting at night upon two oil lamps, one at the Old (now Victoria) Bridge and the other at the Cross (probably situated at what is now Cross Street). By 1801 the population had quadrupled to over 70,000, for whom the Police Commissioners, sanctioned by Parliament in 1792, were striving to improve the facilities of the town, which was expanding rapidly with 'new streets containing many capital houses more distinguished for their internal than their external elegance.' By 1832 the population had reached 180,000 (a tenfold increase well within a century), the principal streets were lit by gas and Everett's plan for this year was the first to show a railway line.

The outstanding event in Manchester during the first quarter of the nineteenth century was what came to be called 'the Peterloo Massacre'. The cause and purpose of the 60,000 men and women who had set out from the towns and villages of what is now the Greater Manchester Metropolitan County to form this historic assembly may be summarised in what one operative wrote to the *Manchester Mercury*: 'Corruption's at the very helm of the state—it sits and rules in the very House of Commons; *this* is the source, the true and only one, of all our sufferings.' And the purpose? 'Why, *reform*,' declared the same writer, 'a radical, complete constitutional *Reform*'; as 'Orator Hunt' put it to the meeting before he was arrested—'the most legal and effectual means of obtaining a *Reform* in the Commons House of Parliament'. This was not incitement to revolution but a genuine desire on the part of working men and women to achieve what today is called 'social justice'. 'We are endeavouring most assiduously,' wrote one of the Oldham men, 'to inform ourselves, and others, by all means in our power, that when we are called upon by circumstances we may be able to act as lovers of our country, and mankind.' The First Reform Act of 1832 enfranchised the large, but hitherto unrepresented, towns, including Manchester, whose inhabitants occupying houses of £10 rateable value were entitled to send two members to Parliament. This extent of enfranchisement applied also to Oldham, Bolton and Stockport while Salford, Bury-and-Radcliffe, Rochdale and Ashton-under-Lyne became entitled to elect one member each for Parliament. Wigan continued, as before 1832, to send one member.

Reform begets reform and that of local government was a natural sequence of the reform of Parliament. Concomitant with the rapid increase in population during the late eighteenth and early nineteenth centuries was the equally rapid development of large-scale industry and commerce. By the 1830s Manchester had become the metropolis of a great manufacturing region in which towns such as Bolton, Bury, Rochdale, Oldham, Ashton-under-Lyne, Stalybridge, Hyde and Stockport were, as one observer noted in the early 1840s, 'manufacturing parts of one great town', and cotton was by far their most important raw material. As J. H. Clapham, the great economic historian, has stated: 'It is not surprising that Britain's foreign trade presented itself almost as a problem in cotton, or that Manchester claimed a great share in the determination of the commercial—and industrial and social—policy of the country.' Yet here was this 'market town' still bound to the apron strings of this grotesquely inadequate system of manorial government. It was indeed 'fast outgrowing its manorial swaddling clothes', as Thomas Swindells once put it. The situation was even more complicated when one realises that there were no fewer than five different authorities competing with each other for the government of the town. They were the Court Leet; the Police Commissioners appointed by Act of Parliament (1792), whose powers were enlarged by a further Act of 1830; the Churchwardens and Overseers of the Parish; the Surveyors of Highways of the township; and the Justices of the Peace of

Lancashire. It was the lack of resident magistrates, able to understand the special problems of the town, which was a source of great danger to the public welfare of Manchester, as was also this hybrid nature of local government a constant threat to its efficiency as 'one of the commercial capitals of Europe'.

The point of complete exasperation was reached in 1837 when Richard Cobden, the Manchester calico printer and radical reformer, finding himself appointed a Juror on the Court Leet at its Michaelmas meeting,[13] 'at the appointed hour, ascending by a flight of steps in Brown Street . . ., reached the door of the manor court-room, which is large, and altogether destitute of furniture, whose row of tall, old-fashioned windows, would, but for the crust of smoke and dirt that covered them, have afforded a cheerful light.'[14] When the proceedings began, he was shocked to find, besides the police constable, exactly seven individuals present, 'and they, one by one, walked listlessly away, leaving the jurors only in the deserted and murky chamber.' When the Jurors set out to choose three persons, resident within the township of Manchester, to fill the offices of Borough-reeve and Constables of Manchester, they found that those nominated were most reluctant to take the oaths of office but 'the honour was at last gently forced upon them.' 'And thus', reported Cobden, 'very appropriately terminated the farce of a mock election of officers to govern the affairs of the town of Manchester', which the *Manchester Guardian* described in a leading article as 'a perfect absurdity'.[15]

The Municipal Corporations Act of 1835 made provision for towns to be granted a charter of incorporation upon application by inhabitant householders to the Privy Council. Among the many advantages which such a charter would bring to Manchester, and to those of its neighbouring partners in industry and commerce which were subsequently to form the urban structure of the Greater Manchester County, Cobden singled out for special distinction 'one of the provisions of the corporation reform act', by which 'no person can be appointed to the office of justice of the peace in any of the boroughs holding quarter sessions, unless he live within the limits prescribed for the residences of the burgesses.' He did so because he was convinced passionately that 'the massacre of the 16th August 1819, could not have occurred, if Manchester had then been incorporated according to the provisions of the present municipal reform act.' 'And why?' he asks. His reason is unequivocal: 'to place for ever the population of our town and neighbourhood beyond the control of a booby squire-archy, who abhor us not more for our love of political freedom, than for those active and intellectual pursuits which contrast so strongly with that mental stupor in which they exist—I had almost said—vegetate.'

The Charter of Incorporation for Manchester, dated 23 October 1838, was received at the Town Hall a few days later, but not before a bitter struggle had been fought out in which petition to the Privy Council was followed rapidly by counter-petition on the part of the Tory-Radical opposition. They must have been exciting days in the township when its walls were plastered with large posters warning, 'Working Men, Beware, The Whigs are at their dirty work again'—a campaign which the *Manchester Guardian* described as 'unworthy artifices and frauds of the enemies of incorporation'. But the granting of the Charter, which incorporated the townships of Manchester, Cheetham, Hulme, Ardwick, Chorlton-on-Medlock and Beswick (population 242,357), and provided for the setting up of a Borough Council consisting of a Mayor, sixteen Aldermen and forty-eight Councillors, was only an initial victory for the incorporators. For four years the opposition conducted a vexatious obstructionist policy in which the Police Commissioners held on to the Town Hall, at the corner of Cross Street and Upper King Street, until the Borough Charters Confirmation Act (1842) re-affirmed the validity of the original Charter for Manchester, as it did, also, for the Charter for Bolton, where similar trouble had been experienced. Yet another two years were to elapse before the Borough Council resolved, in January 1844, that steps should be taken to introduce into an Act of Parliament, 'for the good government and police regulation of the borough', clauses empowering the Council to buy the manorial rights of the manor of Manchester 'and the rights and properties incident thereto', all of which. Sir Oswald Mosley, last lord of the manor, was prepared to sell to the Corporation for the sum of £200,000. So it came about that the last meeting of the ancient Court Leet was held on 15 October 1845, at which the completion of the purchase of the manorial rights was confirmed and at which Richard Cobden, M.P. and foreman of the jury, had the last word in expressing 'the great satisfaction which he and his fellow-jurors felt at the termination of the rights and privileges of this Court, which had lasted, he believed, for many centuries, and which was admirably suited to the times in which it was established, but which all parties

21

admitted was quite unsuited to the wants and requirements of the present day'.[16]

The battle was won, and not only for Manchester. Stockport had already been incorporated as a borough in 1835 and Bolton in the same year as Manchester. In due course, future partners in the Greater Manchester County won their municipal spurs—Salford in 1844, Oldham in 1849, Rochdale in 1856 and Bury in 1876. Wigan is the oldest and proudest borough of them all, having been granted a royal charter over 700 years ago.

Chapter 3

'Heard from every cottage door'

The country round Manchester, which Dr John Aikin described in 1795 'with a particular account of its towns and chief villages', had long been noted for its 'cottons'. In the preamble to an Act of Parliament of 1542, which was primarily concerned with the privilege of sanctuary, Manchester is described as 'a long time well inhabited, distinguished in its trade both in linens and woollens, whereby the inhabitants have obtained riches and wealthy living and have employed many artificers'.[1] There is also a reference to the 'straight and true dealing' of its inhabitants who were, however, finding the presence of rogues in the town seeking sanctuary menacing to the welfare of their linen yarn laid out in the fields for bleaching and their woollen cloth hung out on tenter-frames to dry after fulling. As this temptation was too much for the local thieves who, in their vandalism, were interfering with the increasing manufacture of the town, its privilege of sanctuary was transferred to Chester, where possibly the temptations were less ready to hand.

Fulling (that is, the cleansing and thickening of the cloth) and bleaching were two of the processes carried out by the mercer or clothier on the spot, as it were, for there had been a fulling mill on the Irk since 1282. John Leland, the Tudor antiquary, on his tour of England, entered Lancashire in 1540 and recorded that the villages round Bolton 'do make cottons'. Nearly half a century later, William Camden wrote of Manchester in his book *Britannia* that 'in the foregoing age, this town was of far greater account both for certain woollen cloths there wrought, and in great request, commonly called Manchester Cottons.' Thus the word 'cottons', used in this context, denotes coarse woollen cloths. The first use of cotton itself in a textile fabric appears to have been in combination with flax yarn in the making of fustians. It is authoritatively considered that the first manufacture of fustians in Lancashire was at the beginning of the seventeenth century, when the name of George Arnould appears in the Lancashire Quarter Sessions Records in 1601 as 'fustian weaver of Bolton'.[2]

The two essential figures of the domestic system or industry were the farmer-weaver and the merchant or clothier. The former carried out the basic processes—preparation of the raw material, carding or combing, spinning of the yarn and the weaving of the cloth were all effected by the farmer and his family in their own home. The merchant or clothier undertook the finishing processes—the fulling of the cloth, scouring and dyeing—all of which, needing more equipment, involved more capital investment and tended to be more concentrated. When the cloth was ready for marketing, the merchant had a variety of outlets for its sale: the great national fairs, such as Bartholomew Fair in London or Stourbridge Fair in Cambridge; agents in the ports of Chester, Liverpool or Hull; or the great cloth marts in London. It was mainly to London that the Lancashire clothiers and mercers went, for many had their own agents there and, in some cases, members of their own family. An historic example for Manchester is the Mosley family. While Anthony managed the family business in Manchester, dealing regularly with the fullers in the Irk valley, his brother Nicholas went to London, became an alderman of the Clothworkers' Company, Lord Mayor of the capital in 1599 and was knighted the following year. Manchester's first recorder of its history wrote of him about 1650: 'From a small and low estate, God raysed him up to riches and honour.'[3]

A more illustrious example is the family of 'the best remembered Manchester man of his time'.[4] The Chethams were probably the first of the long succession of Manchester families who rose to wealth through the handling of cotton goods. Their fortunes began with Humphrey Chetham's great-grandfather, Edward, who lived in Crumpsall and in 1541 styled himself 'merchant'. His son, James, who inherited his father's property, described himself as 'yeoman merchant'. His will (he died in 1571) reveals him as a typical Manchester middleman, selling cloth for export at Chester, Liverpool and Hull and buying from those ports the linen yarn and flax which he sold on credit to country weavers. His son, Henry, was also a merchant who traded, among other commodities, in sackcloth, a coarse fabric of flax or hemp.[5] His four sons dealt in both woollens and linen. The eldest was apprenticed to Samuel Tipping, whose father, a Preston man, had set up in Manchester as a clothier. The Chetham and Tipping families were prominent members of the commercial bourgeoisie, which was firmly establishing itself at this time in Manchester. The two families became closely intertwined by ties of marriage and partnership and apprenticeship. Humphrey Chetham was later apprenticed to Samuel Tipping for seven years, at the end of which he joined his brother, George, who was Tipping's representative in

London. Subsequently, George and Humphrey entered into partnership in which they described themselves as 'copartners in the trade of buying and selling fustians and other wares and merchandizes'—the former conducting the family business in London and the latter in Manchester. The family accounts of 1626 (the year of George Chetham's death) show that Humphrey Chetham had dealings with fustian-makers and farmer-weavers in places in the region of Manchester such as Ashton, Hollinwood and Bolton. In so far as these dealings were on a credit basis in that he advanced them the raw cotton and linen yarn, these 'debtors for wool' were economically dependent on him. In these ways, Humphrey Chetham became one of the wealthiest men in Lancashire and sufficiently prominent to be appointed High Sheriff of the county in 1635. The original Chetham's Hospital and the famous Library, founded according to his will of 16 December 1651, bear witness to his native qualities 'of eminent loyalty to his sovereign, and of exemplary piety to God, and charity toward the poor, and a good affection to learning'. Although these merchants dwelt in and operated from Manchester, there were other dealers, variously described as chapmen, mercers, woollen and linen drapers, who operated from neighbouring towns such as Rochdale, Bury, Bolton and Oldham. But it was principally from Manchester that this inward and outward traffic was conducted and it is in this fascinating sphere of the domestic industry that the early links of Manchester with its neighbouring towns and villages of the region may be discerned.

During this early period between the sixteenth and eighteenth centuries, the farmer-weaver families came to rely as much upon their income from spinning and weaving as upon that from agriculture. The most economical and logical means of organising industrial production seemed to be some form of 'domestic' or 'putting-out' system. Its two essential characteristics were firstly, that all or most of the processes of manufacture were carried out in the dwellings of the workers themselves and not in some workshop, mill or factory to which they went as a place of work; and secondly, that these workers did not own the raw materials or semi-finished goods passing through their hands but worked them up for wages, usually piece-rates, paid by an employer who had put out the work to them.[6] As the population grew steadily, there were more farmsteads and many more houses built in the villages and along the valleys of what is now the Greater Manchester

County. Further, the three textile industries were becoming localised. The area which specialised in the woollen manufacture shrank until it lay mainly along the eastern fringe of the county. What woollen lost, linen and fustians gained, although Manchester, as the commercial centre of South-East Lancashire, retained an interest both in the merchanting and distribution of woollen goods and in the fulling, dyeing and finishing processes owing to their dependence on the merchant. All the outlying villages of the great parish of Manchester were given over to linen weaving.[7]

In effect, the farms became more adapted to the requirements of industry. The weaver added a loomhouse, the clothier a dyehouse and the linen weaver a yarncroft where yarn could lie to bleach. Specialisation and division of labour were to be found also in the more common use of occupational descriptions: weaving was ceasing to be regarded as a by-occupation; 'yeoman' was giving place to 'clothier', 'clothmaker', 'chapman' (merchant) or 'webster' (weaver) as a description.[8] Yet the association with the land remained of vital importance. The waste from which turf for fuel was gathered still had its industrial uses, as the inhabitants of the outlying Manchester hamlet of Moston, who gained their living almost entirely by bleaching linen yarn, realised. For this occupation 'doth requyre very moche fyre', they complained, and the waste of the township was their only source of fuel.[9]

The zenith of the old industry, based on domestic production, was reached in the eighteenth century. There were indications of more full-time employment in the industry. Although in many places farming was still combined with weaving, there were cottages in the woollen area which had little or even no land attached to them. There was much more 'putting-out', with the materials remaining in the hands of the merchants, and a decline in the old independent operations of the farmer-weavers. Evidence of the expansion of the industry as markets grew and foreign trade developed is the building of more fulling mills along the east Lancashire streams, especially in the Rochdale and Bury areas and in Rossendale.[10] There is a remarkable, surviving example in the last-named area in Higher Mill at Helmshore, a woollen finishing mill built by the Turner family in 1789. The mill was water-powered by a most impressive wheel which was operating until 1954 and may still be seen in its original position, as too may the fulling stocks, a raising machine where the nap of the cloth was raised by teazles, tentering frames and sulphur ovens for bleaching. The Turners are an example of a family who, by their enterprise and skill, built up one of the largest woollen concerns in the country and, in so doing, converted a scattered rural community into a modern industrial village. Noted for his autocratic methods with his workpeople yet deeply involved in their welfare, William Turner (1793–1852) ruled Helmshore single-handed for nearly thirty years. He provided substantial houses for his workpeople, maintained a good school and built the parish church at Musbury, his most lasting memorial. Today Higher Mill is in the care of a trust which has converted it into a very valuable textile museum.[11]

With the introduction of the new machinery in the later part of the eighteenth century—Hargreaves' spinning jenny (the name is a corruption of 'engine'), Arkwright's water frame and Crompton's mule—both the woollen and cotton industries were eventually affected. From about 1780 spinning mills for the production of woollen yarn were built, especially in the Rossendale and Rochdale areas. With the increasing demand for cotton goods, however, for which the new machines were easier to use, many manufacturers elected to change over from wool to cotton. Thus, for the next thirty or forty years, while the preparatory processes— carding, roving and spinning—were increasingly being operated in water or steam-powered factories, weaving remained essentially a manual process and mainly a domestic process. It has been stated that 'the hand loom weaving of cotton, now often regarded as an old-established industry, was in fact a mushroom growth of the second half of the eighteenth century',[12] the sudden expansion of which 'did not necessarily disrupt the existing pattern of settlement by causing massive migration from the farms and villages to a few advantageously sited towns.'[13]

It would appear that 'although the little country towns of south Lancashire grew markedly in the last decades of the eighteenth century, the expansion of cotton weaving in this period of rapid natural increase in numbers also witnessed a corresponding "thickening" of population in the more remote rural hamlets and villages.' Dr John Aikin, writing in this period, described Stalybridge as 'now a very large and extensive village' and said, 'the greatest part of this village has been built in the last eighteen years';[14] of Middleton he says, 'the village of Middleton is rapidly increasing' and 'though little more than twenty years since, there were scarcely more than twenty houses in the village, there are now

Weavers' cottages in Chesham Place, Bury, with second-floor workshops. The cottages were demolished in 1971

between four and five hundred, which contain more than 2000 inhabitants.' Of 'the new village of Tildsley', he comments: 'This estate had, in the year 1780, only two farmhouses and eight or nine cottages, but now contains 162 houses, a neat chapel and 976 inhabitants, who employ 325 looms in the cotton manufactories.' What Aikin said of Wigan could equally be applied to the towns and villages of what is now the Greater Manchester County: 'The cotton manufactory, as in all other places, intrudes upon the old staple of the place.' This intrusion was to be seen in town, village and hamlet by the building of rows of weavers' cottages to house the new workers who flowed in from so many different sources. This was the great period of the loomshops, which were built in rows of stone-built cottages with the dwelling quarters for the weavers on the lower floors and on the top floor the loomshops from back to front of the house, with long mullioned windows to give extra light and sometimes windows high in the gable ends, providing light for a storage loft above the working floor. These were the domestic workshops which may still be seen in places like Rochdale, Milnrow or Wardle, sentinels of industrial archaeology as they would now be described.

It was in a weaver's cottage in Middleton, such as one of these, that Samuel Bamford, the Lancashire handloom weaver and radical reformer, lived and worked with his uncle and aunt:

'Whilst my life at the bobbin-wheel was wretched on account of the confinement, my poor old aunt had generally a sad time with me. It was scarcely to be expected that a tall, straight, round-limbed young ruffian like myself . . . should sit day by day twirling a wheel and guiding a thread; his long limbs cramped and doubled under a low wooden stool. I accordingly, at times, from a sheer inability to sit still, played all kinds of pranks, keeping my wheel going the while, lest my aunt should have it to say I was playing and neglecting my task. On these occasions I frequently got a rap on the head from a weaver's rod which my aunt would have beside her . . . or (I was) banished into the loom-house amongst the weavers.'[15]

Samuel Bamford was descended from a long line of artisan-craftsmen of the pre-factory era. His great-grandfather, James Bamford, lived at Thornham, near Rochdale, at the beginning of the eighteenth century, 'keeping there a small farm, and making cane reeds for weavers of flannel and coarse cotton'. His grandfather, Daniel, came to reside at Middleton, as a small farmer and weaver, where he lived in 'an old timber and daub house, with thatched roof, low windows and a porch' in 'Back o' th' Brow'. His father was 'a weaver of muslin, at that time considered a fine course of work, and requiring a superior hand', whilst his mother 'found plenty of employment in occasional weaving, in winding bobbins, or pins for my father, and in looking after the house and the children, of whom I was the fourth born.' About 1793, his father took over the management of a 'manufactory of cotton goods' at the new workhouse for the township of Manchester at Strangeways, of which he soon afterwards became the Governor. Two years later, 'several cases of virulent small pox broke out among the children of the house', from which Samuel's mother died. Owing to strained relations at the workhouse and the marriage of his father to a widow with four children, Samuel was sent to live with his uncle William in Middleton in a house which contained 'a loom-shop capable of containing four looms'.[16]

The name of Samuel Bamford has always been closely associated with the events leading to Peterloo, which he himself has graphically recorded for posterity. Following the close of the Napoleonic Wars, a brief boom in textiles was succeeded by sporadic periods of severe economic distress, especially among the weavers and spinners. By the beginning of 1819, the pressure of distress was as hard and insistent as ever, which, for a time, increased the appeal of political Radicalism among the cotton loom weavers. It has been claimed that 'if the weavers' rates had been increased by even 2/- to 3/- in the £ in 1818, there might have been no Peterloo.' Instead, it was the substantial shift of opinion among the handloom weavers in Manchester and the surrounding towns and villages during 1819 which formed the backbone of the movement for peaceful reform,[17] and led to that great assembly which gathered on St Peter's Field, Manchester, on Monday, 16 August. 'It was deemed expedient,' wrote Bamford, 'that this meeting should be as morally effective as possible, and, that it should exhibit a spectacle such as had never before been witnessed in England.'[18] That Peterloo was 'morally effective', if not immediately, as the tragic events of that momentous afternoon so painfully demonstrated, but subsequently in the legislation for parliamentary, municipial and other political reforms, may be accepted. That it was a spectacle such as Bamford desired cannot be doubted: 'I saw the main body proceeding towards St Peter's Field,' wrote the editor of the *Manchester Times*, 'and never saw a gayer spectacle. The "marching order", of which so much was said afterwards, was what we often see now in the processions of Sunday-school children and temperance societies. To our eyes the numerous flags seemed to have been brought to add to the picturesque effect of the pageant.'[19] A contemporary poem describes the scene in this way:

'The Sixteenth day of August Eighteen Hundred and
    Nineteen,
There many thousand people on every road were
    seen,
From Stockport, Oldham, Ashton and other places too,
It was the largest Meeting Reformers ever knew.'

After graphically relating the 'scenes of blood' caused by the military in their attempts 'to force us from the Plain of Peterloo', the outraged artisan concludes on a theme of great hopefulness:

'But soon reform shall spread around for sand the tide
    won't stay,
May all the filth that in our land right soon be washed
    away,
And may sweet harmony from hence in this our land be
    found,
May we be blest with plenty in all the country round.'[20]

This poem and other contemporary sources clearly indicate that the supporters of this historic meeting came that day not only from Manchester and its adjacent townships but from the towns, villages and hamlets which now constitute the Greater Manchester County. Bamford, aware that 'we had frequently been taunted by the press, with our ragged, dirty appearance, at these assemblages' was, with his fellow-leaders, determined that 'these reflections should not be deserved' on 16 August 1819. Accordingly, instructions were issued to the committees forming the contingents that 'Cleanliness, Sobriety, Order and Peace' were to be observed both on the march and at the meeting, and that the last two injunctions were to be provided for by preparatory 'drillings' and 'a prohibition of all weapons of offence or defence'. In such a manner, 'by constant practice and an alert willingness', the contingents set out on that hot morning for St Peter's Field. They came from Newtown, Ardwick, Harpurhey and Blackley in the immediate vicinity, from Middleton, Failsworth, Stockport, and Ashton-under-Lyne, from Oldham, Saddleworth, Lees and Mossley, from Rochdale, Heywood, Milnrow and Wardle, from Bury, Bolton, Radcliffe and Horwich, and possibly smaller contingents from Wigan and the surrounding villages. With local pride, they carried their banners on which were inscribed 'Annual Parliaments', or 'Vote by Ballot', or 'Universal Suffrage', or 'No Corn Laws'. No doubt the outlying contingents joined up with their comrades en route; for example, when the Rochdale party entered Middleton, 'a shout from ten thousand startled the echoes of the woods and dingles.' On they marched through Blackley, Harpurhey and Newtown, swelling their ranks at each township—bearing aloft their banner on which was inscribed 'Liberty And Fraternity' (it may still be seen in Middleton Public Library). The key to the identification of the region from which they came was cotton, and there can be little doubt that the large majority of those who marched so hopefully to form that mammoth assembly on St Peter's Field that day were weavers and spinners with their families. They were historically the very warp and weft of what is now the Greater Manchester County and the names on their banners of the towns, villages and hamlets whence they came are the very stuff of which the new county is spun and woven. That they came from the four corners of the region to impress their unanimous will upon the centre is a matter for modern reflection.

Although this great demonstration resulted in tragedy with the immense crowd brutally dispersed by military force, leaving eleven people killed and about 400 injured, ultimately it was one of the most powerful victories of the people of England and in the end destroyed the old social order.

In the year following Peterloo, the enthusiasm of the handloom weavers for parliamentary reform tended to evaporate due, in the main, to the return of prosperity which brought abundant work and falling prices. The next three years (1820–23) saw the Indian summer of material well-being for the cotton handloom weavers, when life again became reasonably comfortable for them. But by 1826 the gradual introduction of the power-loom into the factories began to affect their livelihood, full-time and part-time alike. A Haslingden weaver commented bitterly:

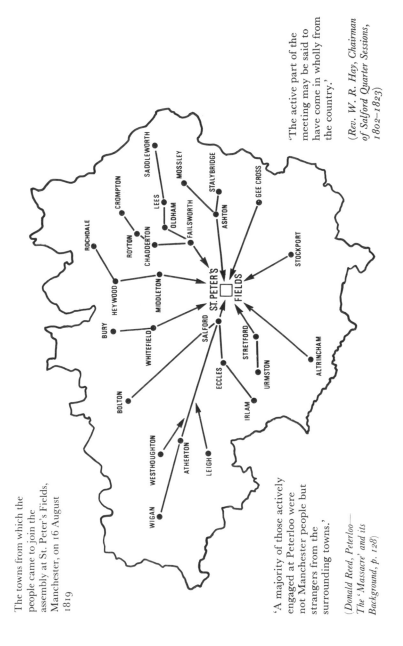

The towns from which the
people came to join the
assembly at St. Peter's Fields,
Manchester, on 16 August
1819

'A majority of those actively
engaged at Peterloo were
not Manchester people but
strangers from the
surrounding towns.'

*(Donald Reed, Peterloo—
The 'Massacre' and its
Background, p. 128)*

'The active part of the
meeting may be said to
have come in wholly from
the country.'

*(Rev. W. R. Hay, Chairman
of Salford Quarter Sessions,
1802–1823)*

SADDLEWORTH
MOSSLEY
CROMPTON
STALYBRIDGE
LEES
GEE CROSS
ROCHDALE
ROYTON
OLDHAM
CHADDERTON
FAILSWORTH
ASHTON
HEYWOOD
MIDDLETON
STOCKPORT
BURY
ST. PETER'S
FIELDS
WHITEFIELD
SALFORD
STRETFORD
BOLTON
ECCLES
URMSTON
ALTRINCHAM
IRLAM
WESTHOUGHTON
ATHERTON
LEIGH
WIGAN

'Cotton weaving got to starvation work in 1826. I don't think anyone could make above 9s. a week, work as hard as they could. Food was dear—salt 4d. a pound, broken sugar 8d., lump sugar 1s. But working people didn't use much sugar. They had porridge and milk. I have had porridge twenty-one times a week . . . All the farmers had loom shops and they fancied the power-loom was going to starve them to death.'[21]

Ultimately it was technology, allied with the economic and social conditions of the period, which broke the handloom weavers. By the mid-1830s they were on the losing side of the textile industry in the Manchester region: ·

'If you go into a loom-shop, where there's three or four
    pairs of looms,
They are all standing empty, encumbrances of the
    rooms;
And if you ask the reason why, the old mother will tell
    you plain,
My daughters have forsaken them, and gone to weave by
    steam.'[22]

The age of the machine had arrived and, according to Carlyle, 'there is no end to machinery.'

Chapter 4

'The grand centre of industry'

Was there a 'golden age' for the Domestic System as compared to the Industrial Revolution? This is a question which has engaged the attention of social and economic historians for many years. It has engaged the minds of others, too, both English and foreign.

When Léon Faucher, described by J. P. Culverwell, a Manchester barrister in the early 1840s, as 'an intelligent French writer', published his classic *Études sur l'Angleterre*, the section on Manchester was regarded by Culverwell as so important as to warrant an English translation, which in due course helped to establish Manchester as the symbol of industrial England but not necessarily as a typical English city. Faucher described Manchester at the beginning of the nineteenth century as 'a town of little dealers and manufacturers who bought unbleached fabrics in Bolton, dyed them, and then hawked them upon horseback, from market to market.'[1] He saw the weaver as 'a sort of domestic manufacturer, who bought his yarn when his family was not able to furnish it, and sold it when woven for a price which remunerated him for the labour and outlay which he had incurred.' Commenting upon the gradual transition of the 'domestic era of manufactures', in which the weaver's time 'was occupied in different occupations, and labour was carried on in an unorganised and desultory manner' so that 'when his shuttle ceased to fly, he turned to his spade or to the plough', he formed the impression that 'society did not suffer much, because the thin and scattered state of the manufacturing population afforded an easier opportunity for alleviating individual poverty . . .' 'But,' proceeds Faucher, 'when manufacturing industry (thanks to the accumulation of capital and the progress of mechanical inventions) constructs monster buildings, and crowds into them machines by thousands, and enrols whole regiments of men, women and children, to work them; when a single capitalist causes all this movement,' then, concludes Faucher, 'the converse of the domestic system is produced', in which 'labour is organised, employment is daily, and as if to evade the loss of time upon the Sunday, it steals from each of the other six days, more energy than human strength can with safety give.'[2] It would appear that, in contrasting the two modes of manufacture in this way, Faucher supports the view of the 'golden age' of the handloom weavers.

Yet Faucher, in his intelligent appraisal of the changing circumstances during the early 1840s of the towns and villages which now constitute the Greater Manchester County, observed that 'the operatives are now convinced that their fate is linked to that of machinery; they now regard them as aids to the labourer, and not as formerly as competitors.' He concludes, 'hence they are reconciled with mechanical power', but adds significantly, 'they are more opposed than ever to the capitalist who puts the power in movement.' He differentiates between the capitalists engaged in rural and urban manufacture, especially in their conduct towards their operatives. For him the former 'rank high as intelligent and benevolent men' and, as examples, he cites the Gregs at Quarry Bank, Styal, the Grants at Bury, the Ashtons at Hyde and the Ashworths at Turton. One almost detects a Gallic streak in his striking statement: 'Industry, as well as war, has its chivalry', by which he infers that the family traditions implicit in the continuing of these industrial establishments 'still deem it an honour to maintain and cherish the colony of operatives formed under the tutelage of their father.' But it is not tradition only which attracts Faucher. In what may be seen as an apocalyptic statement, he expresses his firm conviction that 'the first manufacturer who shall have the courage to invite his workpeople to an interest in the profits of the establishment, will be no sufferer by the experiment', for he 'would establish between himself and his workmen an intimate and permanent union which would be proof against time and circumstances.' One cannot help but feel that here is the germ of an industrial philosophy which is engaging the thoughts of governments, employers and trade unions very much today.

Another foreign observer of Manchester and its neighbouring manufacturing towns in the early 1840s was Friedrich Engels, the revolutionary socialist whose father was a partner in the Manchester cotton firm of Ermen and Engels in Market Street. He was already at odds with his father before his arrival in Manchester towards the end of 1842 and what he saw about him at that unfortunate time of unemployment and industrial unrest seemed to confirm his detestation of the cotton manufacturer as a class, of whom he was already well conditioned to believe the worst. He visited the slums and factories of Manchester, Oldham, Rochdale, Ashton-under-Lyne and other towns of the

Metropolitan County and he buried himself in English newspapers and books. He returned to his native town of Barmen after less than two years' residence in England and proceeded to write on the domestic and working conditions of the English working class. What he wrote was tendentious and unreliable as an historical source in that ironically his work suffered from the very defects of the Whig interpretation of historical method; he selected facts which purported to strengthen his indictment of the 'bourgeois philistines' of his age and unscrupulously suppressed any evidence which did not support his thesis of their innate wickedness. Thus it suited his purpose to idealise the supposed 'golden age' of the weavers of the mid-eighteenth century in England as the origin of the industrial proletariat: the farmers 'enjoyed a comfortable and peaceful existence . . . they were righteous, God-fearing and honest . . . their standard of life was much better than that of the factory today.'

This idyllic conception of the conditions of the weaver's lot in that period has been strongly refuted in a critical Introduction to a new translation of Engels' book:

> 'The view that the period before the Industrial Revolution was a sort of golden age is a myth. Many of the evils of the early factory age were no worse than those of an earlier period. Domestic spinners and weavers in the eighteenth century had been "exploited" by the clothiers as ruthlessly as the factory operatives were "exploited" by the manufacturers in the 1840s. Men, women and children worked long hours for low wages under the domestic system as under the factory system.'[3]

This assessment of comparison has been criticised as 'the commonest error today' on the part of those who 'muddle over the difficult and painful nature of the change in status from artisan to depressed outworker in some such comforting phrases as these.' Yet E. P. Thompson's own answer to this question is not at all convincing, the less so when he poses the equivocal argument: 'After all, if we set up the ninepin of a "golden age" it is not difficult to knock it down.'[4] Perhaps the present 'last word' on this subject may be allowed to the most recent publication on the handloom weavers in which the writer urges that 'it is important to avoid too rosy a picture of conditions in the "golden age" of handloom weaving at the end of the eighteenth century',[5] in which view he is supported by a slightly earlier admonition that 'although all sections of the weavers suffered diminution of income, many of them were earning but a modest sum to begin with. The weavers in all branches of the manufacture did not experience a descent from great prosperity to adversity.'[6]

Although the social consequences of the Industrial Revolution in its crucial stages may not have been quite so appalling as Engels chose to depict them, they were dreadful enough to pierce the consciences of many thoughtful men and women in the 1830s who had a concern 'in promoting the progress of social improvement in the manufacturing population by which they are surrounded', as the Manchester Statistical Society, founded in 1833, set out to achieve. Prominent among them was Dr James Phillips Kay who was born at Bamford, Rochdale, in 1804. As Senior Physician to the Ardwick and Ancoats Dispensary, he came into close contact with those who lived in the slums of Manchester and worked in its factories and mills. As a result of his investigations among them, he traced some of the diseases to which they were prone to the conditions under which they worked, and his experience of the cholera epidemic in 1832 in Manchester convinced him that medical and social science must co-operate in striving to eliminate the evils to be found in 'the most loathsome haunts of poverty and vice'.[7] He later accepted the post of Assistant Poor Law Commissioner in East Anglia which brought him into contact with Edwin Chadwick, a native of Longsight, Manchester, who was at that time Secretary of the Poor Law Commission. The vital problem of public health was undertaken almost nationally as a crusade by Chadwick and it was he who prepared the way for local action by the first Public Health Act of 1848, of which he was both the inspirer and the draftsman. Sir Robert Peel, father of the Prime Minister, founded a small cotton-printing factory in 1770 in a ruined cornmill near Bury and later, as a result, had business interests in Manchester; over thirty years later, he sponsored the first Factory Act, which aimed at protecting the health and morals of pauper apprentices sent from London and the southern workhouses to the northern mills and, later, the Factory Act of 1819, which forbade night-work for children in cotton mills. These Acts prepared the way for the more effective factory reforms of Michael Sadler in 1833 and of Lord Shaftesbury in 1847.

Concomitant with these reforms, initiated by men of the Manchester region, to alleviate the sufferings and to raise the living standards of the workers not only locally, possibly their original concern, but also nationally, were the efforts being made by the new Borough Councils, enfranchised by the Municipal Corporations Act of 1835. The first Manchester Borough Council consisted, on the whole, of self-made men who had exercised their talents successfully in industry and commerce and were, in the main, united in politics and religion. These councillors now applied their knowledge of public affairs and their business experience to the task of making their newly incorporated Manchester a place worthy of human habitation. Having fought a hard battle for their civic independence, as has been noted, they were moved by a strong sense of public duty towards their less fortunate townsmen, and the zeal with which they took up the challenge of their civic responsibility, consonant with their newly-acquired freedom, set a standard of municipal achievement which their Metropolitan successors of today will do well to emulate. It has been well said that 'the bourgeois Manchester, which he (Engels) hated and despised, had gone a good way towards cleaning up the frightful things which he described so vividly, of its own momentum, even before it would have been possible for its people to read his book.'[8]

In any assessment of the historical evolution of the Greater Manchester County as the first industrial society, one is bound to encounter the fundamental question of whether, during the period of the Industrial Revolution (c. 1780–c. 1850), the benefits of material gain outweighed the incidence of human misery involved in producing them. It is not difficult to find evidence in the British Parliamentary Papers and other sources of this period of heart-rending descriptions of the sometimes appalling conditions under which mill and factory workers operated. In 1844 Léon Faucher almost dramatically posed the following questions:

'Are the disorders which manifest themselves in the large centres of industry, a necessary consequence of the manufacturing system? Are we to consider them as accidental features, or as a regular phenomenon of production? Is it not possible to spin and weave cotton, wool, or silk, in large quantities, and at a cheap rate, by the powerful aid of machinery, without conjuring up at the same time, those frightful consequences which now result from it, and which are the destruction of the family tie, slavery, premature decay, and demoralization of children, drunkenness of the men, prostitution of the women, and an universal decay of morality? Or, are not these the inevitable sufferings which always accompany the birth of a new era in social progress?'

He notes, also, of the small manufacturing towns surrounding Manchester: 'Here is no commercial movement, no luxury, little or no fleeting population; nothing which interferes with the internal economy of their management, yet the same disorders are manifested as in the larger town of Manchester.' As in the manner of the politician answering his own questions, Faucher was convinced that 'industry is evidently in a state of anarchy, but it will, sooner or later, make a better use of its liberty' for 'all the great *facts* achieved by a progressive civilization have increased the happiness as well as the intelligence of mankind.'[9] It is, indeed, in the facts of statistics, if one may adopt so contentious a term, that the evidence lies for the answers to this difficult question. Despite the pessimistic view of the Hammonds and Arnold Toynbee, who believed that conditions of urban life had deteriorated under industrialisation, most economic historians today are convinced that the industrial revolution in England has benefited the workers, not only in the long but also in the short run. Between 1780 and 1850 the average real income per head increased, the consumption of food and other consumer goods per head increased and, with the growing government intervention in economic and social life, the working and domestic conditions were both raised and protected. This is not to say that there was no dire poverty at times, especially during the cyclical slumps which produced serious unemployment, but it is to say that the industrial revolution in England not only brought greater wealth to the working classes, especially the skilled artisans, it also brought opportunities for social and political reforms of a far-reaching nature. Herbert Butterfield has written of this period: 'For two thousand years the general appearance of the world and the activities of men had varied astonishingly little . . . Now, however, change became so quick as to be perceptible to the naked eye, and the face of the earth and the activities of men were to alter more in a century than they had previously done in a thousand years.'[10]

In comparison, it may perhaps be not irrelevant to refer to that astonishing fifth century of the ancient world when the city-states of Greece, and particularly the Athenians, laid the foundations, in their practice and speculation, of European political philosophy. In like manner, this tremendous movement of the Industrial

Revolution gripped the towns and villages, large and small, of what is now the Greater Manchester County in such a way as to make the region the very power-house industrially of the modern world. This is what Disraeli was after when, proclaiming 'What Art was to the ancient world, Science is to the modern', he asserted in 1844 that 'rightly understood, Manchester is as great a human exploit as Athens.'[11] It is in this cosmic context that one may evaluate in their proper perspective the 'many accounts of the dark side of this Industrial Revolution, accounts in which some writers have indulged their repressions by dwelling largely on factory cruelties and sexual misdemeanours.' There is another side of the coin to the gloomy portrayal of the 'depressed and degraded factory slaves depicted in the highly coloured and often tendentious accounts of mill conditions which proliferated in the 1830s and 1840s'.[12]

At the centre of the triumphs and tribulations of the Industrial Revolution in this region stood Manchester. In the early stages of its development, the manufacturer worked hard and lived frugally:

'He used to be in his warehouse before six in the morning, accompanied by his children and apprentices. At seven they all came in to breakfast, which consisted of one large dish of water-pottage, made of oatmeal, water and a little salt, boiled thick, and poured into a dish. At the side was a pan or bason of milk, and the master and apprentices, each with a wooden spoon in his hand, without loss of time, dipped into the same dish, and thence into the milk pan; and as soon as it was finished they all returned to their work.'[13]

By the middle of the eighteenth century he was reaching out for orders in every market town in England and acquiring for himself some of the advantages which wealth brings. At about this time there were some three or four carriages kept in the town. By the end of the century, with the rapid expansion of industry through the textile inventions, the merchants of Manchester were extending their own activities correspondingly. They sent out their agents into every part of Europe and invested their profits from these enterprises in mechanised cotton spinning. It was mainly through the enterprise and astute adaptability of these merchant-manufacturers, with their agents abroad, that the value of British exports of cotton goods rose from £45,986 in 1751 to £200,000 in

1764 and to nearly £5½ millions by the end of the century. Their success aroused so much interest and wonder among the merchants of the Continent that it attracted, from the late 1770s, a small number of foreign visitors to Manchester, at first to seek out information and to spy out industrial secrets, but later to settle in the town as merchants and manufacturers. This two-way traffic was noted by a medical contemporary with some pride:

'Within the last twenty or thirty years the vast increase of foreign trade has caused many of the Manchester manufacturers to travel abroad, and agents or partners to be fixed for a considerable time on the Continent, as well as foreigners to reside at Manchester. And the town has now in every respect assumed the style and manners of one of the commercial capitals of Europe.'[14]

This inception of the cosmopolitan growth of Manchester, so fortunate for its future prosperity and cultural character, will be treated at length in a subsequent chapter. Joseph Aston, another native of the town, at that time attributed 'the cause of the prosperity of Manchester' to 'the ingenuity and industry of its inhabitants',[15] while James Ogden regarded the adaptability of the Manchester merchant as 'a peculiar felicity (which) has attended the trade of this town so that when any branch of it has failed, the industry and invention of manufacturers have been so much the more excited to introduce others whereon to employ their capitals and encourage the ingenuity of their workmen.'[16] The modern counterpart in the cotton industry would seem to be those progressive firms which have directed their resources into the production of 'man-made fibres', whether they be in Manchester or in the cotton towns of the Metropolitan County.

By the end of the eighteenth century, the demand for textile machinery created by the cotton spinning mills in the Manchester area promoted the establishment of the engineering industries. G. H. Tupling, the leading authority in his day on local history in the county, has shown that the adoption of machinery in the Lancashire textile industries and the application of steam to manufacture 'brought into existence a new type of craftsman in metal—the engineer, the maker of engines and machinery'—who, in many respects, derived his skill and experience from the metal-smelting and metal-using crafts 'practised by Lancashire men for varying periods during the past 700 years.'[17] That there was great activity during the last quarter of the eighteenth century among the long-established metal-working trades in Manchester is testified by Dr John Aikin, who recorded at the time that 'to the ironmongers shops, which are greatly increased of late, are generally annexed smithies, where many articles are made, even to nails.' He referred, also, to 'a considerable iron foundry established in Salford, in which are cast most of the articles wanted in Manchester and its neighbourhood.' 'Mr Sharrard' (correctly 'Sherratt'), one of the two partners owning this large iron foundry, is described as 'a very ingenious and able engineer, who has improved upon and brought the steam engine to great perfection. Most of those that are used and set up in and about Manchester are of their make and fitting up.'[18] While in the early 1770s the term 'engineer' does not appear in the directories of Manchester and Salford, modern investigation into the beginnings of engineering in Lancashire reveals that 'the tremendous growth of the Lancashire cotton industry, from about 1770 onwards, based upon the mechanical inventions of Hargreaves, Arkwright, Crompton and Cartwright, powered by water-wheels and steam engines, gave rise to an equally rapid development of mechanical engineering.' As a direct result of this development, 'Lancashire soon came to manufacture not only cotton, but also cotton machinery, steam engines, boilers, machine tools and, later on, railway locomotives, iron bridges, gas-work plant, and a vast range of other engineering products.'[19]

It is upon these foundations that the great engineering industry of Manchester and its neighbouring towns was built in the nineteenth century, and probably the greatest inventor and practitioner of them all was Sir Joseph Whitworth. When he started business as a toolmaker in Chorlton Street, Manchester, in 1833, a fitter who could work to one tenth of an inch was looked upon as a skilled workman. Whitworth eventually constructed a machine capable of detecting differences of less than one-millionth of an inch. Yet his greatest contribution to modern manufacture was his 'scheme for standardizing screws, screw threads and other mechanical essentials', which came to be universally adopted. Men such as Whitworth typify the long succession of great engineers and enterprising businessmen who have made Manchester the metropolis of a great engineering industry, the diverse nature of which in its production may be seen in many towns of the Greater Manchester

County—Thomas Robinson & Son Ltd., Woodworkers and Flourmilling Engineers, Rochdale; Robert Hall & Sons, Bury; Hick, Hargreaves & Co., Steam Engine Engineers, Bolton; Platt Brothers & Co. Ltd., of Werneth near Oldham, who produced more textile machinery than the total American output in this field; and, probably most famous of them all, Mather & Platt Ltd., Engineers, Newton Heath, Manchester.

During the 1840s and early 1850s Manchester changed from being a town in which industry and commerce were of equal importance to one in which commerce and services rose to paramount importance to act as the heart of a region vibrant with industrial activities. A well-known handbook of the time noted that 'within the last few years Mosley Street contained only private dwelling-houses: it is now converted almost entirely into warehouses; and the increasing business of the town is rapidly converting all the principal dwelling-houses which exist in that neighbourhood into mercantile establishments, and is driving most of the respectable inhabitants into the suburbs.'[20] It has been estimated that within twelve miles of the Manchester Royal Exchange were situated 280 cotton towns and villages, all dependent in varying degrees on Manchester's commercial expertise. Such towns as Bolton, Bury, Rochdale, Oldham, Ashton-under-Lyne, Stalybridge, Hyde and Stockport were regarded in the mid-1840s as 'the manufacturing parts of one great town'. Although these neighbouring towns were, and are today, rightly jealous of their civic pride and independence, with each of them containing its own measure of commercial and servicing functions which today are becoming more evident than formerly, they were in the mid-nineteenth century still predominantly manufacturing towns. This was revealed statistically for the first time in the 1841 Census of Great Britain, the third volume of which is devoted entirely to the *Occupation Abstract*. This includes, under the heading of the County of Lancaster, a very extensive and detailed classification of the inhabitants of the towns in which the exact employment of every individual person is stated. It is a volume worthy of study.

Market Street in Manchester, regionally famous today for its shopping facilities, through which it claims to have the richest retail trade in Britain, was regarded in the 1840s as 'the heart of the system'. 'Here,' commented one observer in 1844, 'we have around us the wholesale warehouses and offices wherein is contracted all the business between the dealers, the manufacturers, the

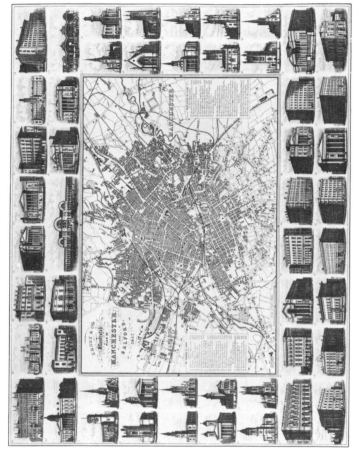

Ernst & Co's Illustrated Plan of Manchester and Salford (1857)

spinners, the bleachers, the calico-printers, etc., whether of Manchester or any of the surrounding towns.' For him, in particular, Mosley Street epitomised 'the whole scheme of things':

'Here almost every house is occupied in the way stated; no manufactures are carried on, no retail shops exhibit the manufactured goods, but every house and almost every floor of every house constitutes the business establishment of some large manufacturing firm... A bargain is struck, say, for 10,000 pieces of calico, as per sample, and this may be done in a small room between the manufacturer and the dealer, while the goods are perhaps at that moment being manufactured at Bolton, or Ashton, or Stockport.'[21]

It must not be thought, however, that at that time Manchester was a very large town, judged by modern standards. When the Charter incorporating the six townships was received at the Town Hall on 1 November 1838, the municipal Borough thus formed contained a population of 242,357 with an area of 4,393 acres. When the title of City was conferred upon the Borough in 1853, its population had risen to just over 300,000 and there was to be no further extension of its boundaries until another thirty years had elapsed. The city was still small enough for most of it to be reached on foot in fifteen or twenty minutes from any other part.

Even more relevant is the changing nature, from about 1850, of the centre of the city. Although Manchester remained an outstanding manufacturing town, the mills in the city centre gradually moved out to make way for the growing commercial and servicing activities. This city core, covering about one square mile, emerged as the distributing centre for raw cotton and manufactured goods. In this way the servicing of the industries of South-East Lancashire became the paramount function of the city. This is clearly shown on p. 45 in the *Illustrated Plan of Manchester and Salford*, published in 1857, for it is in the frieze to this plan that the changing scale of the city centre is abundantly illustrated. The great warehouses and offices, the city churches, the Royal Manchester Institution, the Athenaeum, the new Free Trade Hall and the great Art Treasures Exhibition Hall (geographically out of place but topically most relevant)—all are there and, although differing stylistically, display collectively an impressive solidity. This, then, was the nucleus of the metropolitan core which in due course came to

46

provide the main facilities of banking, insurance, merchanting, stockbroking, newspaper production, shopping and entertainment for Britain's leading industrial region. This is the partnership of the metropolis and its neighbouring towns which has been primarily responsible for the formation of the Greater Manchester County.[22]

It has long been an axiom of history time-charts designed to depict the evolution of transport through the ages that when Napoleon Bonaparte crossed the Alps in 1796 to invade Italy, he used no faster form of transport than did Hannibal when he crossed the Alps in 218 B.C. to invade Italy, over 2,000 years earlier. Naturally, the speed at which a horse can maintain its momentum depends to a great degree upon the nature of the ground surface along which he pursues his course. It is not surprising, therefore, that for many centuries the traveller in England, as elsewhere, had, owing to the state of the roads, to submit himself to both tedium and hazard. It was equally so for the conveyor of goods by packhorse who, when he could, chose the bridle paths along the river valleys such as those of the Irwell, Irk, Medlock, Roche and Rossendale. Although the stage coach had been introduced in 1640 and the first Turnpike Act had been passed in 1663, little progress was made in road-travel and for commerce the packhorse still bore the brunt of the burden. 'When the Manchester trade began to extend,' recorded Aikin in 1795, 'the chapmen used to keep gangs of packhorses, and accompany them to the principal towns with goods in packs, which they opened and sold to shop-keepers, lodging what was unsold in small stores at the inns.' It has been said that 'the greatest condemnation of the roads was the increasing use made of coastal shipment and river navigation.'[23] It was for this reason that the Mersey and Irwell Navigation, promoted by a company of Manchester and Liverpool merchants in 1736, was the first attempt to utilise what nature had provided for Manchester's outlet to the sea. Thus came into being the wharf at the end of Quay Street, at that time only a lane bordered by fields, at which ships of up to fifty tons could dock and ply between Manchester and Liverpool. At the other end of the town the mail coach from London arrived at the Bull's Head Inn three times a week, on Mondays, Thursdays and Saturdays. It had taken that coach four-and-a-half days to reach Manchester and it had probably travelled along the turnpike road through Buxton, Chapel-en-le-Frith and Stockport, described in the Act of 1724 as 'the nearest road from London to Manchester'.[24] The town's first

Post Office was lodged at the Bull's Head Inn and the public was advised 'to Bring the Letters the night Before the going out of the Post because the accounts and Bags are usually made up overnight.'[25]

By the middle of the eighteenth century the increasing demands of industry produced the impetus to transport changes and began what has been termed the 'Transport Revolution'. Due to the enterprise of John Palmer, who introduced in 1784 new mail coaches for passengers, with far greater regularity and swiftness than their predecessors, the innovations of John Metcalfe ('Blind Jack of Knaresborough'), who was responsible for turnpiking many of the roads in Lancashire and Yorkshire, followed later by the even more expert road-making and bridge-building of Thomas Telford and John McAdam, road, and consequently coach, transport improved. By 1800 the main roads out of Manchester to Stretford, Wilmslow, Stockport, Ashton, Oldham, Bury, Bolton and Wigan had been turnpiked. In 1816, Joseph Aston proudly wrote:

'In the year 1754, a Flying Coach was advertised, and boasted, that "However incredible it may appear, this coach will actually (barring accidents) arrive in London in four days and a half, after leaving Manchester"!! The mail coaches now constantly travel that distance in thirty hours; and on several occasions, when Bonaparte was tottering to his ruin, and on the news of the terminating battle of Waterloo, the Traveller, the Defiance, and the Telegraph coaches came down in eighteen hours!'[26]

For all these achievements of turnpikes and coach travel, the real revolution in transport was the advent of canals, chiefly intended to move the heavy, bulky goods with which road transport at that time could not cope either effectively or cheaply. Although Berry's Sankey Brook Navigation, mainly built by 1757, may claim the distinction of being England's first modern canal, it was the dual rôle of the Duke of Bridgewater's Canal, from Worsley to Manchester for the transport of coal and from Manchester to Runcorn and the sea for general goods and passengers, which fired the imagination of the age and started a revolution in canal construction. By 1804, Manchester was linked by means of other canals to Rochdale, Ashton-under-Lyne, Oldham, Bury and Bolton, all of which gave further access to Yorkshire and the Midlands. By 1830, few places in England were more than ten miles from navigable water. The 'Canal Age' had arrived and the canals of England became 'the lifeline of the Industrial Revolution',[27] and remained so until the 1850s. By then, however, steam, which had earlier broadened the bounds of location for mills and factories in the wider valleys where Bolton, Bury, Rochdale and Oldham are situated, had also directed the transport revolution into new channels. Before it impelled ships across the oceans of the world, it provided a new and spectacular means of transport for the land—the railway. It is again significant that the first steam-drawn passenger railway in the world had its original terminus within what is now the Greater Manchester County, namely Liverpool Road Station, Manchester. Further, it was Manchester merchants who in 1824 strongly supported the issue of the first prospectus for the promotion of a 'Liverpool and Manchester Railroad Company', which was naturally hotly contested by the canal companies and the wealthy landowners. During the years from 1800 to 1820 industry and trade had been expanding rapidly in the Manchester area, but the transport of raw cotton to the mills from the Port of Liverpool was causing serious problems. Not only were the canal-owners charging increasingly high rates for conveyance and the Port of Liverpool exorbitant harbour dues, but the delivery of raw cotton to the Manchester manufacturers was taking over a fortnight. Fortunately, Parliament sanctioned the construction of the railway in 1826 and the following year the colossal undertaking of the construction of a permanent way began. On 15 September 1830, the first steam-driven passenger train in the world entered Liverpool Road Station, Manchester, to the shouts of 'No Corn Laws' and 'Vote by Ballot' from the mechanics and artisans present. This famous station, almost unaltered, is still there, and one hopes it will remain for all to see as one of the historic monuments of the early railway system which radiated from Manchester to the towns and villages of what is now the Metropolitan County.

One of the great advantages of the greatly improved facilities of communication afforded by road, canal and railway at this time was the decentralisation of manufactures. As Faucher put it, 'a factory may now be established close to a coal mine, or by a canal, which shall convey to it fuel, without losing the advantages of proximity, to a great market . . . Distance is daily becoming cancelled, and the economy of time is everywhere facilitated.' But more than this: 'There is therefore no longer any reason for struggling for a few feet of land in the midst of some filthy purlieu, and at the risk of the general health.'[28] Most of all: 'Manchester, like a diligent spider, is placed in the centre of the web, and sends forth roads and railways towards its auxiliaries, formerly villages, but now towns, which serve as outposts to the grand centre of industry.'[29]

Are the canals of the Metropolitan County, still there for all to meditate upon their invaluable contribution to this region throughout the Industrial Revolution, condemned to a moribund existence? For nearly a century, their gaily-coloured boats daily conveyed the merchandise of the 'First Industrial Society' which obtained thereby great wealth. Today some of these canals are providing recreation and pleasure to many thousands of enthusiasts, young and not so young. So considerable has the rejuvenation of the canals in this happy form of leisure become, that in September 1967 the Minister of Transport presented to Parliament a report entitled *British Waterways: Recreation and Amenity*. In it the Minister announced that it had been decided that more than 1,400 miles of waterways should remain open for pleasure-cruising and that 'the British Waterways Board will be given the new and positive duty of maintaining these waterways to a standard of navigation suitable for powered pleasure craft.' In this 'new charter for the waterways', the Minister has sought to 'encourage voluntary efforts to develop the amenity network of waterways' so as 'to add a restored waterway to the network' if such an occasion arises. That such an occasion should be seen to arise prompted the boys and girls of Audenshaw Grammar School to take the rightful step of forming a Canal Restoration Society with the object of restoring and opening up the Ashton Canal, a member of the famous Cheshire Ring. On 26 April 1974, it was reported that: 'The Minister responsible for Sport, Mr Denis Howell, will officially re-open on May 13 the Lower Peak Forest and Ashton Canals, running from the North-east Cheshire into the heart of Manchester and almost completing the "Cheshire Ring" canal system which enthusiasts have wanted restored for many years.'[30] The report adds, 'in fact, the two canals have been open since April 1', which is the day when the Greater Manchester County came into being. Evidently, more than 100,000 tons of rubbish had to be taken out of the Ashton Canal alone, and much of this was done by volunteers. As the Transport Act of 1968 gives

Members of the Peak Forest Canal Society restoring the Ashton Canal in
September 1968

local authorities the chance to co-operate in improving waterways in their areas, it is to be hoped that the Greater Manchester Council, rich in its heritage of canals which once served the area so vitally and well, may take this opportunity, amid its manifold problems of public transport and recreation, to restore this 'priceless asset' in such a way as to help its citizens, especially the young, to enjoy the waterways and 'help in seeing that they are fully, imaginatively and adventurously used.' In this respect it is good to know that the Council has chosen this important feature of the new County as the subject for its first official venture in historical publication.[31]

Chapter 5

'The very symbol of civilisation'

There is an important facet of Manchester during the Industrial Revolution, in company with its adjoining towns, which is commensurate with its remarkable industrial and commercial expansion. It is the first flowering of cultural activities during this momentous period, which Manchester has never since abandoned. To the literary and historically-minded men such as Dickens, Disraeli and Carlyle it was clearly evident, but much less so, if at all, to the distinguished visitors from Europe and America. A visitor to Manchester from the latter continent in 1825 came to this conclusion:

'The whole community seems to be absorbed in business. The citizens of Manchester, taking them collectively, are not very polished or very hospitable. They are in general uncourteous to strangers. Money seems to be their idol, the god they adore, and in worshipping their deity they devote but a small portion of their time to those liberal pursuits which expand the mind.'[1]

In view of these forthright strictures, one wonders which particular Mancunians this American businessman met. Alexis de Tocqueville, the French liberal aristocrat of the early nineteenth century who was attracted by the new forces making for democracy in America and Britain, described his impressions of the Manchester he saw, in 1835, in this way:

'The footsteps of a busy crowd, the crunching wheels of machinery, the shriek of steam from boilers, the regular beat of the looms, the heavy rumbles of carts, those are the noises from which you can never escape in the sombre half-light of these streets. You will never hear the clatter of hoofs as the rich man drives back home or out on expeditions of pleasure. Never the gay shouts of people amusing themselves, or music heralding a holiday.'[2]

Is this Gallic view a misguided exaggeration influenced by the prevalent over-emphasis on the evils of the industrial revolution, or was it a timely criticism in that the people of Manchester were so bound up with industrial and commercial enterprises that they had neither the time nor inclination to enjoy the pursuit of culture? A compatriot of de Tocqueville, who visited Manchester some ten years later, supported him in his criticism: 'Manchester has a Statistical Society; and chemistry is held in honour; but literature and the arts are a dead letter.'[3]

Faucher's translator made this comment on this particular censure:

'The almost exclusive occupation of the inhabitants of Manchester, in manufacturing and commercial pursuits, is unfavourable to the cultivation of those branches of literature and of the arts which require leisure, and retired studious habits ... But, although Manchester society may not be fitted to produce or cherish the development of this class of talent, it is not slow to appreciate it and to patronize it. There are few communities in the world which are more emphatically reading communities, than those of Manchester and the manufacturing districts ... Its literary institutions are numerous, and possessed of extensive modern libraries.'[4]

There is clearly a problem here to solve for those who wish to assess and appreciate the ethos of Manchester and its neighbouring towns and villages during the period of the Industrial Revolution. Is engagement in the occupations of industry and commerce antipathetic to the pursuit of culture? Matthew Arnold had strong views on this subject:

'If culture consists in becoming something rather than in having something ... it is clear that culture has a very important function to fulfil for mankind. And this function is particularly important in our modern world, of which the whole civilisation is, to a much greater degree than the civilisation of Greece and Rome, mechanical and external, and tends constantly to become more so ... Faith in machinery is our besetting danger; often in machinery most absurdly disproportioned to the end which this machinery is to serve ... And thus culture begets a dissatisfaction which is of the highest possible value in stemming the common tide of men's thoughts in a wealthy and industrial community ...'[5]

Shortly after Arnold embarked upon his long and distinguished career as one of Her Majesty's Inspectors of Schools, a group of influential citizens of Manchester held a meeting under civic auspices in 1856 to consider a proposal, made to them by the Prince Consort, that Manchester should hold an exhibition of art treasures designed to complement the successful Crystal Palace Exhibition (1851) at which the gifts of science and technology were displayed to the civilised world. A guarantee fund, to which ninety-two Manchester men of commerce speedily contributed over £62,000, enabled the organisers to erect within ten months on a site at Old Trafford a great exhibition hall of corrugated iron and glass in close proximity to the new railway station. Into this hall and other buildings were placed over 2,000 paintings by old and modern masters, and nearly 1,000 water-colours, and sections were devoted to drawings, engravings, photographs, sculptures and architectural drawings. In addition, there were 10,000 examples of the 'ornamental' arts—furniture, ceramics, glass, metalwork, ivories, enamels, arms and armour. Altogether 16,000 objects of art were borrowed from private collections throughout the United Kingdom. It was not only a triumph of organisation and local enterprise, it was also a unique demonstration of the artistic wealth on the walls and in the precincts of British palaces, castles and mansions, which had been garnered during the Grand Tours of Europe since the eighteenth century.

This largest single exhibition of artistic treasures that the world had known was officially opened by the Prince Consort on 5 May 1857 and was visited by Queen Victoria and other royal personages. The exhibition remained open for nearly six months, during which time it was seen by over 1,300,000 visitors from all over Great Britain. For the majority of these, from Lancashire, Yorkshire and the Midlands, 349 special railway excursions were run. Mr Charles Hallé was engaged by the Executive Committee of the Exhibition to conduct daily the augmented Gentlemen's Concert Orchestra which, under its patronage, gave its first concert on 22 October of that year in the Free Trade Hall—a harbinger for its future. The total cost of this outstanding artistic achievement of Victorian Manchester was just over £110,000, which was entirely covered by the receipts—no doubt a source of pride and satisfaction to the Mancunian.

In 1957 the City of Manchester Art Gallery presented a most attractive exhibition of 'European Old Masters' to celebrate the

Manchester Art Treasures Exhibition, 1857

centenary of this great Art Treasures Exhibition without in any way attempting to emulate it. Indeed, it could not have done so for, as the Director, S. D. Cleveland, reported, 'The centenary is significant as a reminder, not only of a great exhibition of artistic wealth but also, more forcibly, of the impoverishment and irreplaceable losses to collectors overseas which have taken place in the last 100 years.'[6] Thus, as a timely reflection on the modern position of the artistic heritage of the nation, 'a series of pictures has been got together of a standard which it is hoped will be thought worthy to celebrate the achievement of our nineteenth century forbears.'[7]

What was happening in Manchester during that *annus mirabilis* of the Art Treasures Exhibition at Old Trafford did not go unnoticed. A well-known national journal of that day devoted a long article to 'this great capital of the north of England', containing this significant passage:

'Its smoke may be dense, and its mud may be ultra-muddy; but not any nor all of these things can prevent the image of the great city from rising before us as the very symbol of civilisation ... That commerce has had no unduly materialising influence upon those engaged in it here, that vast building at Old Trafford which rose at their bidding, and whose glorious contents were collected under their auspices, presents sufficient proof.'[8]

As if the reader of the journal may still require further proof, it proceeds to ask: 'And how is this general intelligence and cultivation to be explained?' An important contributory factor was considered to be the founding by public subscription of a free library in a building in Campfield (near the present Opera House in Quay Street) a year before Parliament passed the Public Libraries Act (1850):

'When the question of the free-library system was first discussed, Manchester was one of the first towns to demand the institution; and amid long mean streets stands one of the noblest efforts made in the cause of human culture. Here a large and handsome ground-floor hall is filled with desks and tables devoted to periodical literature; and the poorest wanderer may drop in and acquaint himself with the chief events and great discussions of the day. A staircase, profusely adorned with excellent engravings, leads to a large room containing a library of reference, the valuable books of which are freely handed to any applicant without question or introduction.'

In a noteworthy conclusion, the journal refers to

'a certain completeness in the minds of Manchester, which recognises the mutual dependence of the physical and intellectual nature; its devotion at once to commerce and industry, to science and art; its attention to the requirements of those who can afford to purchase comfort, and the wants of those who have nothing to pay . . . Herein, indeed, in this universality of genius which cares for everything, and overlooks or neglects nothing, lies the great secret of its success.'

Lest it be thought that this was unwarranted praise amounting almost to adulation, albeit from a highly reputable national journal, consider what the worldly and highly intelligent Disraeli had to say about Manchester in his *Coningsby* in 1844. His aristocratic representative of 'The New Generation', meeting a stranger in the coffee-room of his hotel, was asked, 'Pleased with Manchester, I dare say?' to which Coningsby replied, 'I think in the whole course of my life I never saw so much to admire.' With a certain condescension the stranger commented: 'We have all of us a very great respect for Manchester, in course; look upon her as a sort of mother, and all that sort of thing.' Almost innocently Coningsby observed, 'I thought her only fault might be she was too much in advance of the rest of the country', to which the stranger, stung into parochial pride, retorted, 'If you want to see life, go to Stalybridge or Bolton. There's high pressure.'[9] In that conversation are revealed one of the great strengths and, at the same time, one of the great problems for the Greater Manchester Council and its officers. But in the 1840s, Manchester was not a typical city of the Industrial Revolution. Its real interest lies in its individuality and just as much in its cultural as in its industrial and commercial achievements. It has been indicated that the influence of the Industrial Revolution upon art and literature has been hardly explored as yet. In this respect, R. H. Tawney has pointed out that 'we know at present next to nothing of the relations between the artistic achievements of an epoch and the character of its economic life.'[11] In a profoundly interesting study of the relationship

58

between culture and society since the last decades of the eighteenth century, Raymond Williams, well known as a book-reviewer for the *Guardian*, sets out to demonstrate that the idea of culture, and indeed the word itself in its general modern usage, came into being in this country during the period of the Industrial Revolution. Matthew Arnold, who regarded 'the men of culture' as 'the true apostles of equality', placed the highest possible values upon culture as 'that which saves the future, as one may hope, from being vulgarised'. He considered it also as 'a study of perfection . . . in an inward condition of the mind and spirit'. With the rapid changes in society during the Industrial Revolution, the pursuit of culture seemed to offer 'a different and superior social idea' as opposed to that of 'the cash-nexus', so that by the end of the nineteenth century it came to mean 'a whole way of life, material, intellectual and spiritual'.[12] Perhaps this partly explains that delightful description of the German community in Manchester as those who 'mingled Beethoven and Brahms with business in Portland Street'.

But it was not this German community, musical as it was, which initiated the cultivation of the Apollon art in Manchester and its neighbouring towns. Music-making seems to have been an instinctive desire among the natives of this region as early as the days of Shakespeare, when the Manchester Court Leet appointed and maintained an official band of musicians called 'town waits'. According to the Court's Records, their duties were 'to play music at all and every wedding and dinners in this town', and to play 'morning and evening together, according as others have been heretofore accustomed to do'. Thursday (as with the Hallé) seems to have been a special night for music-making in Manchester, when the waits were required 'to play through this town . . . according to the ancient custom'. During the winter (though not, in this respect, as with the Hallé) the waits fulfilled the dual functions of musician and policeman as they were expected to watch over the town 'by their walking and going abroad in the night'. When Bonnie Prince Charlie set out from Scotland in 1745 to claim the English throne, it is said that his supporters in the Manchester region promoted public concerts as a cover for their secret Jacobite meetings. One of them was John Byrom, author of 'Christians, awake'. In about 1770, twenty-four amateur musicians met in a large room in a Market Street tavern to establish the Gentlemen's Concerts Society which, within ten years, had its own concert hall, believed to be the first of its kind in the North. When the Society built a new hall in 1831 (where the Midland Hotel now stands), a London music magazine, called *Harmonicon*, reported that 'the community of Manchester have in fact, and in the opinion of the public at large, been constantly in advance of all other parts of the Kingdom in their musical taste and knowledge.'[13] But not only Manchester. A few years before the young Charles Hallé appeared on the scene, the manufacturing districts of what is now the Greater Manchester County were described as:

'distinguished for the successful cultivation of two pursuits, viz: music and mathematics. And, it is to be observed that of the various styles of music, Sacred music has always enjoyed the especial preference of the working classes. The oratorios of Handel and of Haydn, are as household words, familiar to them from childhood; and no difficulty is ever found in selecting from amongst the factory operatives, choirs capable of doing justice to these immortal compositions.'[14]

This love of song and music was regularly demonstrated in the churches and chapels both of the towns and of the smallest villages of the region. Wigan and Bolton have had a strong musical tradition since the early nineteenth century while Shaw, near Rochdale, was long noted for its excellent choir. In the villages of the Rossendale valley, players used to meet in each other's houses for rehearsals which culminated in the long-awaited performance itself at the anniversary service. Those who have had the good fortune to live in a town such as Rochdale before the Second World War will know well the excitement and friendly gossip which surrounded the Christmas or Easter performance of the Messiah, without which the year would have been bereft of one of its precious jewels. On a larger scale, it has been recorded that in 1843 'the first great meeting of the Lancashire and Cheshire Workmen's Singing Classes was held in the Free Trade Hall on 10th June', when there were '1,500 performers, led by Mr John Hullah, inventor of the system'.[15] It is an interesting indication of the value placed upon the function of vocal music in the towns and villages of the region that the sponsors of these singing classes were motivated by 'the very general desire amongst the humbler classes to enjoy musical entertainment' away from 'the dangerous associations of the dram-shops and musical saloons'.[16] This laudable attempt to rescue music from the gin shops, the proprietors of which were exploiting music to advertise their dens, must have pleased a foreign visitor who noted that 'the games hitherto carried on in these places not being sufficient, the proprietors have added music, dancing and exhibitions, as additional attractions . . .'[17] While one wholly supports the view that, in regard to the working classes of the towns of the region, such as Bolton, Rochdale, Oldham, Bury and Stockport, 'music was in the soul of the people' in the 1840s, 'sweetening the toil of the day',[18] much would seem to depend upon the location and circumstances in which it was being practised. This would explain why the Mechanic's Institute movement, backed by many prominent industrialists in the region, enlarged its provisions for 'the instruction of the working classes in the principles of the arts they practise' to include classes for vocal music and even 'concerts of a superior character', both vocal and instrumental.[19]

The latter form found its supreme expression in the brass band. In the mid-nineteenth century a veritable fever of 'sounding brass and tinkling cymbals' swept the Manchester region. Locally, keen rivalry arose between the towns, such as one witnesses today among professional soccer teams, but without their regrettable incidents. Nationally the grand contest of brass bands started in 1900 at the Crystal Palace. One of the earliest examples of the appeal of sounding brass was at Stalybridge, where in 1815 a band performed at the pace-egging festival just before Easter and was engaged to play at foundation-stone ceremonies. It was even invited to provide music for Orator Hunt on St Peter's Field but had the good fortune to withdraw before the trouble started.[20] One of the earliest examples of local pride in their band was that of the villagers of Whitefield, near Bury, in their Besses O' Th' Barn Band, of whom it has been recorded: '. . . for years past this has been their idol; their one source of bliss and gratification. The intense interest displayed at times being such that it would seem as though their whole life and its future existence depended on the success of their band.'[21]

When the brass band contests were inaugurated at Belle Vue in 1852, there were to be found among the eight competitors names which were almost hallowed in the homes of the artisans of the towns and villages which are now embraced within the Greater Manchester County: Bury Borough Band, Saddleworth Band, Newton Bank Print Works Band of Hyde, and Mossley

R. Grounds. J. Bell.   W. Bogle. G. Pollitt. J. Lownds.   R. Jackson. B. Livesey. W. Jackson. P. Booth. J. N. Hampson. J. Briggs. E. Eastwood.
E. Bleakley.   F. Barlow.   J. Chadwick.   E. Taylor.   P. Lighthowne.   A. Bleakley.

J. Hilton.   A. Dawson.   W. Lawson.   A. Owen.   F. Entwistle. R. Eastwood.   T. Hampson.   J. F. Carter   F. Durham.

Besses O' Th' Barn Old Band, established in 1823

Temperance Band. Among the famous ensembles at the end of the century were Baxendale's Works Band of Manchester, Eccles Borough Band, Milnrow Public Band, Bolton Victoria Hall Band, Oldham Rifles Band, and The Crooke Band, near Wigan. Large contests were held from time to time at the Pomona Gardens in Salford, at which the sum of £50 was awarded to the winners of the first prize.[22] These, and other, bands numbered their enthusiasts by the thousands, for whom they became important not only in the development of their musical taste but also in the widening of their social contacts. Employers themselves gradually became aware of the potentialities of the movement and wholeheartedly entered into the formation of a works' band by buying instruments and providing a room for practice. They saw the movement as a novel kind of advertisement for the products of their factory or mill and, to forward this worthy cause, they offered employment at advantageous terms to a budding musician in order to assist in creating a band which would receive favourable notice, in much the same way as a sporting employer would announce, 'Slubber wanted—left-arm medium-paced bowler preferred'—in order to strengthen the town or village cricket team.

It has been said that 'nothing in the whole gamut of the social life of the lower strata during the nineteenth century can have given so much pleasure, so much mental and spiritual relief, to millions of people as choral singing and the brass band.'[23] To none did this apply more genuinely than to the men and women who toiled 'from early morn till half the night hath flown' in the mills and factories of what is now the Greater Manchester County. Their desire to give expression to their feelings in song and instrumental music in what leisure time they had would seem to have been a natural consequence of the soulless conditions under which they worked. That there was an innate love of music among the folk of the towns and villages surrounding Manchester and in the metropolis itself cannot be doubted. This is why Charles Hallé, despite his initial despair over the standard of performance by the Gentlemen's Concerts Orchestra, and other early setbacks, decided to remain in Manchester 'to accomplish a revolution in fact', as he wryly put it. This is why, when the Arts Treasures Exhibition closed down in October 1857, he seized his opportunity to keep his orchestra together and embark upon weekly concerts during the autumn and winter 'at my own risk and peril'. And this is why, when he gave the first concert with his orchestra in the Free Trade

Hall on a wet Saturday night on 20 January 1858 and there was but a scanty audience, he was not disheartened.

Charles Hallé had already decided to dedicate his great gifts to spreading an appreciation of music to as wide an audience as possible through a deliberate policy of cheap seats, rather than to a society of subscribers drawn from one class. There were certain strong factors which enabled him to undertake with good hope so bold an experiment in Manchester at that time. First, no other town possessed so large a body of resident instrumental musicians; second, it was a wealthy town containing an unusually large proportion of music-loving men of commerce and industry; third, as Hallé himself stated, 'in Manchester I was most kindly received, especially by the German colony, which was prosperous and important'; and fourth, most important of all for his hopes and ideals, there was in the towns and villages surrounding Manchester an artisan class whose love of music, as has been seen, was innate and of long lineage. It may be claimed that the attributes of this artisan class were not peculiar to the region of Manchester. The towns and villages of Yorkshire, for example, were no less devoted to the pleasures of choral singing and brass bands. That may well be so, but what was particularly fortunate for the region of Manchester was the unusual, and possibly unique, combination of all four factors and especially the last two. It was the complementary nature of these two factors in which the potentialities of the native love of music were reinforced and refined by the influential and cultural character of the German community, whose members, it has been said, not only 'helped Manchester to reach out to the markets of the world', but culturally also 'brought the arts of Europe more freely into the life of the city.' Most fortunate of all was the fact that, as the *Manchester Guardian*'s notice of that historic first Hallé Concert stated, 'no other town possesses a resident musician of Mr Hallé's calibre.'[24] It was he who blended these four factors into a harmony which gave the region of Manchester the first permanent professional orchestra in Great Britain. How Sir Charles Hallé selflessly devoted the latter half of his long life in the region of Manchester to 'the art which I profess has been a sort of religion to me all my life' has been eloquently and factually described in a work beautifully published to commemorate the centenary of the Hallé Orchestra, or the ''Allé Band' as it was affectionately known at that time among his artisan supporters.[25] On the day of his funeral in 1895, all the flags in Manchester flew at half-mast and thousands of people from the towns and villages of the region lined the streets from his home at Greenheys to Weaste Cemetery in Salford to bid farewell to their beloved Mancunian. Among the many honours which Hallé received during his life, probably none moved him more than the simple letters of gratitude which he received from the mill and factory workers of the towns and villages around Manchester to whom he had revealed the ineffable beauties of music. Among Hallé's private belongings, his son came across two yards of white flannel, carefully folded and preserved, which a grateful listener, who simply signed himself 'Operative', had sent the great conductor in 1873 as a 'small token' of his appreciation of 'such a display of talent'. In that small but evocative incident lies the quintessence of the new Greater Manchester County, provided it remains faithful and true to its historical character.

How Gustav Behrens, member of the shipping house of Sir Jacob Behrens and Sons in Chepstow Street, and firm friend of Charles Hallé, knowing well the responsibility which wealth entails, resolved that the Hallé Orchestra should remain intact and the concerts continue; how he, with the loyal support of Henry Simon, founder of the Simon Engineering Group at Cheadle Heath, and James Forsyth, Hallé's business manager, ultimately secured the services of Dr Hans Richter, acknowledged as the world's greatest conductor and at that time in charge of the Vienna Opera, is a fascinating demonstration of Gustav Behrens' conviction that 'only the best is good enough for Manchester.'[26] It took him four years of patient and dogged diplomacy to bring Richter to his beloved city as conductor of the Hallé Orchestra, now under the control and ownership of the Hallé Concerts Society, founded in 1899. How, at the end of the period of transition from the days of privilege to the dawning of the Welfare State, the Hallé Concerts Society resolved to meet the growing challenge of a great new public, musically brought into being by the wireless and an enlightened municipal education, by placing the orchestra on a full-time basis with a permanent conductor and thereby 'putting the Hallé on top where it used to be and where it rightly belongs', as Philip Godlee, Chairman of its Committee, forthrightly stated, is the exciting prelude to the Golden Age of Barbirolli.[27] From the very start, this conductor was inspired by what he regarded as 'a very great mission—that the name and fame of this great orchestra shall not, under my guidance, achieve less honour in the future than it has done in the past.'[28] Sir John Barbirolli honoured these words to the end of his life and was supported wholeheartedly by his faithful audience, especially in his home-based region. 'In Manchester,' he once said, 'I have found an audience willing to walk hand-in-hand with me and explore great music. The wonderful new audience we have built at Belle Vue is of my own class, the lower middle class. The way they have turned out in snow and fog has mattered to me a great deal.' It would have been interesting to have analysed where the members of those great Belle Vue audiences, each of 6,000 capacity, came from in those thrilling days for the Hallé; there can be little doubt that a large proportion would be found to have come in their local coaches, as for a brass band festival, from Oldham, Bolton, Bury, Rochdale, Ashton, Stalybridge, Stockport and other towns and villages of what today is Greater Manchester. Indeed, one of the great fruits of the reign of Barbirolli has been the building-up of financial support, large and small, from the local authorities of the surrounding area. During the financial year 1971/72 as many as forty-eight local authorities now within the Greater Manchester County contributed to the Lancashire and Cheshire Local Authorities' Scheme which the Hallé shared with the Royal Liverpool Philharmonic Orchestra.

It is not without significance that when the leading Manchester architect of the mid-nineteenth century, Edward Walters, designed the Free Trade Hall, he placed in the spandrels between the nine ground-floor arches the coats-of-arms of neighbouring towns— Liverpool, Rochdale, Oldham, Bolton, Stockport, Ashton-under-Lyne and Wigan, with those of Manchester and Salford in the centre. Apart from Liverpool, which has shared with the Hallé the contributions of the Local Authorities' Scheme, these towns hold a leading position in eight of the Districts of the Greater Manchester County. When, almost a century later, the City Architect of Manchester designed the restoration and re-planning of the old Hall, he decided to include for display on the upper panels of the main walls above the Side Circles the coats-of-arms in full colours of the following neighbouring towns—Salford, Stockport, Bolton, Oldham, Rochdale, Bury, Stretford, Sale and Ashton-under-Lyne, while the City of Manchester coat-of-arms was displayed in full colours as the central feature of the wall behind the platform. Thus, of the ten Districts of the new County, only that of Wigan is unfortunately unrepresented. Here, then, in the old and the new

66

Halls, has been incorporated in heraldic form the clear recognition not only of the regional function of the Free Trade Hall but also of the ten major towns which form the foundations of the Greater Manchester County. It is good to know that the ancient device of chivalry has heralded the basic structure of the new County.

What has drawn these Lancashire folk, young and old, to the Hallé Orchestra, to claim it as their own when it comes within reasonable distance of their homes? One thing is clear from the Local Authorities' Scheme—that the Hallé may be Manchester-based but it is regionally owned. What drew Barbirolli from rich and safe New York to war-engulfed Manchester and induced him, in spite of all temptations, to remain a Mancunian for the rest of his life, as it did Adolph Brodsky who came from Berlin in 1895 to lead the Hallé Orchestra for a year's trial to see how he liked it and stayed until his death in 1929? Perhaps Paul Hindemith, the eminent composer, found the answer when, after conducting the Hallé for the first time in his life in 1958, he remarked, 'I had only been working with them for two minutes when I knew: "Here are musicians with a background, a strongly rooted cultural tradition."' [29] A Hallé concert today is still a powerful example of tradition in action. The orchestra has only a few players who were there when Barbirolli announced his mission at that first concert under his baton at Bradford in 1943; yet the same warmth and friendly atmosphere, the same natural enthusiasm and northern character are there. It attracts audiences to its Manchester concerts which have an average level of 93% Free Trade Hall capacity (some 2,500).[30] One wonders what Hallé, Richter, Hamilton Harty, Beecham and Barbirolli think of the multitude of youngsters, from all parts of the Manchester region, as they look upon them from the walls of the main foyer of the Free Trade Hall. It is fitting that the Greater Manchester Council has now assumed responsibility for the major financial grant of the former local authorities' contributions, for the Hallé, with its great international reputation and its proud position as the fourth oldest orchestra in the world, yet remains the same homespun Hallé, as securely woven into the texture of the Greater Manchester community as are 'City' and 'United' and the other great soccer teams of the region, and as is Lancashire cricket at Old Trafford.

Within eight years of the final closing of the doors of the Art Treasures Exhibition, another great art established its home at Old Trafford, and this time permanently. Before attaining county status, Manchester Cricket Club was at Stretford and participated in the summer game with many other clubs of Lancashire and Cheshire. When the Lancashire County Cricket Club was formed in 1864—the year when Wisden published his first Cricketers' Almanac—the Manchester Club's ground at Old Trafford became its headquarters. Its first official county match took place on three days in July 1865 when there was a small gathering of enthusiasts, much as there is today, to watch Middlesex play the home team, who defeated the southerners by sixty-two runs. For the first twenty years the Lancashire club was led by one of its greatest amateurs, A. N. Hornby, partnered by a great professional, R. G. Barlow, who, as a Bolton schoolboy, used to practise with a bat hewn from a chunk of wood while the ball was pieced together with cloth and string. These two stalwarts were the heroes of the Old Trafford crowd, among whom was a medical student from Owens College who, escaping from his studies, gloried in the cricketing days in the sun. Years later, Francis Thompson wrote wistfully of those happy days at Old Trafford:

'And a ghostly batsman plays to the bowling of a ghost,
And I look through my tears at a soundless-clapping host
As the run-stealers flicker to and fro.
O my Hornby and my Barlow long ago!'

When Gloucestershire first visited the ground in 1878, a crowd of 20,000 came on the Saturday to see W. G. Grace. Some came by carriage, others on horseback, while those who alighted at Old Trafford station used a path through the fields. Among them were the supporters of the more democratic, but keenly competitive, clubs which, fourteen years later, came to form the backbone of the Central Lancashire Cricket League when it was founded in 1892. Yorkshire, then as now, were the great rivals. One can imagine the scene at Old Trafford in 1875 when Yorkshire set Lancashire in their second innings to score 146, all of which were wiped off by Hornby and Barlow without fall of a wicket. It has been said that when the Battle of the Roses starts at Old Trafford or Headingley, the players greet each other with 'Good morning' and thereafter say only 'How's that?' for three days. But the atmosphere is not always like that at Old Trafford. The pervading spirit of the place is hospitable and warm, while the shrewd Lancashire wit has often relieved a moment of tension. When Warwick Armstrong, captain of the formidable Australian team of 1921, sat his twenty-two stone bulk on the Old Trafford pitch by way of protest at some incident in play, he was invited by a local spectator to 'give the pitch a roll'! It is in this spirit that one delights in reading the Lancashire County Cricket Club's Centenary Brochure.[31]

But for down-to-earth and hard-hitting cricket one needs to be present at one of the Saturday afternoon matches of the local clubs whose grounds are situated in the towns and villages of Lancashire and Cheshire. There are in all some fifty-six Leagues, which regulate and control the fixtures of these clubs, many of which are associated with a church or chapel, a mill or factory. The players are amateurs, but some of the wealthy and old-established clubs engage a well-known professional. In pre-war days Rochdale had Cecil Parkin, the famous England and Lancashire medium-fast bowler and a comedian much loved by the crowd, while Nelson, reputed to be the richest cricket club in England, brought Learie Constantine from the West Indies, who so distinguished himself in club and Imperial cricket that he opened up for himself a notable career in diplomacy and a place in the peerage. Naturally the professional, by his prowess with bat and ball, is expected to draw the crowd who pay to enter the ground in order to see their home team trounce the visitors from the neighbouring town. There is no place for a chivalrous knock-about here and 'may the best team win'. Theirs *is* the best team and it must prove itself so. That is why the amateurs must not leave all the glory (and a round-the-ground collection) solely to the professional. They want their 'talent money' too, for a good performance and a continuing place in the team. These Lancashire club matches are not, and never have been, urbane social gatherings; they are hard-fought contests not only between rival teams but between rival towns, each with its closely-knit community. These intrinsic qualities, with their savour of unceasing conflict, are probably most clearly in evidence in the Central Lancashire Cricket League. Founded in 1892, this League contains fourteen clubs all of which now reside within the Greater Manchester County. They were all playing clubs when the League was formed and over half of them were well established before the Lancashire County Cricket Club came into being. Their very names are reminiscent of the days of the handloom weaver.[32]

Rochdale	(1824)	Littleborough	(1859)
Oldham	(1852)	Werneth	(1864)
Middleton	(1852)	Crompton	(1865)
Stockport	(1855)	Royton	(1868)
Milnrow	(1856)	Heywood	(1892)
Ashton	(1857)	Radcliffe	(1892)
Castleton Moor	(1857)	Walsden	(1892)

There are three old-established clubs of the Metropolitan County in the Lancashire and Cheshire Cricket League—Swinton (1862), Thornham (1868) and Stalybridge (1879)—while Wigan, founded in 1848, has its place in the Manchester and District Cricket Association, which contains in all thirty-nine clubs, most of which are now within the Metropolitan County. Some of the larger towns have their own District Leagues as, for example, Rochdale and District Cricket League containing sixteen clubs, some of which are works clubs (e.g. Turner Brothers Asbestos Company); Oldham and District Cricket Alliance; Denton and District Cricket League with four chapel clubs—Levenshulme Wesley Fellowship, Springhead Congregational, Stalybridge St Paul's & Stalybridge Unitarians; Bolton and District Cricket Association with a First and Second Division. The South Lancashire Cricket League, founded in 1904, comprises twenty-six clubs, most of which belong to well-known works—Avro, Chloride, C.W.S., Fairey Engineering, Ferranti, Hans Renold Social Union, Massey-Ferguson, Mather and Platt, Norwest Gas, Prestwich Hospital and Watneys.

One of the most illuminating features of some of the Leagues is the inclusion of clubs representing a resident immigrant community. The Bolton Association has two clubs, the Bolton Indians and the Bolton West Indians, founded in 1966 and 1965 respectively; the Denton League also has two based on Ashton, called Aazad and Bharat. No doubt these and other clubs of the immigrant communities, whose welcome presence in the towns of the Metropolitan County plays an important rôle in a later chapter, have contributed a richness of colour and a variety of cricket to the life of the clubs and equally have assimilated the serious business of the game which is the hall-mark of the Leagues. Not for them 'a

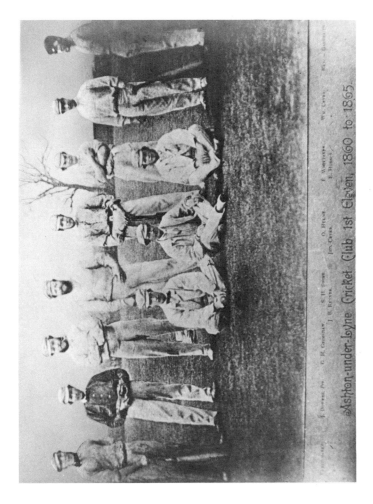

Eleven proud cricketers pose for a very early photograph

team of splendid sporting chaps', but 'eleven lads who enjoy a good fight' as the Yorkshireman, Brian Close, once defined 'what cricket really needs'.[33] Herein lies a great and venerable tradition of cricket natively moulded for the Greater Manchester County. Its Council would do well to note the reciprocal nature of the relationship between the County Cricket Club and those of the towns and villages in their Leagues. While Old Trafford was important to the League Clubs, they in turn were equally important to Old Trafford.

Chapter 6

'Towards the creation of an educated and happy democracy'

If the purpose of the theatre is to act as a mirror of life, then for the early evidence of drama and spectacle in the region of Manchester 'we see through a glass darkly'. Unfortunately, there is now no trace of the medieval mystery or miracle plays which were probably enacted in at least some of the towns of the Metropolitan County. The nearest evidence is at Chester where in 1951 the Cheshire Community Council presented an abridged form of the original twenty-four plays of the Medieval Cycle. A more homely revival was that of a mumming play for pace-eggers (pace = pascha, meaning Easter, as in paschal) entitled *The Play of St George, The Knights and The Dragon*.[1] The text of this play comprises extracts from eleven 'old-time' mummers' plays performed in various parts of Great Britain. Before the War, the boys of Rochdale Grammar School presented the play annually, with suitable gusto, just before Easter both on the old Market Place and in the Town Hall. It is good to record that, when in 1965 the Balderstone Upper School replaced the Grammar School, it resolved to continue this local tradition by a series of performances in various parts of the town, culminating in the magnificent Town Hall Square of Rochdale. It is said that bands of young children still perform 'regularly, but carelessly' a much abridged version of the pace-egg play in the streets of the town, introducing by tradition an extra character called 'Dirty Bet' who, in the form of a bedraggled old woman, winds up the play in Shakespearean fashion with the appropriate couplet.

The first local play-bill advertising organised entertainment on the public stage in Manchester is that relating to *The Recruiting Officer*—a play performed about 1743 at the Exchange in the Market Square.[2] The first public announcement of a new theatre in Manchester appeared in 1753, when reference was made to 'the theatre at the Upper end of King Street'.[3] It was usually called the Marsden Street Theatre, at which dramatic performances provided by provincial touring companies alternated with cockfighting, the popular sport of the day for both the gentry and the working-classes.[4] By the 1760s theatrical companies from Dublin and London were performing in the Riding School at Salford and in Hill-gate, Stockport. Evidently at this time Salford was theatrically ahead of Manchester, for it erected in 1761 what came to be called Blackfriars Bridge, to encourage playgoers from the Manchester side of the Irwell.[5] When the Marsden Street Theatre finally closed its doors in May 1775 with its last two performances of *The Bold Stroke for a Wife* and *High Life below Stairs*, the first of the Theatre Royals, situated at the junction of Spring Gardens and York Street, was opened. The atmosphere of this theatre has been described by a German resident as 'graceful, warm and comfortable and the scenes, curtains and effect-machines very good indeed. The gallery is here, as everywhere in England, unbearably unashamed; they throw apples, pomegranates, nut-shells on the stage, in the pit and in the boxes; they cry out and make a lot of noise.' This lively description ends with a timeless comment on theatre audiences: 'Of battles and murders are they especially fond.'[6]

By the end of the eighteenth century, just before the second Theatre Royal was built in Fountain Street, some towns in the Manchester region, such as Rochdale, Wigan and Stockport, had established their own theatres. In Rochdale the first theatre was established in 1790 in a vacated Wesleyan chapel in Toad Lane. Some of the famous artistes of their day, such as the Kembles, Miss Farren, and Grimaldi, probably the greatest English clown, performed at this theatre, which was greatly patronised by the gentry of the district.[7] When the third Theatre Royal in Peter Street, Manchester, first opened its doors in 1845, it must have provided a colourful and romantic scene, with its five great gas chandeliers, to those who entered its auditorium. Yet the year before, Léon Faucher had written in most disparaging terms of the reputation of the theatre in the Manchester region: 'The theatre does nothing to purify and elevate the taste, and furnishes little but what is necessary to attract the crowd habituated to gross pursuits.'[8] Even his liberal-minded translator supports him: 'Yet, after all, the theatre in its present state cannot be defended as a moral institution. It might be worse, certainly, but is still bad ... The more moral portion of the community, therefore, shun it, and wisely so, as fraught with immoral tendencies.' Whether members of the working class in the region were in a position to frequent the theatre (a seat in the gallery cost one shilling at that time) may be judged, with certain possible reservations, by what another very knowledgeable contemporary had to say: 'At present the entire labouring population of Manchester is without any season of recreation and

74

is ignorant of all amusements excepting that very small portion which frequents the theatre'[9]—an estimate which probably applied even more rigorously to the towns in the region of Manchester.

By this time, pantomime had become closely associated with Christmas and thirty years later assumed the entire presentation of an evening's performance. While in Manchester three separate productions could be seen, towns in the region, such as Oldham and Bolton, had their own resident pantomimes. No doubt, the presence of Charles Dickens, who appeared in two performances in the Free Trade Hall of Wilkie Collins' drama, *The Frozen Deep*, at which afterwards the author spoke of 'the extraordinary intelligence and enthusiasm of the great audience', and likewise, the presence of the young Henry Irving at the Theatre Royal in 1860 in a notable season of Shakespeare's plays, when he found that both audience and critics were 'more discriminating and consequently more severe' than any he had known, are an eloquent testimony to the rising artistic standards in the Manchester theatre on both sides of the footlights. In the last decade of the century, the new revolutionary drama of Ibsen and Shaw prompted the forming of an Independent Theatre Committee and even the prospect of an endowed theatre in Manchester—an excellent, but sad, example of hope still deferred.

It was a wealthy London-born producer who brought to Manchester its brief but most fruitful golden age of drama. When Miss Horniman was in Dublin, helping the Irish Players to establish the Abbey Theatre in that attractive city, she began to realise the wide possibilities of a drama rooted in local customs and beliefs, expressed in the homely idiom of its own soil. She came over to Manchester and in September 1907, started her own company in the Gentlemen's Concert Hall in the Midland Hotel. The following spring, she bought the old Comedy Theatre in Peter Street; the theatre had been built in 1884 by the Salford-born architect and actor, Alfred Darbyshire, who had once played Polonius to the Hamlet of Henry Irving in the theatre at Bury.[10] Renaming her theatre 'The Gaiety', Miss Horniman resolved to revive the impact of drama upon the region of Manchester by adopting the repertory system so that quick and regular changes of programme would give scope to new authors, especially regional authors, and would prepare for them an informed audience instructed in the most important developments of contemporary drama. Equipped with a permanent stock company of producer and players who were prepared to settle in Manchester in their own theatre, she conspired to establish a Lancashire school of dramatists: 'If Lancashire playwrights will send their plays to me I shall pledge myself to read them through. Let them write . . . about their friends and enemies—about real life.' They did, both nationally and locally. The plays of Shaw, Masefield, St John Ervine and Barrie were soon in her repertoire. Most popular of all was John Galsworthy, whose plays on the social and industrial problems of the day, such as *The Silver Box* and *Strife*, had an immediate impact upon the Gaiety audiences. Equally, the plays of Allan Monkhouse, Stanley Houghton, Harold Brighouse and the theatre's first protégé, Charles McEvoy, laid the foundation of the Manchester School of Drama with its native, earthy flavour— the 'kitchen sink' of its day, every bit as strong and compelling as John Osborne's plays fifty years later. Her players, led by a Manchester man, Iden Payne, included young, dedicated artistes such as Mona Limerick, Sybil Thorndike, Lewis Casson and Basil Dean.

Probably the secret of Miss Horniman's success in these all-too-brief years was the sense of purpose which she inspired in her players. As one said: 'We were most of us young, we received enough to live on and we felt to be doing something that mattered.' It certainly mattered, for what Miss Horniman and her players did was not only to establish the first repertory theatre in Great Britain, but also to create among the working classes of the cotton towns surrounding Manchester a new body of enthusiasts for drama. A young Bolton mill-girl of the period has vividly described in later life what the Gaiety Theatre meant to her and her companions:

'These shaping years also included the gay, gracious days of Miss Horniman's reign at the Gaiety Theatre, Manchester. As a member of a group of young socialists I hoarded my scanty pocket-money, amounting at that time to one penny in the shilling of factory earnings, so that I could afford with them the luxury of a monthly matinée. With a cheap seat in pit or gallery we saw most of the early Shaw and Galsworthy plays, followed by tea in the Clarion Café in Market Street. If the café was crowded, we hived off to the Art Gallery and over tea, brown bread, peaches and cream we animatedly argued and discussed

the philosophy, art or satire of the productions. The whole out-
ing cost about five shillings each, but we returned home like
exultant young gods, tingling and a-thirst with the naïve faith
that if only sufficient human beings could witness good drama
and comedy it might change the world. In those days
Manchester seemed the mecca and home of culture.'[11]

Alice Foley's concluding thoughts must have been echoed by many
a young devotee of the Gaiety in those halcyon years of great and
inspiring drama not only for Mancunians but also for those of the
neighbouring towns who, like her, were wise enough to hoard their
scanty pocket money for a visit to Miss Horniman's theatre. It has
been said by someone more elevated in academic circles that 'to
live in Manchester from 1908 to 1914 was to feel oneself—and perhaps to feel oneself a little too self-consciously—in the very workshop of the new drama.'[12]

Although, in due course, all England had seen Miss Horniman's
Gaiety players, who visited London annually and had twice toured
Canada and the United States, eventually her great theatrical
enterprise became 'a casualty of Manchester's withdrawal into
Cheshire'.[13] In 1921 Miss Horniman gave up her attempts to
finance the Gaiety which, as a result, 'passed into the darkness of a
picture house.'[14] Even that has gone now and in its place stands
what Dame Sybil Thorndike, with supreme contempt, once described as 'a block of offices'. But the tradition which Miss
Horniman and her players courageously established and sustained
in Edwardian Manchester now lives on in the repertory theatre
movement, and nowhere more brightly today than in the larger
towns of the Greater Manchester County.

The Library Theatre in Manchester, originally founded in 1934
by the City Libraries Committee for amateur companies and for
lectures, has since 1947, under the direction of a most enterprising
City Librarian, presented offerings of a high, artistic standard by
professional repertory companies. A complementary, alternating
repertory company has now been added at the Forum Theatre in
the newly-built Wythenshawe Civic Centre. One recalls with infi-
nite pleasure the Library Theatre's outstanding production in 1958
of *Hindle Wakes*, especially designed to celebrate the golden jubilee
of Miss Horniman's founding of the repertory theatre. More
recently, the charmingly intimate University Theatre, built in
1965 as part of the facilities of the Manchester University Drama

Department, has opened up promising prospects for adventurous productions in the art of drama. Providing opportunities for theatre-in-the-round or proscenium productions, this comfortable, small theatre has already demonstrated in its plays, both classical and modern, its ability 'to pierce and stun and elevate' its audiences, as Sybil Thorndike characteristically defined the essential function of the live theatre when she officially (and graciously) opened this one. Perhaps its greatest service to the region of Manchester lay in its providing a temporary home for a most promising and exciting theatrical venture, the '69 Company. Founded by a Council of enlightened citizens and a Board of distinguished artistic directors, this Company has presented a season of plays, concerts and recitals—all in a temporary 'wooden O', built on the floor of the Great Hall of the Royal Exchange to accommodate an audience of 450. Now an ingeniously planned and designed permanent structure of multi-coloured steel and glass, with seats for 700, has replaced the temporary auditorium. This complex and highly individual structure is the new home of the Royal Exchange Theatre Company, which has already opened its first full season. With kiosks, a bar, a coffee-bar, a restaurant and art exhibitions in and around the Great Hall, Mr Michael Elliott, the resident artistic director, hopes 'it will buzz with life throughout the day.'

This great, artistic challenge, which would have warmed the hearts of Miss Horniman and her players, is being generously supported financially by the Arts Council of Great Britain, the Greater Manchester Council and the Corporation of Manchester. The promoters have already launched a new appeal in the Greater Manchester region. They are right to do so, for the historical setting to this appeal is both compelling and fascinating. This third Royal Exchange building, until recently known as 'the parliament house of the lords of cotton', is situated on land which was for centuries the scene of Manchester's three-day annual fair. It is conceivable (but not yet proven) that at this fair a local medieval mystery play was performed on Acresfield. What we do know is that for the past century merchants and factors, directly or indirectly concerned with textiles of one sort or another, came in their hundreds from every town of what is now the Greater Manchester County into this Great Hall, especially on 'Change Day, when, it has been recorded, 'they move noiselessly from one part of the room to another guided as if by some hidden instinct to the precise

The Royal Exchange Theatre, opened in September 1976

person in the crowd with whom they have business to transact.'[15] It is most appropriate that this Royal Exchange Theatre Company, in its ambitious and attractive venture for the whole region, should call upon the support, both now and in the future, of the citizens of the Metropolitan County. Those who were fortunate enough to attend *The Three Portraits of Schubert* at the Royal Exchange in January 1974 will not readily forget the extraordinary way in which the artistes, despite (or perhaps because of) the rigours of an economic crisis and the consequent lack of heating, yet created an atmosphere of chamber music worthy of pre-war Vienna. If the successors to the 69 Theatre Company can recreate and maintain that standard, then it augurs well for the future of drama in the Metropolitan County.

In this respect Bolton, with its enterprising Octagon Theatre, has already shown the way. Conscious of the lack in the early 1960s of a professional 'live' theatre, the independently-minded citizens of Bolton set about repairing this serious omission. Within less than twelve months, sufficient funds were raised by public donations and grants from Bolton Corporation, the Arts Council and other interested bodies to enable the Borough Architect to design and have built an intimate modern theatre in a style described by Nikolaus Pevsner as 'neatly and crisply done'. Opened in 1967, the Octagon is claimed to be notable on two counts: it was the first professional theatre to be built in the North-West since the war; and it was the first professional 'flexible' theatre to be built in this country, that is, it was designed so that three different types of stage—theatre in the round, 'thrust stage' and 'open end'—could be used as desired. With its resident professional company, the theatre has presented a wide variety of plays, ranging from Elizabethan to modern and including full-blooded melodrama performed with great gusto. Attracting audiences from a wide area, the Octagon has also been used for jazz sessions, folk-singing concerts and other community events, while its players have both introduced drama into the schools and encouraged staff and pupils to make use of the facilities of the theatre. Altogether the Octagon has become more and more an integral part of the District's social life and, like the Manchester Ship Canal, exemplifies in its private and municipal support the virtues of a 'mixed economy'.

When C. P. Scott, the great editor of the *Manchester Guardian*, once wrote, in a notable leader on the function of a newspaper, that 'comment is free, but facts are sacred', he enunciated a great

The Octagon Theatre, Bolton

truth. To obtain the facts and to find honest comment on them, it is necessary to have free access to information. This is essentially the function of libraries and in them Manchester, on behalf of the region surrounding it, is undoubtedly rich. There are three great libraries in the city and a private library of distinction called The Portico. The earliest, Chetham's Library, was founded in 1653 in accordance with the wishes, expressed in his will, of Humphrey Chetham, a Manchester merchant to whom reference has already been made. Housed in the city's most historic building, this Library is one of the oldest of its kind in Europe and still retains its seventeenth-century furnishings. Today Chetham's is still there, as its Founder desired, 'for the use of Scholars, and others well affected, to resort unto'. It is especially useful for those who wish to study the topography and local history of the north-west of England and, in particular, the older material relating to the towns and villages of the Greater Manchester County.

The second, the Portico Library, arose out of the dissatisfaction of two Manchester businessmen who lamented that there was 'no institution in this large and opulent town, uniting the advantage of a newsroom and library on an extensive and liberal plan.'[16] Eventually such a library was founded by private subscription in 1806 in Mosley Street which at that time consisted of many elegant houses of men important in Manchester society. The Portico, in which the library was, and still is, housed, was designed by Thomas Harrison, the outstanding provincial architect of the eighteenth century. It is claimed to be one of the first Greek Revival buildings in England and has been authoritatively described as 'the most refined little building in Manchester'. Its membership, and particularly its officers, have included many distinguished men. The Library's first Secretary was Peter Mark Roget, who was practising at that time at the Manchester Infirmary. As his *Thesaurus of English Words and Phrases*, begun in 1805 (first published in 1852), arose out of 'a system of verbal classification' which 'might help to supply my own deficiencies',[17] it is likely that some of the early preparation for his well-known book was undertaken at the Portico Library. The first minute-book records 'that Mr Dalton be requested to superintend the going of the clock, and in consideration of his undertaking this office, that he be offered free admission to the rooms and library.' The eminent Manchester scientist evidently fulfilled this appointed duty until his death in 1844. The Chairman of the committee for the whole of that period

The Portico Library in Mosley Street, Manchester, in the 1820s

was the Reverend William Gaskell, of Cross Street Chapel, whose literary wife, commenting upon the Library's rules, once said: 'With a struggle and a fight I can see all Quarterlies 3 months after they are published; until then they lie on the Portico table for gentlemen to see. I think I will go in for Women's Rights', thus anticipating by nearly forty years Emmeline Pankhurst and her movement for women's suffrage in the Manchester region. Since the First World War, conditions for the Portico have not been easy but it still attracts an interesting variety of new members, both professional and commercial, in Manchester and its neighbouring towns of the Metropolitan County.

The great municipal Central Library in St Peter's Square originated from a Free Library founded by public subscription in 1850. With the passing of the Public Libraries and Museums Act in that year, this Library was handed over to the Corporation 'to be thereafter maintained as one of the permanent public institutions of the borough ...'[18] Thus came into being the first rate-supported public lending and reference library in England established under the Act. As one of the largest municipal libraries in Europe, it serves a very wide region and is used each day by over 5,000 people. One of its most valued assets is the Henry Watson Music Library, originally a private collection but owned and administered by the City Libraries Committee since the death of Dr Watson in 1911. One of its important services to the new Metropolitan County is the lending of sets of choral and orchestral music to organisations and societies of its towns and villages. Over ten years ago, the late Mr D. I. Colley, the City Librarian, expressed his convictions in these words:

'Throughout their long history, those who have controlled the libraries of Manchester have always held firmly to the belief that free access to published material is an essential adjunct for a full life, and the continuation of this policy will ensure that the libraries, separately and in co-operation, will continue to make their very considerable contribution to the vitality of the Greater Manchester area and towards the creation of an educated and happy democracy.'[19]

This great truth, and the continuation of this policy for fulfilling it, will be readily endorsed by all Mr Colley's colleagues in the municipal libraries of the Metropolitan County. An indication of the practical value of the Central Library's services to the County is exemplified in a pilot study undertaken professionally at its Commercial Library, in which it was revealed that 'more telephone enquiries come from the area within twenty miles of Manchester (52%) than from the City itself (41%).'[20] In more respects than one, therefore, this great repository of knowledge and of the sources of wisdom, as indicated around the dome of its Great Hall, may well be the Central Library of a great and unitary region, such as the Greater Manchester County undoubtedly is, rather than merely of the city which originally founded and still maintains it.

The most recent, and internationally the most renowned, of these libraries is the John Rylands Library in Deansgate, which was opened for readers on the first day of this century. Born of the wealth of a Manchester merchant, this Library is known to scholars in every land, for it is a priceless treasure-house of books and manuscripts kept and cared for in a beautiful Gothic building. In its Bible Room there are copies of all the earliest and most famous texts and versions of the Bible, and in the Early Printed Book Room there are over 3,000 volumes printed before 1501. The treasures of the Manuscript Department must be seen to be believed. There are records on clay, bark, bamboo, papyrus, parchment and paper representing over fifty different languages and cultures. There are breath-taking examples of Eastern and Western illuminated manuscripts and, perhaps most precious of all, the papyrus fragment of St John's Gospel (dated A.D. 100–150), the earliest known piece of the New Testament written in any language. In July 1972 the Library merged with the University and is now known as the John Rylands University Library of Manchester. As such, it continues to serve the scholars of the Metropolitan County who may wish to use it for purposes of research and reference. In these respects it confers a privilege upon all.

In 1965 Alderman Sir Maurice Pariser proposed to the Manchester City Council a scheme for a new Arts Centre in the Princess Street area, which would contain an opera house, a theatre, a modern cinema and an extension to the City Art Gallery. The scheme was approved in principle, and was supported by the Arts Council, the Minister for the Arts, and the Earl of Harewood, who described it as 'splendid and imaginative'. But a succession of national economic crises has since then entirely frustrated attempts to launch the scheme, and a national reorganisation of local government has taken place. Do the ghosts of Miss Horniman and the Lancashire-born Sir Thomas Beecham haunt the members of the City Council today, for both believed that a wealthy city like Manchester could afford the finest theatre and opera house in Europe? Perhaps the Greater Manchester Council, inspired by the region's long tradition of education and performance in music and the other arts, may one day, in a more propitious economic climate than at present obtains, be in a position to take up again a scheme such as Sir Maurice Pariser so well envisaged. The challenge is there.

Chapter 7

'A state of electric communication of ideas'

Dr Robert Vaughan, a distinguished Congregationalist divine of the mid-nineteenth century, wrote a long treatise in which he set out to show that 'only in urban surroundings is the highest kind of civilisation possible.' To support his argument he appealed to the entire range of recorded history. He was well qualified to do this, for he was appointed in 1834 to the Chair of History at University College, London, and, nine years later, became President and Professor of Theology at Lancashire Independent College in Withington, at that time outside but in close proximity to the newly-created Borough of Manchester. In this important work,[1] Dr Vaughan discusses many factors which impinge upon urban society, such as its relation to science, art and literature, to intelligence, morals and religion. In certain respects, he anticipated the monumental work of Arnold Toynbee,[2] in that he analysed what he described as 'the conflict between feudalism and civilisation in modern society', as exemplified in the attempts of the ruling class in the post-Napoleonic war period to withhold personal and political liberty from the citizens of the rapidly growing manufacturing towns. In this context, he came to the conclusion that 'commercial greatness is the only powerful state of things that can possibly come into the place of military greatness.' In like manner, he may be seen to have anticipated R. H. Tawney who, in a well-known work,[3] demonstrated that there is some connection between the Puritan and the bourgeois virtues. 'The strength of Protestantism', wrote Dr Vaughan, 'is a strength on the side of industry, of human improvement and of the civilisation which leads to the formation of great cities. The genius of Protestantism is the genius of all pacific and manly enterprise. So long as it exists, it must exist as a potent agency in favour of the higher culture of cities.'[4] What particularly irked Dr Vaughan was the facile nature of William Cowper's well-known assumption, 'God made the country, and man made the town', which seemed to him to imply that 'in prosecuting the higher arts which flourish in cities, man is not so much in his place as in attending to the more limited arts which relate to pasturage and cattle.' Vaughan had no doubt that 'man is constituted to realise his destiny from his association with man, more than from any contact with places.' For such a realisation, he requires 'civil freedom which is the result mainly of civil association, and it is in the nature of such freedom to contribute both to intelligence and virtue.' To substantiate his claim that this freedom is used to advantage, at least in the realm of literature and the arts, 'much more among traders and artisans than among farmers and peasants', he cites a speech of John Bright of Rochdale, in which he said:

'I went, the other day, at Edinburgh through the establishment of William and Robert Chambers. The former told us that they sell 60,000 copies weekly of the *Journal*, and that 59,000 of these copies find their way into the manufacturing districts and not more than 1,000 copies are sold in the agricultural districts of Great Britain and Ireland. He said, moreover, that Liverpool, Manchester, and the district of which we are the centre, consume more than half of the 60,000 copies sold; and that Manchester itself reads more of Chambers' *Journal* than the whole population of Ireland.'[5]

If it is true, as Dr Vaughan succinctly states, that 'men are losers in intelligence in proportion as they are losers in the habit of association', then the men of Manchester and of its neighbouring towns during the late eighteenth and early nineteenth centuries would stand comparison with any in the land in their 'habit of association' and, consequently, as gainers in intelligence. Within a period of just over fifty years (1780–1835), no fewer than nine learned societies and academic institutions were founded in Manchester, all of which were, in the widest sense, educational ventures at the service of the towns and villages of what is now the Metropolitan County and even further afield. A distinguished Irish contemporary, who knew the manufacturing districts of Lancashire well from close, personal investigation, commented in 1842: 'Individually I believe that no men alive have done more for the patronage of art, science and literature, than the northern manufacturers, and particularly the men of Manchester ... in supporting the numerous literary and scientific institutions in the town and its neighbourhood.'[6] A description of each of these societies and institutions, in chronological order of foundation, is not without value.

Literary and Philosophical Society (1781)

Dr Thomas Percival used to invite some of his medical colleagues and friends to his home in King Street in order to converse on subjects of a literary and philosophical nature. They decided to form themselves into a kind of weekly club which held its first meetings in the Assembly Coffee House in Exchange Buildings. At that time there were twenty-five members, but by the end of their first year, when they moved into the Cross Street Chapel Room, their numbers had increased to fifty-three. As nearly half of the original members were honorary physicians and surgeons to the Manchester Infirmary, four of whom were Fellows of the Royal Society, it was natural that they should establish their permanent home in 1799 in George Street, close to Piccadilly. John Dalton joined the Society in 1794 and during fifty years' membership he read 116 papers to the Society, was its Secretary from 1800 to 1808 and its President from 1819 until his death in 1844. It has been said that with the announcement of his Atomic Theory and its subsequent development, John Dalton brought great prestige to the Society.[7] Similarly, James Prescott Joule, who was born in Salford and came under Dalton's tuition in the George Street House, became famous both for his researches on electro-magnetism and for his determination of the mechanical equivalent of heat. As a member of the Society, he conducted all his researches in the neighbourhood of Manchester and was regarded as one of the outstanding figures in the realm of science. The technical inventions of the latter half of the eighteenth century had not only revolutionised economic life, they had also transformed the quality of human life itself. It was this tremendous factor of the effects of the new mechanical machinery upon human society which prompted a contemporary local historian to describe the Society as one which had brought Manchester 'almost as much into the notice of philosophers and men of letters, as its manufactures have into that of merchants and manufacturers and financiers'.[8] It was this compassionate approach to the vital, human problems of the industrial era which in its early days gave a compelling sense of urgency to the papers read by members to the Society. Its founder, Dr Thomas Percival, delivered a paper on 'The State of the Population in Manchester and other adjacent places' (a highly relevant topic for the Greater Manchester Council today), which anticipated our modern sanitary laws.

More significantly, Robert Owen presented a paper entitled 'Thoughts on the Connection between Universal Happiness and Practical Mechanics', out of which arose his experiments in education and his 'kingdom' at New Lanark. Most significant of all, John Kennedy, a leading Manchester machine-maker and cotton spinner and a partner in the great firm of McConnel and Kennedy, read a paper of penetrating insight in 1826 on 'Observations in the Influence of Machinery upon the Working Classes of the Community'.[9]

A modern economic historian once posed the question, 'Who can say how much the master cotton-spinners gained from their contact with Thomas Percival and John Dalton in the Literary and Philosophical Society of Manchester?' What these members, and others with them in the manufacturing towns which now form the basis of the Greater Manchester County, were experiencing, was not only an industrial revolution but also a revolution of ideas. 'If', as has been said, 'it registered an advance in understanding of, and control over, Nature, it also saw the beginning of a new attitude to the problems of human society.'[10] It is in this perspective that the influence of the Society must be seen as penetrating far beyond the town of its birth and residence. An analysis of the list of ordinary members in July 1971, in accordance with the Society's records, reveals that, out of a total of 523 members, no fewer than 160 reside outside Manchester in nearly all the towns of the new Metropolitan County. The 'Lit and Phil', as it is affectionately called, is the oldest provincial society of its kind, with a continuous history, in Great Britain and nationally is preceded only by the Royal Society.

College of Arts and Science (1783)

It has often been asked how not only the leading engineers and cotton spinners but, more particularly, the common engine-erectors and ordinary millwrights in the eighteenth century acquired their knowledge of mathematics, mechanics and machine-drawing. They were undoubtedly influenced by the itinerant lecturers who regularly visited the principal towns in the later eighteenth century and gave lectures on science and mechanics, often with what today would be called 'visual aids' in the form of working models and scientific apparatus.[11] Some of these lecturers held a part-time connection with the short-lived Manchester

College of Arts and Science, the foundation of which arose out of a paper presented in April 1783 to the Literary and Philosophical Society by Dr Thomas Barnes, the eminent Unitarian minister of Cross Street Chapel and one of the first two secretaries of the Society. The title of the paper was 'A Plan for the Improvement and Extension of Liberal Education in Manchester', in which Dr Barnes pleaded eloquently and forcefully for 'a plan of liberal education for young men designed for civil and active life, whether in trade or any of the professions.' To achieve this he advocated the establishment of a college in Manchester in which 'the happy art might be learned of connecting together, Liberal Science and Commercial Industry', and stipulated that there was to be no political or religious exclusiveness as 'science and arts are of no political or religious party.' Although the College, with its Governors drawn from the nine officers of the Literary and Philosophical Society, started with high hopes, it had but a brief existence, lasting only four years.

The Manchester Academy (1786)

When the Act of Uniformity of 1662 decreed that every clergyman and schoolmaster must subscribe to a declaration that 'he would conform to the Liturgies by Law established' and when, a decade later, the Test Act similarly decreed that the doors of the Universities of Oxford and Cambridge would be open only to those who did so conform, those who dissented on principle realised the necessity of providing higher education for non-conformists in general and, in particular, for maintaining the supply of scholarly men for their ministry. This especially applied to the region now called the Greater Manchester County, for its manufacturing towns were, in the main, strongholds of Nonconformity and sturdy supporters of the movement for intellectual freedom which became enshrined in the Dissenting Academies of the eighteenth century. One of the most distinguished was a very close neighbour—the Warrington Academy, open to young men of all religious opinions preparing for ministerial or civil life. Its most distinguished teacher was Dr Joseph Priestley, the eminent scientist, who contended that 'the chief and proper subject of education is not to form a shining and popular character, but an useful one ...' When this famous Academy which, so it was reported, 'bore no mean witness to the principle that men and not money make an academy',[12] had to close its doors in 1786, three of its alumni, Dr Thomas Percival, Dr Thomas Barnes, and the Rev. Ralph Harrison of Cross Street Chapel, founded the Manchester Academy which inherited from Warrington its library of 3,000 volumes and its fine traditions. Described by a contemporary local historian as 'a College for the education of Dissenters in the higher branches of science and literature', it was established here in 1786, and 'a handsome building erected for the purpose in Mosley Street'.[13] Among the 'characters of the first respectability and talent' who taught at the College was John Dalton, who had twenty-four pupils for mathematics, mechanics, geometry, algebra, book-keeping, natural philosophy and chemistry. He is said, according to the social reformer, Robert Owen, to have first broached his Atomic Theory at a meeting in the Academy.[14] In 1804 the Academy was transferred to York, where it became known as 'Manchester College'. Under this name it moved in 1853 to London, where it became the first Dissenter's College to be affiliated with the University of London. It finally moved in 1889 to Oxford, where it remains as a theological college under the same name. In its origin, therefore, it takes its honourable place among the Dissenting Academies which 'did for England in the eighteenth century something of what the Universities did for Scotland.'[15] Even more important for the future of this region, these Academies, in their zeal for intellectual liberty and freedom from ecclesiastical exclusiveness, made the way clear for the modern civic universities, a movement which locally is to be amplified.

The Natural History Society (1821)

When a Stockport handloom weaver, named John Jennison, acquired in 1836 a whitewashed cottage in Hyde Road, Gorton, to which he attached a small tea-garden and a modest zoo of parrots and monkeys, he could hardly have realised that he was embarking upon an enterprise which a century later was described as 'a most successful lung to Greater Manchester'.[16] Belle Vue, with its great Zoological Collections and extensive Gardens today, a mecca of its kind for the citizens of the Metropolitan County, originally met a very real need when parks and open spaces 'for the health and convenience of the inhabitants' were virtually non-existent. It is the more remarkable, then, that the Manchester Society for the

Promotion of Natural History began in rooms in St Ann's Place in 1821 with a small museum of natural objects. In 1835 the Society opened a larger museum in Peter Street. Despite a tribute to 'its great services to science long before the days of science classes and technical institutions',[17] it is not surprising that, with an admission fee of ten guineas and an annual subscription of two guineas, the Society reported in 1839 that 'not one individual has applied for admission as being of the working class.'[18]

Nearly thirty years later the Society decided, as it found itself unable to maintain the collections properly, to hand over the valuable contents of its museum to the governors of Owens College, who accepted the collections in trust for the benefit of the students and the public. In 1868 the Society held its last meeting and eventually sold its building to the YMCA. Happily, Museum Street still remains as a reminder of the earlier building. The new Manchester Museum moved with the College in 1873 to its premises in Oxford Road, and in 1888 finally moved into its present buildings, which have twice been extended in accommodation. This Museum has thus been established for the promotion of life and earth science studies, together with the study of archaeology, Egyptology, ethnology and numismatics. It has been jointly controlled by the University and the City and is under the management of a committee appointed in accordance with regulations made by the University.[19] Negotiations have been taking place between the University, the Manchester City Council and the Greater Manchester Council to enable the rich resources of the Manchester Museum to be at the service of all towns and villages in the Metropolitan County, as indeed are the municipal museums and art galleries of all the Districts.

The Royal Manchester Institution (1824)

In 1823 three Manchester artists visited an Exhibition of Paintings and Works of Art of the Northern Establishment of Arts held at Leeds. On returning home, they asked themselves, 'Why can we not have such an exhibition in our own Town?'[20] They at once set about organising a general meeting at the Exchange Rooms, at which the following resolution was passed unanimously:

'That the diffusion of a taste for the Fine Arts in this populous and opulent district, by establishing a collection of the best

93

models that can be obtained in Paintings and Sculpture, and by opening a channel through which the works of meritorious artists may be brought before the Public, and the encouragement of literary and scientific pursuits by facilitating the delivery of popular courses of public lectures, are objects highly desirable and important.'

Following the customary Anglo-Saxon procedure, a Committee was at once set up with the object of 'establishing in Manchester an Institution for the Fine Arts'. Its reasons for doing so are stated in sound, Nonconformist middle-class terms which must undoubtedly have found a willing response from their fellows in the manufacturing towns of the region:

'An alliance between Commerce and the Liberal Arts is at once natural and salutary. The wishes of mankind increase with the means of gratifying them; and the superfluous wealth, which is the fruit of an extensive and flourishing trade, finds an object in those elegant productions of human genius and skill which minister to the luxury of the imagination. Nor do the Arts fail to reward the patronage which is extended to them; they bestow an intellectual grace upon society; they refine the taste and soften the manners; they not only furnish employment for the riches which must otherwise accumulate in useless abundance, but provide a counter-acting influence to the gross and sordid spirit, which is too often the result of an undivided attention to mercenary pursuits.'[21]

With this fanfare of high-minded sentiment, 'The Manchester Institution for the Promotion of Literature, Science and the Arts' was established and Royal Patronage sought and appropriately obtained through the good offices of the Home Secretary, Robert Peel. With remarkable astuteness, they engaged Charles Barry, the rising architect who later designed the new Houses of Parliament, to provide them with a building, for which they bought an excellent site in Mosley Street, described then as 'the handsomest street in Manchester'. Thus they provided Manchester with its 'most noble building of the period immediately preceding the accession of Victoria . . . a work of art and mind'.[22]

Barry's other 'Greek' building, *Buile Hill*, now used as the Salford Natural History Museum, was originally designed as a

The Royal Manchester Institution (1825), with the Athenaeum (1839) in the background

villa for Thomas Potter, first Mayor of Manchester and Chairman of the Royal Manchester Institution. The activities of the Institution mainly took the form of exhibitions and lectures, with conversaziones in the winter, which were very popular. Various rooms were used by societies such as the Choral, Medical, Architectural, Geological and Pathological Societies. The Regional College of Art, which is now a constituent member of the Manchester Polytechnic, originated from the School of Design which, from its beginning, met in the Royal Manchester Institution. In 1880 certain influential members of the Institution, including the architect, Thomas Worthington (who was born in Salford Crescent and designed the Albert Memorial in 1862), and George Faulkner, proposed that the building and its contents should be given to the Manchester Corporation to be maintained as a public art gallery under certain conditions relating to the purchase of works of art, a trust which the Corporation has honoured to the present day. Thus came into being, in 1883, the City Art Gallery.

The Royal Manchester Institution, however, continued its service to the community for another ninety years until its final dissolution in 1973. The walls of several Manchester hospitals have been adorned by paintings presented by the Institution, while the corridors and classrooms of many schools have carried artistic productions of students of the Municipal College of Art. Probably its greatest function has been its insistence upon the highest standards in civic design and environment. In a striking passage upon the value of the Institution as an advisory body, a prominent member of recent years has written:

'The Royal Manchester Institution seeks to encourage the ideal of a Manchester imaginatively planned, where forethought and design will ensure spacious squares, broad streets, dignified and well-designed buildings, a city with a clean atmosphere, smoothly flowing traffic, green belts, gracious parks, with well-planned homes and generous provision for the encouragement of music and the Arts, a city, in short, in which Mancunians may take a new kind of pride.'[23]

But this is not only for Manchester. In a beautiful essay dealing with cities, Lord Crawford, in 1929, wrote of Manchester and its neighbouring towns in this way: 'It is a city surrounded by a constellation of towns and villages. Here the term city is justified by scale, and by its close relations with smaller communities, perhaps nascent cities themselves, in the neighbourhood, all connected by commerce and personal affinities . . .'[24] The Royal Manchester Institution has officially ended its distinguished service to the region of Manchester but, in a very real sense, its aims still inspire its successors in the County Planning Office, the County Recreation and Arts Committee, and the Arts Section of the Literary and Philosophical Society, where its remaining members have found their new home.

The Royal School of Medicine (1824)

Until 1793 it had been customary for medical students in the Manchester region to begin their career as apprentices sometimes as early as sixteen years of age and to be indentured for periods of five or seven years. For this training, fees of from 300 to 500 guineas were paid. The apprentice received theoretical instruction from his master at his house, and his clinical experience by assisting him in his practice in medicine, surgery and midwifery. With the rapid enlargement of the Infirmary in the last two decades of the eighteenth century, it became possible for the Hospital itself to undertake the teaching of students and to work side by side with individual surgeons. In 1824 Thomas Turner, a surgeon, founded a School of Medicine in a makeshift building close to the Infirmary. Turner was officially permitted to call it 'The Manchester Royal School of Medicine', although the name was more grandiose than the rooms and technical equipment justified. Yet it was the first complete Medical School in the Manchester region, and it was there John Dalton delivered his course of lectures. He began his evening lecture at 7 o'clock and continued for two or even three hours, by which time his students, hearing the Infirmary bell ringing, would creep quietly away to their supper. At this time there were four medical schools—all private ventures —operating in Manchester, but it was Thomas Turner's Royal School of Medicine, acquired by Owens College at the end of six years of negotiation, which came into the possession of the Medical School Building in Coupland Street in 1874. With the granting of University status to Owens College in 1880, medical degrees were conferred for the first time in 1883. The great story of the Manchester University Medical School had begun.[25]

The Mechanics' Institution (1824)

It was natural that, when industry and science had become complementary to each other in the eighteenth century, the masters of the factories and mills, at least the more enlightened of them, should realise the advantages, both to themselves and to their employees, of enabling young men to receive practical instruction in the application of science to the mechanical and manufacturing arts. So it appeared, too, in the early nineteenth century to the philosophic Radical and educational reformer, Henry Brougham. To him it seemed that the conditions of life in a manufacturing town, the great number of working people herded together and dependent for their livelihood and the well-being of their occupations upon the technical progress of industry, provided an ideal situation for education along the lines of a man's occupation. By 1824 he realised that 'this is the moment beyond all doubt, best fitted for the attempt when wages are good, and the aspect of things peaceful.'[26] The practical aspect from the national point of view was forcefully expressed the following year by a Manchester man addressing an audience in Stockport:

'It is to our manufactures that we owe our national prosperity. It is by our manufactures that we must maintain it. We have at present got the start of other nations, and we must take care that they do not come up to us. Our prosperity has excited an active competition ... there is certainly no way of proceeding by which we may keep in advance of our national competitors, more certainly than by enlightening the mechanics.'[27]

It was in the counties of Lancashire and Yorkshire that the right conditions were to be found for the establishing of mechanics' institutes, and nowhere more fruitfully than in the area now contained by the Greater Manchester County. It was especially in the smaller towns that the right soil was to be found for this educational enterprise. They had retained their individuality and local pride, which fostered in their citizens that independent character and the habits of thrift and doggedness which are an essential part of the self-made scholar of the working class. Furthermore, it was in the cotton-spinning and weaving industries that the application of science to mechanical art had had its most outstanding successes. It is not, therefore, surprising that, by 1825, at least six

Mechanics' Institutions had been founded in Ashton-under-Lyne, Bolton, Manchester, Stalybridge, Stockport and Wigan, while three more were founded later at Bury (1837), Miles Platting (1836) and Salford (1838). In addition to these, there were kindred institutions such as the Dukinfield Village Library (1833), and the People's Institute, Rochdale (1845), while a new type of institution called the Lyceum was established at Salford, Oldham, Ancoats and Chorlton-on-Medlock.

The Manchester Mechanics' Institution was the first of the large provincial establishments. It was founded at a meeting held at the Bridgewater Arms, which was situated in High Street. The Institution was initiated by men of commerce and industry, who had a particular preoccupation with technical developments yet were drawn, also, by natural inclination to philanthropic and intellectual activities (several of them were members of the Literary and Philosophical Society). Their aims, clearly stated in the preamble to the rules, eloquently testify to their belief in the relation of principle to practice in the history of industrial progress:

'The Manchester Mechanics' Institution is formed for the purpose of enabling Mechanics and Artisans, of whatever trade they may be, to become acquainted with such branches of science as are of practical application in the exercise of that trade; that they may possess a more thorough knowledge of their business, acquire a greater degree of skill in the practice of it, and be qualified to make improvements and even new inventions in the Arts which they respectively profess . . . There is no Art which does not depend, more or less, on scientific principles, and to teach what these are, and to point out their practical application, will form the chief objects of this Institution.'[28]

An interesting feature of the Institution was its possession of a building, opened in 1827 in Cooper Street (which flanks the back of the Town Hall), which was described as 'the first erected in this country to include accommodation for all the objects of a Mechanics' Institution'. Such was 'the commencement of an institution', reported the editor of the *Manchester Times*, 'which, after being subject to many vicissitudes, has become one of the most popular and most useful of its class, combining the diffusion of very valuable and solid information with the promotion of rational and refining recreation, at the cheapest possible rate.'[29]

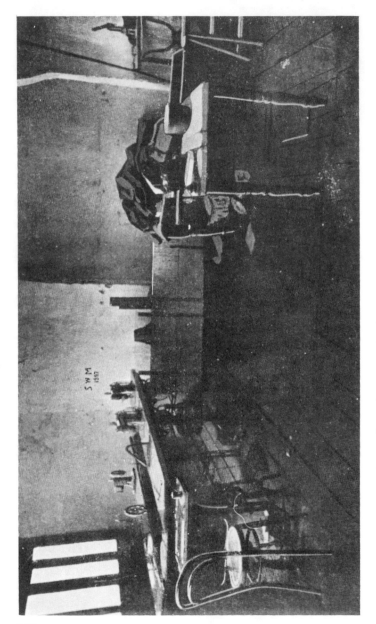

A garret in Shepley Street, Stalybridge, the first home of the Mechanics' Institution (1825-42)

Just as the Dissenting Academies prepared the way for the modern civic universities of the late nineteenth and early twentieth century, so the Mechanics' Institutions, or at least some of them, laid the foundation for the development of the modern technical schools and colleges. This particularly applied in the region of what is now the Greater Manchester County where, it has been said, 'nearly every village in the manufacturing districts has its mechanics' institute.'[30] Indeed, it may be claimed that the modern Colleges of Technology which have played an indispensable rôle in the provision of scientific and technical education in Oldham, Bolton, Bury, Rochdale, Stockport, Wigan and other manufacturing towns of the Metropolitan County owe their origin to the widespreading influence of the local Mechanics' Institute. That in Manchester entered, about 1883, upon a remarkable progression of adaptation to new needs and circumstances. From its transformation into a technical school, it became in 1902 a new Municipal School of Technology and in 1918 a Municipal College of Technology and a constituent part of the University of Manchester. In 1955 the College received its Royal Charter, making it independent of the City as The Manchester College of Science and Technology. It is now the University of Manchester Institute of Science and Technology. As it celebrates its 150th Anniversary of its origin, the aims of UMIST, as it is now called, have undoubtedly broadened well beyond those of its more parochial progenitor. Yet its primary function is still that of enabling its students 'to become acquainted with such branches of science as are of practical application in the exercise of their trade.' One would like to think that, while recognising its bounden duty to students from many parts of the world, this now-famous Institute is still there to serve the manifold needs of the manufacturing towns of the Greater Manchester County in whose soil it has been nurtured.

The Manchester Statistical Society (1833)

Samuel Robinson, a master cotton-spinner and philanthropist, founded in 1833 The Dukinfield Village Library in the hope that the working men of Dukinfield would have 'the good sense to avail themselves of the advantages they possess in the present day beyond any former period', and that 'the higher classes may take a generous interest in the moral and social improvement of the lower.' As the Statistical Society had just been founded in the same year, Robinson took the opportunity at a meeting of his Village Library to wish its sponsors every success 'in their endeavours to improve the condition of the industrial classes by an accurate investigation of the causes which produce our social evils . . .'[31] In these laudable sentiments, sincerely expressed by a manufacturer who passionately desired closer and better relations between different classes of society, one may detect the kind of aspirations which moved those practical-minded citizens who resolved 'to assist in promoting the progress of social improvement in the manufacturing population by which they are surrounded.' They were essentially men of affairs: Samuel Robinson's brother-in-law, Sir Benjamin Heywood, was a well-known Manchester banker and an M.P. for the County; Richard Cobden, calico-printer and political reformer, who led the fight for the incorporation of the Borough; William Neild, who came as a country lad to the Manchester textile business in which he became a partner; Thomas Potter, whose father was a yeoman farmer at Tadcaster, was the first Mayor of Manchester; the Gregs, founders of the Quarry Bank Mill and the country factory community at Styal, Cheshire; and Samuel Robinson himself. There was no leisured class in Manchester or its neighbouring manufacturing towns in those days. The employers lived near their business-houses, factories or mills and worked almost as long hours as their employees, for whom many of them had a real concern. It has already been noticed that the founding of the Statistical Society was, in the main, due to the revelations made by Dr James Kay of the evil conditions, morally and physically, under which those employed in the cotton manufacture in Manchester lived and worked. It was natural, therefore, that the first major report of the Society was on the 'Condition of the Working Classes in 1834, 1835 and 1836'. It was, however, its investigation into 'the state of the Day, Sunday, Charity and Infant schools in the Borough of Manchester' which brought the Society's methods to the attention of the nation. Its 'Report on the State of Education in the Borough of Manchester (1834)' was acclaimed by the Central Society for Education as the first truly scientific investigation into this important sphere. So relevant was this investigation by the Society that it was resolved to apply its methods to Salford, Bolton, Bury and other towns. It was subsequently found that the state of elementary education in Manchester compared unfavourably with that in Salford and

Bury, but favourably with that in Bolton, which was definitely worse.[32] The Manchester Statistical Society was the first of its kind in England and, as a result of its pioneer work, similar associations have been established in other parts of the country. The Society has continued to function to this day 'for the discussion of subjects of political and social economy and for the promotion of statistical enquiries to the total exclusion of party politics'. Its '*Reports*' are still of great value, not only to the citizens of Manchester but also to those of the Districts of the Metropolitan County whose interests it has always served.

The Athenaeum (1835)

It is perhaps significant that in the year in which the Municipal Corporations Act was passed (1835), which three years later enabled Manchester to assume the status of Incorporated Borough, the founding of the Manchester Athenaeum took place. The common factor of those two events was the altruistic driving force of Richard Cobden, who desired in this new institution to promote the education and widen the cultural horizons of the new young middle class—the clerks and salesmen who worked in the warehouses, offices and banks of Manchester and the neighbouring towns. Speaking at the official opening of the new building on 28 October 1839, Cobden said of the Athenaeum: 'It offers to young men by means of its classes and societies all the advantages that could be afforded by the national universities themselves'—an interesting comment from one whose home in Quay Street was to become twelve years later the birthplace of the University of Manchester. The Athenaeum Building, one of the finest in the City, was designed in the style of the Italian Renaissance by Sir Charles Barry, at that time the most important architect in England. It secured, within four years of its opening, a membership of over one thousand, which included a number of the 'broad cloth' members of the Mechanics' Institution who transferred their allegiance to 'our own offspring', as Sir Benjamin Heywood magnanimously described the new institution. The Athenaeum had much to offer 'the class of superior mercantile servants and young men':[33] a good library and a reading room with a wide variety of newspapers and periodicals, an attractive programme of lectures, classes in languages, a discussion society and a gymnasium. Charles Dickens presided over one of its soirées in 1843 and, in the autumn of the following year, Benjamin Disraeli, who had visited Manchester before and was fascinated by its vitality and alarmed by its problems, addressed the members of the Athenaeum on 'The Acquirement of Knowledge'. Evidently not only the youth of Manchester was present, for Disraeli gracefully welcomed 'the presence of deputations from many societies in this county, who acknowledge a sympathy and an analogy of pursuit with the Athenaeum of Manchester', which clearly indicates that the Club had affinities with the towns of the region. In a moving and eloquent peroration in which he presented to his youthful audience the idea that 'human happiness is dependent on the cultivation of the mind', in pursuit of which he regarded the Manchester Athenaeum as 'part of that great educational movement which is the noble and ennobling characteristic of the age in which we live', Disraeli appealed 'to the youth of Manchester, representing the civic youth of this great county and this great district' to remember that 'they will some day succeed to the high places of this great community' and that 'when they have wealth, when they have authority, when they have power, let it not be said that they were deficient in public virtue and public spirit.'[34]

The Club continued to serve the community of the region until its centenary in 1935. By then, however, a rapid decline had set in, comparable to that of the cotton industry, upon the prosperity of which it had been originally founded. Fortunately, the Athenaeum building, sold to the Manchester Corporation in 1939, has taken upon itself a new rôle in the cultural and educational activities of post-war Manchester. As a dignified and most useful Annexe to the City Art Gallery, it houses in the public rooms on the ground floor displays of pottery, including the beautiful Greg Collection of Ceramics, and the Assheton Silver Collection. Three rooms on the first floor are used as the headquarters of the Athenaeum Education Service of the Manchester Education Committee, which provides a wealth of facilities in the halls, museums and art galleries of the City.

Of the literary and/or scientific societies which have served the intellectual interests of the other Districts of the Metropolitan County, that of Rochdale is the oldest extant. In 1878 a group of young students in the Science Classes, held under the educational scheme of the Equitable Pioneers Society, expressed a desire to have the opportunity of discussing together the subjects they were studying. An interested friend of the students, W. H. Pennington, took up the project and developed it on broad lines as a town Society. Later in the year Canon Molesworth, descendant of an old Rochdale family, on being invited to become the first President, suggested the inclusion of literature in the subjects. On 9 November 1878, the Rochdale Literary and Scientific Society came into being. The activities of the Society from the beginning have taken the form of a programme of fortnightly lectures during the winter months on both local and general topics of a literary or broadly scientific nature. Thus, in the first full session of 1879–1880, a paper was given on 'The Problem of the Roman Road over Blackstone Edge', which is in the vicinity of Rochdale. Considerable excitement must have been caused in the town when Lieut. C. W. Royds, a member of a distinguished Rochdale family, gave to the Society one evening his personal reminiscences of life in the Antarctic during Captain Scott's great Expedition in 1912, which created another 'epic of the snows'. Each session an endowment called the 'Pearson Lecture' enabled the Council to invite a distinguished scholar to address the Society as, for example, when Lord Rutherford discoursed on his epoch-making researches on 'Radio-activity'. One remembers, almost with awe, another such occasion when Professor P. M. S. Blackett demonstrated to a fascinated audience the mysteries of 'Cosmic Rays'—an important sphere of science in which this modest and humane scholar was a pioneer. What he was discovering at that time in the late 1930s came to play a vital rôle in 1941 in the Battle of the Atlantic and the preservation of the Western Approaches, in which 'the stranglehold of the magnetic mine was only loosened and kept from closing by triumphs of British science and ingenuity.'[35] Each year, in the summer months, excursions have taken place, some in connection with local investigations, others of a literary or historical nature further afield. The Society has published regularly, every two or three years since 1888, its own *Transactions*, which were proudly exchanged with those of many other learned societies of kindred interests and standing. Although the *Transactions* have not been published since 1960, the Society continues to serve the Rochdale Metropolitan Borough and has, as its younger neighbour, the Castleton Literary Society.

It has been said that 'where there is great vigour there will be much doing, and great diversity of judgement, both in regard to what it may be best to do, and as to the best mode of doing it.'[36] In 1836 the Manchester Statistical Society invited Harry Longueville

Jones, a former Dean and Fellow of Magdalene College, Cambridge, to read his paper entitled 'Plan of a University for the Town of Manchester'.[37] This was not the first time that such a plan had been proposed for Manchester. In 1640, Lord Halifax presented to the Long Parliament a Petition declaring how much the north of England suffered through lack of a university, as a result of which 'many ripe and hopeful wits' were 'utterly lost for want of education'. It proceeded to nominate Manchester as 'the fittest place for such a foundation, it being almost the centre of these northern parts'. The significant features of the Petition are its insistence on the regional nature of the proposed university and its expectation of regional support—a clear historical forecast of the present developing relationship of the Greater Manchester Council and Manchester University. The second attempt was Dr Thomas Barnes' advocacy in 1783 of 'A Plan for the Improvement and Extension of Liberal Education in Manchester'. It was the establishing of the second Manchester Academy in 1786 that revealed the spirit which inspired these projects and carried the conception of a university in Manchester a step nearer the goal. The great merit of H. L. Jones' Plan, however, lay not in the novelty of his ideas but in translating into a practical structure a group of purposes of which Manchester had been for some time increasingly conscious, namely the need for a modern University possessing full intellectual freedom and directly associated with the life and work of the region. It was these purposes which the John Owens bequest of nearly £100,000 was intended to fulfil. It is significant that certain of the Trustees whom Owens nominated in his will of May 1845 were members of the committee which had considered the carrying out of Jones' Plan immediately after its publication.[38]

It was John Owens' wish 'to found within the said parliamentary borough of Manchester ... an institution for providing or aiding the means of instructing and improving young persons of the male sex ... in such branches of learning and science as are now ... taught in the English Universities.' For whom geographically was the institution originally intended? John Owens clearly indicated what he had in mind:

'If the number of applicants for admission to such institution as students shall be more than adequate to the means of the institution, a preference shall in all cases be given to the children of parents residing ... within the limits now comprised in the parliamentary borough of Manchester, or within two miles from any part of such limits; and secondly, to the children of parents residing . . . within the limits comprised in the parliamentary district or division of south Lancashire; but subject as aforesaid, the said institution shall be open to all applicants for admission, without respect to place of birth, and without distinction of rank or condition in society.'

There are two conclusions to be drawn: one, that John Owens intended to bring University education to the young men of the region, that is Manchester and south Lancashire; two, that once this condition had been satisfied, such education was open to all young men wherever they may live and whatever their 'condition in society'. It is relevant to observe, also, that the Trustees, whose privileged duty it was to translate John Owens' ideals into a working organisation, realised that, in his insistence on identifying the college with its environment, they should make provision for students 'not intending to go through the regular course' but who could attend classes in such subjects as would be useful for their training as 'engineers, machinists and other pursuits in practical science'. For this and other cognate purposes, the Trustees considered it 'expedient to appoint a Professor of Chemistry . . . with a view to afford greater facilities than at present exist in this neighbourhood, for obtaining instruction in a branch of science of so much local importance as well as general interest.' One can see how 'Owens and the Tech' came into being in their own good time. One can see, too, how the regional concept held its own ground, in more senses than one, when, during the crucial decade of 1863–73, the movement for the extension of Owens College both academically and physically took place. Overcrowding had become so apparent by 1864 in the 'building located in a squalid and noisy slum', as A. F. Tout once described Quay Street, that the Trustees decided to appoint a small committee to investigate the possibilities of finding more accommodation. The problem had become even more urgent as the Manchester Natural History Society and the Geological Society, both possessing valuable collections, as has already been noticed, were in a state of rapid decline, while the Royal School of Medicine was ripe to be taken in hand as the College's School of Medicine. Clearly the opportunity was there for expansion and so were the men, both lay and professional, to match it.

An early factor which had spurred the committee in its efforts to find more accommodation was the failure to establish in 1863 a department of civil engineering, vital to South Lancashire, because of lack of space:

> 'We think that Owens College contains the nucleus of a very efficient school of these branches of Art and Science, and that such a school attached to the College would be warmly welcomed, not only by Manchester, but by the many populous and busy manufacturing towns around and would give us a hold on those towns which would react beneficially on the other branches of the College.'[39]

When, in the winter of 1866–7, the Trustees set up the New Buildings Committee, it was resolved at a large and influential public meeting to call upon 'the public of the district to unite for the purpose of developing the College on a more comprehensive scale and in appropriate and convenient buildings.' As a result, local committees were set up in Bolton and Oldham, which did useful work in the raising of funds, but regrettably the other towns of the cotton district, with the exception of Stockport, did not show much enthusiasm for the cause.[40] By 1869 sufficient funds had been raised to encourage Murray Gladstone, Chairman of the Site Committee and a cousin of W. E. Gladstone, to purchase secretly a large and cheap site of about four acres, in his own name and at his own risk, which became the area in Oxford Road on which Alfred Waterhouse, R.A., designed the nucleus of the future Victoria University of Manchester.

One of the greatest Chancellors of the University was Lord Crawford (1923–1947), a superb example of English aristocracy at its best. He also included in his titles that of Baron Wigan, an early nineteenth-century creation in which he took a rightful pride. 'I have heard the whisper of prejudice, directed against Wigan and quite unjustly', he once wrote. 'Wigan is a great personality with a homely face.'[41] His ancestral home, Haigh Hall, was there near his coal pits (he used to describe himself as a Lancashire coal merchant). In his home he had his magnificent Bibliotheca Lindesiana, the library accumulated over a long period by his family and comprising 100,000 volumes and over 6,000 choice manuscripts. This was the manuscript collection acquired by Mrs Rylands which today forms the nucleus of the wonderful collection in the Manuscript Department of the John Rylands University Library of Manchester in Deansgate. Lord Crawford once invited the Governors of the John Rylands and certain of the University Professors to see his library at Haigh Hall. In the party was Professor Daniels, a thorough Lancastrian who had worked in a pit in his youth and was a product of Ruskin College and Manchester University. At the end of the visit, Lord and Lady Crawford waved their guests an informal farewell. Daniels, an ardent Radical, turned to a colleague and said, 'You know, it's worth five centuries of breeding to breed two like those',[42] a comment which epitomises the Lancastrian's natural respect and even affection for an aristocratic family whose members justify their place in the community not simply on what they claim to be but on what they do for that community. Lord Crawford was always concerned about the extent to which Manchester University could contribute to the enrichment of its province and analyse its special needs. He regarded his high and privileged office as one in which he must consistently strengthen the ties between the University and the life of the region, and constantly strive to inspire in the representatives of the towns of the region associated with the University a feeling of fellowship in a high social endeavour. One of these towns is now the Metropolitan Borough of Wigan within the orbit of the Greater Manchester County.

One would like to think that these ideals, which Lord Crawford assiduously upheld throughout his distinguished period as Chancellor, are now the guidelines of the Greater Manchester Council in its relationship with Manchester University. In a very real sense, this is one of the rich, home-spun traditions which the Council has inherited and is now privileged to serve. It is the very nature of these traditions, patiently moulded, often unwittingly, by the human efforts of those men and women who have toiled and spun in the towns and villages of what John Owens called South Lancashire and what now is called the Greater Manchester Metropolitan County, which is what this book is really about. There are indeed 'great truths to tell' on what, over the centuries, has evolved, sometimes almost imperceptibly, to produce this Metropolitan County. Someone once said, probably on seeing the plans for the Manchester Education Precinct, that 'the University today is simply the Owens' idea growing in the way of its own nature to a larger and larger life.' The inner meaning of this inspired observation may equally well apply to the Greater

Manchester County, in whose future our hopes and aspirations lie.

What aroused the minds of the men in the region of Manchester which produced what has been graphically described as 'a state of electric communication of ideas', and out of which arose these great cultural and educational institutions? The triumphs and tribulations of the Industrial Revolution had something to do with it, for the economic and social problems which arose out of them brought home to men the material value of knowledge. This in turn led their social sense to find in the acquirement of knowledge the way to culture and the intellectual gifts of civilisation. Allied with this approach was their moral sense, which saw in the dissemination of knowledge a valuable instrument for promoting the health of society and the progress of mankind. The ideas and intentions behind the founding of the institutions which have been described in this chapter are more significant than the institutions themselves. The most powerful appeal to the Mancunian and his like-minded neighbours was one in which 'the imagination discloses to the intellect a possibility which arouses in him a passion to achieve what he will regard as a moral ideal'—what has been described as 'the fervour of passionate conviction'.[43] A supreme example of the determination of the operatives of the cotton towns surrounding Manchester to uphold a moral ideal in face of unemployment and hunger is in their attitude towards the American Civil War, in which they pledged their support to the North in their fight to end slave labour in the cotton fields and plantations of the Southern Confederacy, from which States most of the raw cotton for their mills and factories came. Despite the resultant Cotton Famine (1862–1864), during which many cotton-workers lived very close to starvation and riots broke out in Stalybridge, Ashton, Dukinfield and Hyde,[44] they held fast in their loyalty to the Northern States. In a message addressed to the 'working men of Manchester' (which geographically should be very broadly interpreted as what today is the Greater Manchester County) Abraham Lincoln described the stand they had made for a moral ideal as 'an instance of sublime Christian heroism'.

The religious attribute contained in the President's message (there is an oversize statue to the great man in commemoration of this historic event in Platt Fields, Manchester) was no accident on his part. H. L. Jones, in noting in 1836 that 'in all directions the circle of Manchester is full of life and intelligence', found also that 'their political sentiments indicate the restless vigour of a rising and strong people; their religious opinions are full of fervour and piety.' This applied in particular to the Nonconformist denominations which had increased steadily both in numbers and influence from the beginning of the nineteenth century until, by 1836, they outnumbered the Anglican churches in Manchester by at least three to one.[45] Indeed, the steadily growing number of Dissenting establishments in Manchester and the neighbouring towns was a cause of increasing disquiet to zealous Anglicans. In the eyes of many of them, dissent from the Established Church implied also dissent from loyalty to the British Constitution. In the minds of the Anglicans, Dissent was virtually equated with sedition against the State. One can imagine that such a plausible doctrine at that time, reminiscent of English thought and government policy in the 'state-ecclesiastical' of Elizabeth I and the Early Stuarts, did not trouble overmuch the consciences of the sturdy, independent Nonconformists of the manufacturing towns of South Lancashire, where their stronghold lay. Nearer to their hearts' desire was a political liberalism which insisted on the sacred rights of the individual who carried a corresponding responsibility to render service to the general progress and well-being of society.

It was in these textile towns that the Sunday School movement remained strong, with the Stockport school, founded in 1784, the greatest of them all, while Bolton also claimed some of the earliest schemes of Sabbath instruction.[46] The most representative chapel of the liberal Christian faith in Manchester was Cross Street Chapel, opened as the Dissenters' Meeting House in 1694. It was the second place of worship erected in Manchester and the parent church of Nonconformity in the town. The scholarly ministers and distinguished members of the congregation have, over two-and-a-half centuries, made a remarkable contribution to the civic and public life and to the intellectual and cultural activities of the town. One enters with reverence the old Chapel Room where, either formally or informally, many of the institutions already referred to had their beginning and where Richard Cobden learnt the art of oratory. Of the original Trustees of Owens College, four were Cross Street Chapel men. The first Secretary of the College was J. P. Aston, a Unitarian lawyer, who drew up John Owens' Will, in which the founder, mindful probably of the earlier Manchester Academies, stipulated that the students, professors, teachers, and others connected with the College should be freed from religious tests, which ultimately in 1904 facilitated the establishing of a faculty of theology. Sir Alfred Hopkinson, first Vice-Chancellor of the University, said in 1930: 'In mid-Victorian days the intellectual aristocracy of South Lancashire was largely Unitarian . . . they took an active part in the local life of the cities, and especially in University education.'[47] In those days, also, 'the approaches to Cross Street Chapel were filled with carriages conveying a wealthy congregation to worship: and to become a pew-holder in a Chapel accommodating twelve hundred people one had to put one's name on a waiting-list.'[48] *Autres temps, autres moeurs!*

Mr Harold Lever, MP for a Manchester constituency, in moving the loyal address to the Crown on 9 November 1965, said: 'In Manchester there are few idealists who have not got a touch of the shrewdness of commerce and, on the other hand, there are very few successful business-men who have not got a view of progressive thought and scholarship.'[49] In these words, the present Chancellor of the Duchy of Lancaster has fittingly summed up the peculiar quality of the generations of industrialists and men of commerce who have moulded the essential character of what is now the Greater Manchester County.

Chapter 8

'As well as foreigners to reside . . .'

In 432 B.C. Pericles, the enlightened ruler of Athens at the height of its power imperially and artistically, proudly said of her: 'We throw our city open to all and never, by the expulsion of strangers, exclude anyone from either learning or observing things.' In A.D. 1783, James Ogden, a native of Manchester, in commenting upon the almost fortuitous open-door policy of the town's somewhat archaic system of government, realised its great advantage to the trade of his birthplace in that it 'has been kept open to strangers of every description, who contribute to its improvement by their ingenuity.'[1] This comparison between the two cities, ancient and modern, is a captivating one. Up to and including the latter half of the eighteenth century the term 'stranger' or 'foreigner' referred to any outsider, either from Scotland, Ireland or Wales, from the neighbouring county or even from the next parish or town. Until very recently one used to hear in the villages of the Rochdale district, such as Wardle, Milnrow or Newhey, those who lived outside the village referred to as 'offcomers'—a sobering thought for the members and officers of the Greater Manchester Council! The Scots, in particular, formed a significant group of immigrants to Manchester and district in the eighteenth century, many of them being men of enterprise and skill. In addition to a number of Scottish surgeons and physicians,[2] engineers such as William Murdoch, John Kennedy and William Galloway found much scope for the development of their talents in Manchester.[3] It is clear from the deliberations of the Court Leet in the autumn meetings of 1788 that the presence and growing influence of these immigrants were causing some concern. The Steward, determined to test the tolerance and impartiality of members, declared: 'It is of no publick consideration whatever what religious persuasion the Borough-reeve, the Constables, or other Officers hold. All we want, and all that are necessary, are sensible, respectable, steady, upright active Officers.'[4] That his injunction was taken to heart may be exemplified by the remarkable career of public service rendered to the town by a German merchant, Charles Frederick Brandt. Described as a fustian manufacturer in Raffald's *Directory* for 1781, he was elected a member of the Literary and Philosophical Society in 1783, appointed a Juror of the Court Leet in 1784 and Boroughreeve in 1799, and elected first President of the Manchester Commercial Society (forerunner of the Chamber of Commerce) in 1793. When he died in 1814, he was revered as 'as loyal and excellent a subject as his Majesty could boast of', for 'his attachment and support to the country have been manifested on every occasion.'[5] Here, then, may be discerned the tolerance and practical sense of the Mancunian in his attitude towards strangers who came into his midst from other parts of Great Britain or from overseas and wanted to serve the town and community.

The variety of merchants and others who came to Manchester from overseas naturally leads one to speculate upon what in particular attracted these foreigners to this region, why they decided to settle in it and what they contributed to the life of the community. Why, for example, did Nathan Meyer Rothschild, third son of the founder of the House in Frankfurt, come here in 1798 at the age of twenty-one to live in Downing Street for seven years? 'As soon as I got to Manchester,' said Nathan, 'I laid out all my money, things were so cheap and I made good profits.' At that time there were fewer than twenty foreign firms in the town: when he died in 1836 on a visit to his native city of Frankfurt there were over a hundred, and three-quarters of them were German business-houses. It is interesting to note that in 1964, nearly 160 years after the founder of N. M. Rothschild & Sons left Manchester, the renowned merchant bankers opened in this city their first branch office outside London. Thus the Rothschilds in England have returned to their first love, Manchester. Germany had been for some time the best European market for British textile goods, but the time was fast approaching when the Far Eastern markets came to absorb every yard of cloth that Manchester and its neighbouring cotton towns could produce. Thus the dealers in the now smaller European markets had virtually to beg for every yard of cloth they needed. They found, in fact, that it was advisable to come to Manchester and set up in business as exporters of cotton goods to their native countries. Although the number of German merchants in the city continued to grow, by far the most impressive increase was among those merchants who came from the Eastern Mediterranean, in particular the Greeks and the Armenians. 'All roads led to Manchester in the 1840s', a modern historian has proclaimed,[6] and this was certainly true for the Levantine merchants for, by 1870, with approximately 200 firms here, they not only outnumbered the Germans (about 150 firms) but constituted the largest group of foreign business houses in Manchester.

Trade was not the only magnet which drew foreigners to the region of Victorian Manchester. The intellectually invigorating climate created during the previous half century, as has been noted, almost rivalled, for many of the liberal-minded Germans in particular, the great industrial and commercial opportunities in the region. Certain professional men, also, both academic and technical, were more than interested in what was going on in Quay Street during the formative years of Owens College, where H. E. Roscoe on the Science and A. W. Ward on the Arts side were creating an intellectual atmosphere inspired by their experience of the academic principles of the German universities. It was in particular the former's pioneer work in the application of research in the physical sciences to the needs of local industries which brought to the College the enthusiastic support of those foreigners who were building up highly successful commercial and industrial organisations in the region, especially those concerned with textiles and engineering. Arthur Schuster, who came as a young man from Frankfurt in 1870 to join the family textile business, studied first as an evening and later as a day student at Owens and in 1888 was appointed to the Langworthy Chair of Physics. Julius Dreschfeld, a Bavarian, who came to Manchester in 1861, was appointed the first Professor of Pathology in Great Britain. It has been said of him that 'he brought to Manchester the European tradition of scientific medicine.'[7] There were benefactors, also, such as C. F. Beyer, co-founder in 1854 of a great locomotive works at Gorton, who gave over £100,000 for the establishment of chairs in science, and Eduard Schunck, son of a distinguished German family, which originally came to Manchester in 1810, who left £20,000 for chemical research. But beyond these material computations, great as they were, it was the fact that these new citizens from the Continent were, as has been eloquently stated, 'as if instinctively, sympathetic supporters of the social and cultural ideas for which the College, and then the University, has stood.' It was not only that they were 'intellectually like-minded', but also that they brought to the region of Manchester 'a range of interest and of aesthetic sensitiveness which hitherto had been much more a casual than a regular item in the life of our successful men of commerce and industry.' In this most valuable way they brought 'a stream of spiritual values which gradually incorporated themselves with the already established moral culture of the native Mancunian.'[8] It was a most felicitous blending of native and foreign gifts which endowed the region of Manchester with its own urbane cultural tradition.

There were some fourteen nationalities whose members came to and settled in Manchester for varying lengths of time during the period 1784 to 1876. They were: German, French, Dutch, Russian, Italian, Spanish, Portuguese, Swiss, Swedish, Danish, Greek, Turkish, Armenian and Arabic. Of these, seven formed distinct and settled communities—Jews, Germans, Greeks, Armenians, Italians, French and Moroccans. Except for the last-named, they have remained as settled communities in Manchester and Salford to such an extent that they are now taken for granted as part of the ethos of the twin cities on the Irwell.

The largest community, the Jewish, may be traced at least to the late eighteenth century, for the *Trade Directory* for 1788 records a Hamilton Levi who is described as a flower-dealer in Long Millgate. By 1794 there were fifteen Ashkenazi families in Shudehill, Withy Grove and Long Millgate, for whom a room was rented in Ainsworth's Court in Long Millgate as a synagogue, and a burial place near St Thomas's Chapel, Pendleton.[9] With the considerable growth of the community it became necessary to build the Great Synagogue in Cheetham Hill Road in 1858, while at the same time the foundation-stone of the Reform Synagogue was laid in Park Place. A later influx of Spanish, Portuguese, Syrian and Corfu merchants—the Sephardi branch of Judaism—into Manchester necessitated the building of their own synagogue in 1874 on Cheetham Hill Road. The closely-knit nature of the Jewish community, which by this time had reached 5,000, is well illustrated by the provision made for the religious education of the young. The first Jewish school was established in rooms rented in 1838 in the Salford Lyceum, but in 1859 moved to Derby Street with 300 children on the roll. By the end of the nineteenth century some 2,400 Jewish children in Manchester were being educated in Hebrew schools. Always noted as a race for the care of its own people, the Jews in Manchester soon established their own charitable institutions. There was a Manchester Jewish Philanthropic Society in 1804, their own Board of Guardians was founded in 1867, the Jewish Ladies Visiting Association in 1884 and the Homes for the Aged in 1898. Nor was this philanthropy confined to their own folk. An outstanding example of an enlightened

The Jews' Synagogue (left foreground) in Cheetham Hill Road, Manchester

Manchester Jewish merchant was Salis Schwabe. Originally a calico-printer in Oldenburg, Schwabe came to Manchester in 1832. Deeply interested in the plight of the insane, he was mainly responsible for raising £25,000 to provide an Asylum for them. He was a generous supporter of the Infirmary and his wife was instrumental in founding the first Froebel Institute in the region.

Another Jew, Dr Louis Borchardt, who had spent two years in a German prison 'for encouraging revolt', was chief physician to the Children's Dispensary which, under his care and direction, developed into the General Hospital and Dispensary for Sick Children at Pendlebury, which has continued to perform outstanding service in this sphere of medicine. In 1862 Dr Borchardt was elected President of the Manchester Medical Society—an indication of the esteem in which he was held by his profession. In the cultural and commercial spheres, the community has provided a wealth of talent and business enterprise which almost speaks for itself. Sir Charles Hallé must have esteemed highly the executant ability of the Jewish musicians. Among the great leaders of his orchestra were Ludwig Strauss, who came from Vienna, Willy Hess who studied under Joachim, and Adolph Brodsky whose name became a legend at the Manchester Royal College of Music and in the rarefied world of chamber music. Among his distinguished players were Siegfried Jacoby, who served the orchestra from its inception in 1858 until Hallé's death in 1895, Samuel and Simon Speelmann and Isidore Cohn.[10] In commerce, Emanuel Freud, half-brother of Sigmund, was a notable cloth merchant, while Ludwig Mond made a most valuable contribution to the founding of the chemical industry in Manchester in his alkali discoveries. He was assisted by Philip Goldschmidt, who twice became Mayor of Manchester, in 1883 and 1885—the first foreign-born citizen to be elected to this office. But the story of this great community goes on.[11]

Not all Jews in Victorian Manchester were German and not all Germans Jewish, but the racial and national overlap was very marked in the Manchester and Salford German communities. For example, one of the most distinguished families of the German community in Victorian Manchester was the Behrens. Descending from an eighteenth-century Jewish family of Hamburg, the Behrens became associated with Manchester through two grandsons. Solomon Levi Behrens came to Manchester in 1809 to represent the interests of the family business in Hamburg. As a merchant-banker he established the firm of S. L. Behrens & Company, which became one of the most respected business houses in Manchester, with close connections with the London House of N. M. Rothschild & Sons. Solomon Levi was one of the first subscribers to young Charles Hallé's chamber concerts in 1849, and used to obtain the household milk from a small farm with cows at the corner of Charlotte Street and Portland Street. The other grandson, Sir Jacob Behrens, came to Leeds in 1834, when he founded the family shipping firm which he transferred to Bradford in 1838. Two years later he sent his brother, Louis, to open the Manchester branch of the business in Chepstow Street. To this Manchester office Charles Hallé was a regular visitor, as he sent his cheques through the firm to his mother in Hagen, Westphalia. This is how he met a young business apprentice, Gustav Behrens, eldest son of Jacob, thus inaugurating a friendship which ultimately had consequences of the utmost importance for the future of the Hallé Orchestra. When Gustav married Fanny Warburg in 1879, Charles Hallé was a frequent and welcome guest at 'Holly Royde', the Behrens' home in Palatine Road, Manchester. When Gustav Behrens died, at the age of ninety, in March 1936, it was said of him that 'no man did more than he to add "sweetness and light" to the rather grim philosophy which governed Manchester's development. He was an example of the good European.'[12] It was thus a happy inspiration when his children presented the family home to the University to enable the Extra-Mural Department to possess its own Residential College— the first institution of its kind in the country, which now has important links with many of the towns of the Greater Manchester County.

Not the least important contribution of the German community was the establishing of the chemical industry, for which Manchester, in the proximity of its coal mines, was ideally placed. Edward Schunck of Kersal laid the foundation for the production of artificial alizarine. Regarded as the pioneer of the manufacture of this chemical from coal tar, Schunck was a Fellow of the Royal Society and a much valued member of the Manchester Literary and Philosophical Society. With the production of sulphuric acid and naphthalene by the Levinsteins at Blackley as early as 1865, Manchester was rightly claimed, twenty years later, by Ivan Levinstein as 'an important chemical centre' at which 'nearly every branch of chemical manufacture is represented.' In 1860 there arrived in Manchester a young Silesian from Switzerland, with no influence other than his engineering diploma from Zürich. Seven years later, Henry Simon laid the first part of his family business by introducing into England a roller flour-milling plant and, in another fourteen years, the second part by installing a by-product coke oven. From these two highly technical enterprises the great Simon Engineering Group at Cheadle Heath, Stockport, grew into one of the leading businesses of its kind in the world. That the native Mancunian in commerce and industry regarded the members of the German community with respect and at times admiration may be deduced from the reports of the Chamber of Commerce. Despite the threat from German industry to Manchester's domination of world trade in textiles, the Chamber recorded its conviction that

'rivals in world commerce we must necessarily be but a commercial rivalry should be no more a barrier to amity between nations than it is between individuals. We frankly admit and admire the wonderful industrial progress made in Germany in the past forty years and it is only reasonable that she should want outlets for her expanding trade and her place in the sun.'[13]

These are liberal sentiments reflecting not only the quiet confidence of the manufacturers of the cotton towns and of the merchants in Manchester in their own ability to maintain their position in the markets of the world but also their cosmopolitan outlook. Evidently something of Richard Cobden's dream sixty years earlier of international peace as a consequence of free trade still lingered on in the communities of Greater Manchester.

The third largest influx of foreigners into Victorian Manchester was that of the Greeks. With the dissolution of the Levant Company in 1825 and the withdrawal of the East India Company's monopoly of the India trade by 1813 and the China trade by 1833, the way was open for the ambitions of the Manchester Chamber of Commerce and for the business acumen of the commercially-minded Greeks, who brought to Manchester an intimate knowledge of the requirements of the consumer. By 1835 there were four Greek merchanting firms in the town and ten years later there were twenty-four. With the repeal of the Corn Laws and the consequent opening up of an expanding two-way traffic with the Levant, the Greek community began to increase rapidly, so that twenty years later there were at least 150 Greek merchant houses in Manchester. Although a large community, the Greeks do not seem to have sought integration with the inhabitants of their adopted City. Greek names do not appear prominently in the records of the Chamber of Commerce, in the civic offices of the municipality nor in the lists of members of the cultural and scientific societies. They lived as a community chiefly in Kersal and Higher Broughton, in which latter district they built their own church of the Greek orthodox faith in 1860 in Bury New Road. Although now a somewhat diminished community, the Greeks continue to dwell in these two districts of Salford.

While the Greeks in the early nineteenth century controlled most of the foreign trade of the Ottoman Empire, the Armenians had a strong hold on the internal trade. As the demand for Lancashire textiles gradually increased in this sphere, the more enterprising Armenians in Constantinople and Smyrna, jealous of their Greek rivals, took their courage into their hands and came to Manchester to procure textiles either for their own firms in the Levant or on commission for others. By 1848 there were three Armenian merchant houses in the city. The success of these pioneers and the events of the Crimean War and the Russo–Turkish War of 1877 encouraged others to follow so that by 1858 there were fifteen Armenian firms established in Manchester, by 1881 there were thirty-one and by the end of the century just over fifty. They shipped cotton textiles, bleached and unbleached, dyed-prints of various types and also certain woollen goods to their markets in Constantinople, Smyrna, Trabizonde and Alexandretta, and through these towns to the whole extent of the Ottoman Empire. In the 1890s Armenians owned several laundries in Manchester, equipped with the most up-to-date machinery and giving excellent service to the Manchester public. The focal point for the Armenian community was, and still is, their church in Upper Brook Street—the first Armenian church in England. With its great Christian traditions from the third century (the Armenians claim to be the first nation to have embraced the Christian faith), the Church symbolises not only the spiritual but also the national unity of this much-persecuted people. With their instinct for preserving national customs and with the growth of the community, the Manchester Armenians formed two associations which continue to this day: the Armenian Ladies Association and the Armenian Association of Manchester. Their social, cultural and philanthropic activities would be an immense credit to any community.[14]

The majority of French and Italians who settled in Victorian Manchester were engaged in business other than merchanting and manufacturing, with the prominent exception of Henry Bronnert, founder of the well-known firm of shipping-merchants. His brother, Dr Emile Bronnert, perfected the processes which led to the commercial use of rayon by the Lancashire cotton industry. Perhaps the most important French contribution to late Victorian Manchester was that of Victor Kastner who established the Department of French Language and Literature at the University in 1895. As a young man, he had been stationmaster at Lyons (a Civil Service post in France) and, later, major domo to the French Ambassador at the Court of St James. When he retired from his Chair at the University in 1909, he was succeeded by his son, Léon Emile Kastner. When the latter completed his long and distinguished service to the University in 1933, he was succeeded by Eugène Vinaver who, for thirty-three years, presided over a Department, the size and variety of which would have astonished its founder. It must be almost a University record to have an academic Department served by only three successive professors over a period of seventy years, a period in which many great changes, social and economic, took place in the University, in the City and in the region which is now the Greater Manchester County.

Azeglio Valgimigli, who came to Manchester in 1881, lectured in Italian Studies at the University and was a founder and the first Secretary of the Manchester Dante Society, has described the Italian community.[15] It would appear that the first Italian merchant to settle in Manchester was C. G. Alberti, who in 1790 had his office at 21 Brazennose Street. The Ronchetti families were early settled as opticians and mathematical instrument-makers and as manufacturers of waterproof garments. C. J. Ronchetti, who is said to have made several of the instruments for John Dalton's experiments, was grandfather of the most famous of the Manchester Italians, Louis Charles Casartelli, who became the fourth Bishop of Salford, lectured in Iranian languages at the University and was President of the Manchester Statistical Society from 1898 to 1900. From 1835 small groups of Italians came to Manchester to earn their living as caterers and ice-cream manufacturers. They gradually settled in Ancoats, and by the end of the century the community numbered about 2,000, some of whom attained fame in their trade. In another sphere, F. O. Ruspini, a Genoese, was the first professional clerk to the Manchester School Board, an office he held from 1871 to 1886. One of the most interesting and valuable members of the community was Dr Andrea Crestadoro, described as 'an Italian by birth, English from choice and librarian through opportunity'.[16] He was educated at the University of Turin, where he eventually became Professor of Natural Philosophy. When he first visited England in 1849, he found life in London so much to his taste that he decided to stay, pursuing his work as an indexer and cataloguer with a particular interest in the British Museum Library, upon which he wrote a small book.[17] He applied the methods he advocated to the cataloguing of the Manchester Free Reference Library, to which he was appointed for this purpose in 1862. Two years later, he was appointed the Chief Librarian of Manchester, in which office he became noted for his organizing ability and for a liberal attitude towards lifting restrictions on the use of libraries.

The Moroccans, a non-Christian and non-European community, began to settle in south Manchester during the latter half of the nineteenth century. They quickly endeared themselves, with their white turbans and gay Eastern dress, to the citizens of Manchester and Salford, and they acquired proficiency in English almost as quickly as they exchanged their oriental slippers for black boots. In business affairs they earned a reputation for honesty and fair dealing.[18] They strictly observed the rules of their Moslem faith and during the long fast of Ramadan most of them did not eat, drink or smoke during the day, an ordeal for anyone when it occurred during a Manchester winter. Owing to changing economic and political conditions in Morocco, this kindly, colourful community began to leave the district of Manchester in the early years of this century.[19]

It may be thought that, up to the end of the nineteenth century, Manchester, and to a lesser extent Salford, had a disproportionate monopoly of these foreigners, who came and settled here in their communities. In view of the lack of evidence of any appreciable number of foreigners migrating to the manufacturing towns of the Metropolitan County and settling there, one has to ask why this is so. The answer lies in the word 'monopoly', which is authoritatively defined as 'exclusive possession of the trade in some commodity' and is derived from two Greek words meaning 'sole seller'.[20] This is precisely what Manchester was in relation to the towns of the region in which the cotton goods were manufactured—what has been well described as 'the metropolis of manufactures'.[21] The foreigners, and especially those from Europe who 'came as suppliants', says Asa Briggs, needed all the cloth they could buy, and the Manchester merchants were there to sell it to them. Better still to be on the spot to do business with those Manchester men. So they remained, either as principals of their own business-houses or as representatives of those at home. When the second great wave of immigrants came in the mid-twentieth century the story is entirely different and for different reasons. Between the two immigrations, however, there is a period of about half a century when the process was of smaller dimension, but of much significance.

When Hitler became Chancellor of Germany in January 1933, the exodus of those who could not tolerate the inhuman and sordid nature of Nazi philosophy began to increase. In this way, some of the most distinguished scholars and scientists of Germany turned to more liberal lands. Such, for example, was Michael Polanyi who left Berlin for the freedom of Manchester University, which he proceeded to serve for twenty-five years as Professor of Chemistry (1933–48) and Professor of Social Studies (1948–58). As the 1930s progressed, the plight of the Jews in Germany and in the countries annexed by Hitler became very serious, particularly after the abortive Munich Agreement in 1938. To help the refugee scholars, an unofficial group of university teachers in England—among whom were many at Manchester University—raised funds and organised assistance. Many Jews fled to this country, among them those who had relatives in the large and influential Jewish community in Manchester. They naturally came here, some to remain when they were found employment by their brethren, others to emigrate to America or to the dominions of the Commonwealth. It is difficult to estimate the number of those who chose to settle in Manchester (very few settled in the smaller towns of the Metropolitan County, mainly because they did not have established Jewish communities), but in 1956, the year of the commemoration of the tercentenary of Oliver Cromwell's liberal-minded decision to allow the Jews to resettle in England (Edward I originally expelled them), it was estimated that there were 30,000 in Manchester. As a community they have made a distinguished contribution to the civic and cultural life of Manchester and a most fruitful one to its commerce and industry. 'We are proud of our Jewish faith and heritage,' said a leading member of the community during this celebration, 'proud too of our deep roots in Manchester, our citizenship, and all that such a status gives and demands.'[22]

It has been estimated that the total population of the Jewish community today in the Greater Manchester County is 39,000, by far the biggest proportion of whom live in the cities of Manchester and Salford.[23] A recent development in foreign relations was the foundation in 1948 by Lord Simon of Wythenshawe of Research Fellowships designed to give scholars of all nationalities special facilities at Manchester University. In 1960 Lady Simon gave her former home, Broomcroft Hall, and its gardens to the University 'to be used as a residence for Simon Fellows and such other senior visitors as the Vice-Chancellor shall from time to time determine'.[24] The Hall is situated at the southern end of Didsbury village and commands lovely views over the fields of the Mersey valley. One of the reciprocal advantages of these generous Research Fellowships is that they regularly bring a number of European and other scholars into the cultural and industrial life of the Greater Manchester County.

With the rapid collapse of Hitler's Germany in the closing months of the Second World War, and during the early years of peace, there was a migration not before experienced of Polish and Eastern European nationals into this country. One of the main factors promoting this process was the determination of the victorious Russian Government either to annex neighbouring lands, as it did with the Baltic States, or at least to impose its Communist ideology upon those States on its borders which at that time it found prudent not to annex, such as Poland, Czechoslovakia and Eastern Germany. There was the further factor of the disbanding of the Polish Army in exile here and of the immigration of refugees from Poland itself and from the Ukraine. All these newcomers to England were known as European Voluntary Workers (E.V.W.s), many of whom spoke little or no English and did not possess relevant skills. The civil rights of these Poles, Ukrainians, Latvians, Lithuanians, Esthonians and Yugoslavs were much restricted and their access to social rights limited. It was only some years later that the British Government accepted the definition of integration as 'not a flattening process of assimilation but as equal opportunity accompanied by cultural diversity, in an atmosphere of mutual tolerance'[25]—a first-rate goal for all immigrants. The Polish community in Manchester today has its Social Club in Cheetham Hill Road, its Ex-Service Men's Club, its Parish Club and its own Travel Office. In Rochdale, with a population of over 500, the community has its Polish Catholic Centre; in Oldham, in addition to its Catholic Centre, there is an Ex-Servicemen's Club; in Bury a Social Centre, and in Ashton-under-Lyne a Social Club. The Ukrainians have in Manchester three Social Clubs and a Saturday School for their children to keep alive their national culture; in Oldham the community has three Clubs, as has also the thousand-strong community in Rochdale, where some members have married Italian immigrants. There are Ukrainian Social Clubs, also, in Stockport and Bury. In Manchester there is a Lithuanian Social Club in Middleton Road. A new generation, children of the parents of the original E.V.W. movement has now grown up, born in Britain and therefore legally entitled to the rights of full British citizenship, educated in British schools and some of them having enjoyed the advantages of higher education. One trusts that they, at least, live in an atmosphere of mutual tolerance and equal opportunity.

The origin of the New Commonwealth waves of immigration to this country is to be found during the years of the Second World War when troops from all parts of the Empire were stationed in Britain. It was not, however, until the early 1950s that the movement of West Indians, Indians, Pakistanis and Africans into Britain assumed substantial proportions. In 1951 the New Commonwealth immigrant population in England and Wales was 336,400; by 1961 it had increased to 659,800 and by 1966 it had reached nearly a million (942,300).[26] It is reckoned that today there are in Britain over two million New Commonwealth immigrants. Why have they come here? There are at least three reasons, the primary one as applying to the majority of immigrants being economic, in order to work. A powerful secondary reason was the presence in Britain of family or of relatives. This is why one finds that in Rochdale, for example, the large Pakistani immigrant community come in the main from the same villages of north-west India and tend to settle in the same quarter in Rochdale. This is so strong a tendency that the Gujarat State is called the 'Lancashire of India'. One can readily find evidence of this familial congregation of immigrants in other Districts of the Greater Manchester County as, for example, in Bolton, Bury and Oldham. The third motive which influenced the immigrants to come to Britain was their desire to live and work in the Mother Country—one might almost say for historical reasons. Those who deplore the 'flood' of immigrants and fear that Britain will become overcrowded as a result of it seem to ignore the fact that in many of the post-war years more people have emigrated from this country than have come into it. In 1972, as many as 233,200 people emigrated from England, while those who entered it numbered 221,900.[27] The imputation that violence is increasing in this country because of the presence of coloured immigrants was officially refuted in 1968 by an Under-Secretary at the Home Office, who declared that 'it is a view commonly held that there is some link between colour and crime. There is absolutely no evidence to substantiate this claim.'[28]

One of the significant features of Commonwealth immigration into the north-west of England is the practical manner in which the medical profession and the National Health Service have assimilated those qualified to enter these vital services to the community. It has been estimated that over 67 per cent of Junior Hospital doctors in this region are Commonwealth immigrants, mainly from India. Similarly, from 30 to 40 per cent of the nurses serving in the hospitals are from the West Indies and Asia. The total population of the Greater Manchester County is at present 2,721,534. Of these it has been estimated that there are some 90,000 resident immigrants who live and work in all the ten Districts. The immigrant population is therefore 3·4% of the total Greater Manchester population. Socially they have their own community centres and sports activities. It has already been noticed, for example, that in the Denton and District Cricket League, in the District of Tameside, there are two Indian clubs with their ground at Ashton-under-Lyne, while the Bolton Association has two clubs, also—the Bolton Indians and the Bolton West Indians. In August 1974, the very large West Indian community in Manchester organised and held a Culture Week at their own Centre in Chorlton-on-Medlock, where an exhibition displaying the art, crafts and literature of the Caribbean and African countries was housed. The organisers stated their purpose as 'to create an awareness in our people in Manchester and also in the host community, of the contribution we have made and are still making to British society, and to give our young people tangible reasons for being proud of their cultural heritage.'[29] These are excellent objectives and entirely in accord with the best traditions

SURVEY OF ESTIMATED IMMIGRANTS IN GREATER MANCHESTER COUNTY (1971-1974)

COUNTY or MUNICIPAL BOROUGH	POPULATION 1971 CENSUS	NEW COMMONWEALTHS 1971 CENSUS		ESTIMATED INCREASED TOTAL 1974	TYPE OF EMPLOYMENT	DISTRICT and ESTIMATED POPULATION 1974
BOLTON C.B.	154,199	7,065 Indian Pakistani West Ind. African	3,940 885 435 1,570	12,500 400+Uganda Asians recently arrived	Mainly textiles	BOLTON 258,000
BURY C.B.	67,849	1,030 Indian Pakistani West Ind. African	225 575 100 55	3,000	Mainly textiles	BURY 200,000
MANCHESTER C.B.	543,650	17,290 Indian Pakistani West Ind. African	2,995 3,440 7,120 2,195	45,000 West Indians now 25,000 Half Indians are Sikhs	Mixed— transport, engineering, catering and other occupations	MANCHESTER 590,000
OLDHAM C.B.	105,913	3,960 Indian Pakistani West Ind. African	500 2,480 535 280	9,500 Mostly Bangladeshis and large increase in West Indians	Mainly textiles	OLDHAM 230,000
ROCHDALE C.B.	91,455	4,435 Indian Pakistani West Ind. African	1,035 2,815 110 290	7,000 Main increase in Pakistanis & some Uganda Asians	Mainly textiles	ROCHDALE 200,000
SALFORD C.B.	130,976	1,325 Indian Pakistani West Ind. African	240 325 180 180	2,500 The area of Salford tends to merge with Cheetham area of Manchester	Mainly textiles	SALFORD 318,000
STOCKPORT C.B.	139,644	835 Indian Pakistani West Ind. African	225 170 130 110	1,300	Mainly textiles	STOCKPORT 350,000
WIGAN C.B.	81,147	215 Indian Pakistani West Ind. African	75 25 15 25	450	Mixed— textiles and coal-mining	WIGAN 301,000
STRETFORD M.B.	54,295	2,590		5,000	Mixed— transport, engineering and catering	TRAFFORD 230,000
MIDDLETON M.B.	53,510	210		400	Mainly textiles	ROCHDALE
ASHTON-U-LYNE	48,952			2,000 Indians, Pakistanis, West Indians	Mainly textiles	TAMESIDE 246,000
HYDE	37,095			1,000 mostly Bangladeshis		
STALYBRIDGE	22,805			200 mostly Indians		

of English liberalism and national tolerance. These characteristics are to be found also in the sensitive sphere of comparative religion—the great majority of New Commonwealth immigrants are not members of the Christian Church. Thus, throughout the Greater Manchester County, where there are Sikhs and Hindus there are temples in which they freely worship; where there are Pakistanis, Indians and Bangladeshis, there are mosques. Among the large West Indian communities there are Pentecostal churches and chapels.[30]

With the publication of the national Census for 1971 and the compiling of more recent estimates, it has been possible to draw up an up-to-date survey of the New Commonwealth immigrants who have settled in the Districts of the Greater Manchester County. The discrepancy in the third column between the sum of the itemised numbers and that of the total is due in the main to the omission of immigrants from the Old Commonwealth (Australia, New Zealand and Canada) and from the Irish Republic (see table, page 128).

The presence of the second generation of children of the New Commonwealth immigrants in the Greater Manchester County has created both a challenge and an opportunity for the District Councils, which are entirely responsible for their education. The immigrant communities themselves are also conscious of the intricacies of this very human problem. The West Indians in Manchester have recently expressed their awareness of the implications involved:

'Many of our children are denied the privilege of learning about their cultural background in British schools, so it is our duty to fill this gap in their development by providing supplementary schools which teach culturally relevant subjects and by getting them involved in cultural activities . . . by plays, poetry, films, art and music.'[31]

The size of the problem may be seen in the table on p. 130, which gives the percentage in January 1972 of immigrant children among all pupils in the primary and secondary schools maintained by four large Metropolitan Boroughs in the Greater Manchester County.[32]

In the remaining six districts the percentage for immigrant children in their maintained primary and secondary schools at that time did not exceed 2 per cent.

	Primary Schools	Secondary Schools	Primary and Secondary Schools
Bolton	7.3	10.2	8.3
Manchester	6.5	4.6	5.8
Oldham	3.6	4.7	4.0
Rochdale	6.3	7.2	6.7

Percentage in Jan. 1972 of immigrant children in schools

As the Local Government Act (1972) rightly placed the responsibility for the provision and maintenance of education upon the District Councils, this has undoubtedly placed upon those Districts in the Greater Manchester County which have proportionately large immigrant communities in their midst a correspondingly big commitment. It has been estimated that in 1973, Manchester Education Committee found itself responsible for the education in its schools of some 6,400 immigrant children, of whom approximately 45 per cent were West Indian children, 27 per cent Pakistani and 8 per cent Indian with the remainder made up of Chinese, Greek Cypriot and African children. In 1974 the number of children of immigrant origin probably exceeded 10 per cent of the school population in Manchester Schools. Evidently half the schools of Manchester have at least 10 per cent of immigrant children on their registers, while some of the Primary schools and large Comprehensive (High) schools have as many as from 40 to 60 per cent of immigrant children. Birley High School, for example, in Hulme, which carries the name of a much honoured Manchester family with a very distinguished record of service to education over the past century, has 40 per cent of its pupils from immigrant, chiefly West Indian, families—and attractive and happy many of them look in this well-equipped modern school.

It is the policy of the Education Committee that pupils, wherever possible, should enrol at local (or neighbourhood) schools. Wherever there is a significant proportion of immigrant children at a school, additional teaching staff are allocated to it in order to reduce the teacher–pupil ratio and thereby cope with particular problems such as English language teaching and learning. For this purpose, some immigrant children are withdrawn from normal

Immigrant and English children working together in a Manchester primary school

classes for a period of time to enable them to receive special tuition in both language and social training from the teacher equipped for this particular work. For such teachers interested in the welfare of immigrant children, the Committee arranges special training courses of its own and encourages them to enrol for courses organised by the Department of Education and Science. For all this the Committee has appointed a Curriculum Development Leader with special responsibility for the education of immigrant children.[33] Clearly much thought has been, and is being, given to the personal and educational problems which are bound to arise for immigrant children in English schools. It is the tradition of Manchester and its neighbouring District Councils of Bolton, Rochdale and Oldham that they are tackling them generously and wholeheartedly.

Immigration rules for this country are very strict today and it is only natural that serious social problems are bound to arise. The extent to which successive governments have recognised the importance of this situation may be judged by the fact that each has appointed a Junior Minister who is responsible to the Home Office for the supervision of these problems. One of the most difficult of these is the type of employment an immigrant is expected to undertake. Often he may have to accept a low-grade job even though he is qualified to do a much better one. This has been well explained by the Community Relations Commission and would seem to have reference to those immigrants in the manufacturing towns of the Greater Manchester County who find at least their first employment in the textile industry:

'Both textile and clothing jobs are widely regarded as low paid and, in addition, the recent large scale adoption of shift work in the textile industry has created a demand for male workers which has largely been met by New Commonwealth immigrants, especially Asians; labouring jobs are not only relatively badly paid but also demand little skill—a feature thought to be characteristic of New Commonwealth workers.'[34]

In a revealing article on the TUC and its policy towards racial discrimination, the Labour Correspondent of a 'high quality' Sunday newspaper has pointed out that the trade union movement, after years of prevarication, 'is at least taking positive steps to eliminate racial discrimination from its own ranks.'[35] It is recognised that most immigrants are still in low-paid jobs, that they and foreign workers now make up almost 5 per cent of the work force and, feeling established in Britain, they now protest at industrial conditions they had previously accepted. In other words, white workers have accepted non-whites in their places of employment but not in the better jobs. Many of the immigrant workers, knowing that they have qualifications greater than their present jobs require, resent the fact that they do not get deserved promotion or training for the better paid jobs in factories. The TUC, realising the potential dangers of these fractious factors in industry, is evidently now ready to recommend that unions should incorporate clauses on equal opportunity into their collective agreements, thereby committing members and managements to protect the rights of minority immigrant workers.

As so often happens, one disadvantage tends to promote a chain of disadvantages. Because many of the New Commonwealth immigrants are in low-paid jobs, they cannot obtain for their families the housing conditions they would like to have, nor can they participate in the social amenities they would like to enjoy. These are real handicaps, and even causes of grievance, for many self-respecting immigrant workers, and they feel them keenly. And it is precisely in these respects that the mid-twentieth century immigrant differs from the foreigner who came to Manchester in the nineteenth century to obtain his share of the products of the textile industry and decided to settle here. He, unlike his twentieth-century counterpart, was an employer, as principal or agent of his own business; as such, he was able to secure for himself the housing and living conditions to which he aspired; above all, he was accepted by the society of which he regarded himself a member by birth and standing, and was, as a consequence, able to enjoy the civic and social amenities which were freely his. Yet it is interesting and encouraging to know that the New Commonwealth immigrants who have come to Manchester and its neighbouring towns of the Metropolitan County, having settled here, are not keen to move elsewhere in England.[36] It is, perhaps, not too much to assume that the region of Manchester, traditionally used to receiving foreigners, has a reputation for the kind of hospitality which the natural courtesy and innate kindliness of its inhabitants have for nearly two centuries promoted. Inheriting, as it does, such a distinctive tradition, the new Greater Manchester County would do well to recognise and maintain so great a truth.

Chapter 9

'Growing in the way of their own nature'

Manchester

On Wednesday 22 May 1974 a ceremony took place at the Manchester Town Hall at which HRH The Prince of Wales presented to the Lord Mayor a new Charter under the Queen's Sign Manual, which conferred upon the District of Manchester the status of a borough, henceforth to be known as the Metropolitan Borough of Manchester. His Royal Highness also presented Letters Patent in which HM The Queen conferred upon the Borough of Manchester the status of a City. This grant of Letters Patent also declared and directed that 'the Mayor and Deputy Mayor of the said City shall respectively be entitled to the style of Lord Mayor and Deputy Lord Mayor of Manchester and enjoy and use all and singular the rights privileges and advantages to the degree of a Lord Mayor and Deputy Lord Mayor . . .' It was an historic and very pleasant ceremony, at the conclusion of which the Lord Mayor expressed his gratitude to the Prince for enabling him to feel that he was no longer like a bridegroom emerging from the church without his marriage certificate, to which the Prince of Wales at once replied that he was happy to have the opportunity of legitimising the position of his host.

Why, as Manchester had already been incorporated as a borough in 1838 and had received the title of City in 1853, did this ceremony take place? By the Local Government Act of 1972, which effected nationally an almost complete reorganisation of the structure of local government, Manchester was due to lose not only its title of City but also its status as a borough. As, however, the Act was not due to become fully operative until 1 April 1974, on which day the Greater Manchester Metropolitan County became a reality, the opportuniy was given under a special section of the Act for the Manchester City Council to petition the Queen, as indeed other Councils similarly placed were entitled to do, for the restoration of its city and borough status. This Manchester did at the appropriate time and the result was this ceremony. It has to be remembered that the royal grant of the status of city does not in itself confer upon its Chief Magistrate the title of Lord Mayor. This title was not conferred upon the Mayor of Manchester until 1893, which explains why the Letters Patent presented at this ceremony specifically endowed upon the Mayor, as he then was, his entitlement to the style of Lord Mayor.

Salford

But Manchester was not the only place within the newly-created Metropolitan County to petition the Queen for the restoration of its status as a city and borough. Salford, its independent-minded neighbour, had been incorporated as a borough in 1844 and had also had conferred upon it in 1926 the title of City, although its Chief Magistrate remains as Mayor. But the City Council of Salford was in the exalted position of being able to petition Her Majesty not only in her capacity as the Duke of Lancaster but also as lord of the manor of Salford, as has earlier been noted. When, in the reign of William Rufus, 'a stroke of a Norman baron's pen' divorced Manchester and Salford, it was not Salford which became separated from Manchester, it was Manchester, humbler in its line of lords, which became separated from Salford. As the royal demesne manor, Salford was at the head of the Hundred named after it and had its own Court of Record. This Court, known as the Salford Hundred Court of Record, continued to function as a Civil Court until 1 January 1972 when, with other ancient Courts of a like nature throughout the country, it was abolished and replaced by the Unified Court Service. Salford, then, is a place of antiquity and, locally, was more important than Manchester in the early stages of their growth. In 1228 Henry III granted a fair and market to the town, and two years later Randle de Blundeville, sixth earl of Chester, gave a charter to its burgesses, the substance of which was taken as a model by Thomas Grelley when he granted his charter just over seventy years later to the burgesses of Manchester. The Salford charter enabled its enrolled burgesses to have a burgage of one acre, for which they had to pay 'twelve pence a year' and which entitled them to free pasture in the woods and on the plain. Craftsmen such as shoemakers, skinners and fullers were given the commercial advantage of being protected from competitors living beyond the bounds of the manor.

From the early Middle Ages, Salford was rich in its manor houses, for it has been estimated that within five miles' radius of Ordsall Hall, probably the best known, there were nearly three dozen manor houses.[1] In the fourteenth century Ordsall Hall was the seat of Sir John Radcliffe, with whose family it remained for the next three hundred years. Part of the Hall which he built may be seen today in the Star Chamber and the room above it. These rooms and the subsequent reconstruction of the Hall and its surroundings were bought by Salford Corporation in 1959 from the Egerton Trustees, with the object of restoring and adapting it as a museum. As a direct result of this enlightened municipal enterprise, one is able to enjoy in Salford an excellent example of late medieval and Tudor domestic architecture, well cared for and in the very centre of a great industrial region. It is eminently worth visiting. There were at least four other historic Halls in Salford: Broughton Hall, owned by the Earl of Derby, which eventually passed into the hands of the Clowes family; Pendleton Old Hall, which owned land valuable for its water and mineral rights; Kersal Hall and Kersal Cell, important half-timbered houses with estates in the Irwell valley.[2]

In the opening stages of the Civil War, Salford and Manchester took opposite sides. Their only physical link was Salford Bridge, predecessor of Victoria Bridge, which joined the two towns over the River Irwell, described 130 years ago as 'the most hard-worked and over-tasked stream in the universe'.[3] The two towns at this period were very small in comparison with modern standards. If one crossed the Old Bridge to enter Salford, to the right would be Greengate with its famous hostelry, the Bull's Head, at the end of which was the market place, with its black and white timbered houses, the village green and the Courthouse with its pillory and stocks. A few minutes' walk from the market place in any direction brought a citizen of Salford into open fields with focal points in scattered villages and hamlets. Farther afield, larger clusters of houses denoted Pendleton and Irlam's-o' th'-Height on the Bolton road and Tetlow Fold (in the region of Cheetham Hill) on the Bury road.[4]

By the end of the eighteenth century, this country setting was gradually being converted into a scene of industrial activity which eventually marked out Salford as one of Britain's most important centres of the engineering, textile, chemical and distribution industries, employing some 70,000 people in over 1,000 enterprises. This change from a rural to an industrial town has greatly altered almost the whole of the landscape of Salford. Equally, its population has grown from 12,600 in 1812 to 176,400 in 1952. Whether, if any of the several attempts to amalgamate Salford and Manchester had succeeded, the prospects for the two close neighbours would have been better in general, it is difficult to decide. Certainly Salford itself has consistently been against such a move. It is a proud city, which has been governed for some years by a vigorous and courageous City Council, whose record of achievement in housing, public health, education and the social services will stand comparison with any other city of similar size. It claims to be the first city in the world to make a total survey of the circumstances, living conditions and needs of every old age pensioner within its boundaries, as a result of which its civic report on this survey has aroused international interest and enquiry. Casting its eyes upon its larger neighbour, Salford has often wondered whether, if it had pursued an expansionist policy (what it calls almost contemptuously 'municipal colonialism') during the past hundred years, it might conceivably have been just as large and as powerful as its sister city, Manchester. Having preferred to 'cultivate its own garden', it now hopefully sees a new future in its position as the focal point of a Metropolitan District within the Greater Manchester County, in which capacity it will be linked, on a friendly basis, with a number of its neighbours 'to their mutual advantage'.[5] It regards its position in this District as a strategic one, in as much as its neighbouring towns will provide a ready market for its industrial and consumer products while the excellent rail and road services between the various towns will promote a great and expanding home market. Salford has no doubts about its future.

During the last two decades of the nineteenth century, important reforms in the machinery of local government took place. The Local Government Act of 1888 set up popularly elected County Councils to replace the ancient administration of counties by the Justices of the Peace sitting at Quarter Sessions, a class largely made up of the landed gentry, to whom, as has been noted, Richard Cobden in the 1830s so eloquently and strongly took exception. To further the course of urban democracy, all towns of over 50,000 inhabitants were separated from the county jurisdiction and were given their own local self-government as County Boroughs. Six years later, another Act completed the process by setting up Borough, Urban District, Rural District and Parish Councils, all based on direct popular election. The new Greater Manchester County embraces some seventy former local Councils, ranging from County Boroughs to Rural District Councils, all of which lost their status with the coming into force of the Local Government Act of 1972. However, the eight County Boroughs involved in this process have all succeeded in recovering their status, a new one called Metropolitan Borough. Each of these new Boroughs has given its name to, and embraces, the District in which it is situated, while Trafford and Tameside, to complete the ten Districts into which the Metropolitan County is divided, assume new names of historical and geographical origin respectively. Thus Manchester and Salford are not the only boroughs to recover their status in the Metropolitan County. The six other former County Boroughs have done so and it is proposed to extend to them and to Trafford and Tameside due recognition as follows:

Metropolitan Borough of Wigan

The original site of this town has been generally identified with the Roman station of Coccium, as mentioned in the *Antonine Itinerary* of the second century A.D. The derivation of the name Wigan is not positively known, but it is generally considered to be of Saxon origin. At the time of the Norman Conquest, Wigan was included in the barony of Newton. In 1245 Henry III granted a royal charter to the town, incorporating it as a borough with its own guild and trading rights. At the end of the Middle Ages there were only four boroughs in Lancashire possessing royal charters—Lancaster, Liverpool, Preston and Wigan. They ruled themselves through their mayors, aldermen and burgesses and they held their own courts-leet and their regular markets and fairs, from which they drew considerable fees and rents. Guilds of merchants organised their trade and industry and from the reign of Edward I each was entitled to be represented by 'two worthy burgesses' in the House of Commons. At this time Wigan emerged as an important market town. In the Tudor period coal was mined extensively. Leland recorded that 'Mr Bradshaw hath a place called Hawe [Haigh] a myle from Wigan; he hath found much canel like sea-coale in his ground, very profitable to him.' During the Civil War, Wigan was prominent as the central garrison for the Royalists in the county, in which it staunchly maintained its long-held reputation as the 'ancient and loyal town'. The Royalists were finally defeated at the battle of Wigan Lane in 1651, after which their leader, the Earl of Derby, having fought for Charles II at Worcester, was captured, tried at Chester and condemned to die at Bolton. A far more profitable occupation for Wigan at this time was the introduction of the English porcelain industry into the town as a result of experiments by John Dwight with the local clays. This was accompanied by clockmaking at the end of the century.

But undoubtedly Wigan's main industry was coal-mining, for its immense coal formations extended for miles in every direction. Coal-getting was even a domestic matter, for it has been said that 'a coal-mine in the backyard was not uncommon in Wigan.'[6] To facilitate the transport of coal, a canal was constructed in 1727 parallel to the River Douglas, on which Wigan is situated. In 1772 this canal was continued to Liverpool and flats of coal were transported into the heart of the town. Subsequently this canal was incorporated into the new Leeds and Liverpool Canal, whose wharf at Wigan became known as 'Wigan Pier'. Side by side with coal-mining, the textile industry began with the making of woollen garments from cloth woven on hand looms. By the end of the eighteenth century Wigan had its own Cloth Hall as its textile industry gradually expanded and became nationally known. At this time Wigan was a town of contrasts; textiles and mining industries on the one hand and agriculture on the other were carried on in the midst of the town. Wigan even enjoyed a brief spell as a spa until its springs of chalybeate water became contaminated by coal workings and eventually drained away. It was the coming of the railways to Wigan in 1831 which inaugurated its great modern industrial era. In view of its position on the great South Lancashire coalfield, Wigan soon possessed large ironworks. Its mining industry rapidly progressed with the application of steam to the winding-engine and ventilation-fan which enabled coal to be wound from greater depths. Formed in 1865, the Wigan Coal and Iron Co. Ltd. soon replaced the small coal-owner and the yeoman who dug his coal. Miners from the Wigan coalfield began to play an increasingly important rôle in the trades union association, while the Earl of Crawford, who inherited the great Haigh estates through his marriage in 1780 to Elizabeth Bradshaigh Dalrymple, took up residence in Haigh Hall as the most prominent owner of coal mines in the district. Both he and his son did much to promote the industry in Wigan. In 1861 the Corporation of Wigan bought the manorial rights and the centre of the town surrounding the old market place. It was at this point that the Wigan and District Mining and Technical College was founded, one of the oldest of its kind in Britain, and it was about this time that its cultural, social and civic activities began to develop strongly, activities which, in a very real sense, find their counterpart today in this 'progressive and proud town'.[7]

Metropolitan Borough of Bolton

Historically, what is now the District of Bolton has had the closest affinity with Manchester from the beginning, inasmuch as the lord of the manor's forest of Horwich, within the original Barony of

Manchester, was situated in what is now the north-west corner of the new District. Following the bestowal of the manor of Bolton by William I upon Roger the Poitevin, it eventually passed by marriage to the Derby family, who in 1251 obtained the grant of a royal charter for the establishment of a market and fair in the town. Two years later, Bolton (or Bolton-le-Moors as it was then named) received a charter from the same family, which in its privileges followed closely those conferred upon the burgesses of Salford by Randle de Blundeville, Earl of Chester, some twenty-three years earlier.[8] Bolton early played its part in the 'manufacture of stuffs called Manchester cottons', as the Elizabethan antiquary, William Camden, described the coarse woollen cloths. An earlier chronicler, John Leland, said of the villages round Bolton that they 'do make cottons'. At first the wool came from the local clip, the sheep reared on the slopes of the Pennines in the vicinity of Bolton, but by the sixteenth century wool had to be bought from other parts of England and flax was imported from Ireland. Thus, as with other towns in South-East Lancashire, Bolton became the focal point of the domestic industry for the surrounding villages for which, in a larger sense, Manchester was the main centre in the marketing of the linen and woollen goods which they produced.

Nor was learning neglected. Robert Lever in 1641 founded his school at Bolton-le-Moors for instruction, not only in grammar and classical subjects, but also in 'writing, arithmetic, geography, navigation, mathematics and modern languages', thus conforming to the educational trend of the times, when thinkers and practical men alike were stimulated by a strong desire to curtail the time devoted to Greek and Latin in order to find a place within the school curriculum for what John Locke called 'real knowledge'.[9] At this time, Bolton and Manchester were the twin centres of Lancashire Puritanism. They were undoubtedly encouraged and influenced in their religious beliefs by the strong connection between the textile merchants in the towns of South-East Lancashire and the Puritan merchants in London. This subtle affinity of trade and Puritanism naturally tended to place the Lancashire textile towns on the side of the Parliamentarians from the outset of the Civil War, and Bolton was no exception. When, in 1644, Prince Rupert savagely attacked the town on his march through Cheshire and South-East Lancashire, its Puritan inhabitants suffered so severely that eventually the Royalist leader, the Earl of Derby, captured after the 'crowning mercy' of Cromwell's victory at Worcester, was wrongfully made to pay the price for Rupert's massacre by his execution in October 1651 at the market cross in the centre of Bolton.

By 1700 each textile district in the region of Manchester was specialising in the production of one type of cloth: Stockport and Ashton-under-Lyne produced almost all the linen cloth made; most woollens and worsted were manufactured in Bury and Rochdale; Bolton and Blackburn were centres for fustians. During the eighteenth century there were big increases in production, especially of cotton cloth. Between 1741 and 1750 the annual consumption of raw cotton was doubled, by 1780 it was again doubled, and between 1780 and 1787 it rose from five to twenty-two million pounds weight. Even the wars with France did little to retard this remarkable rate of development.[10] It was new machines, which used power and necessitated the steady replacement of the domestic system by the factory system of manufacture, which achieved this textile revolution. To this revolution Bolton made two cardinal contributions. The first was the Water Frame, invented in 1769 by Sir Richard Arkwright, who 'passed a great part of his life in the humble station of a barber in the town of Bolton.'[11] Arkwright was a go-getter and a ruthless organiser, the first of the industrialists who built up an immense fortune by organising industrial production on a very large scale. By 1780 there were twenty Water Frame factories and ten years later there were no fewer than one hundred and fifty.[12] The first cotton mill in Manchester was built by Arkwright just off Miller's Lane. Examples of his Water Frame may be seen at the Higher Mill, Helmshore Museum, near Bury, and at the North Western Museum of Science and Industry, Grosvenor Street, Manchester. The second of Bolton's great contributions was the 'Muslin Wheel' or 'Mule', which Samuel Crompton invented in great secrecy in the Hall in th' Wood at Tonge Moor, near Bolton. Crompton was born in a cottage situated among an isolated little community at Firwood Fold, just off what is now Crompton Way. A few years later his father took a few rooms on the upper floor of Hall in th' Wood, an attractive black and white sixteenth-century manor-house which at this time had been divided into tenements. Crompton's Mule, combining ideas from Hargreaves' 'Jenny' and Arkwright's 'Water Frame', achieved the great 'breakthrough' in 1780 for the cotton spinning industry, which went on to expand tremendously, so much so that spinning pushed so far ahead of weaving for decades that yarn itself became for a time an important export from England. Unlike Arkwright, however, Crompton did not make a fortune out of his great invention, for 'some gentlemen in Manchester purchased the invention for £100 and made it public.'[13] Fortunately his fame is enshrined in the manor-house where he spent two intensive years developing his 'Mule'—Hall in th' Wood, which was rescued from decay in 1899 and carefully restored by the first Lord Leverhulme, who generously presented it to his native town, where it is now maintained by the Bolton Corporation as a folk museum. To find an example of Crompton's 'Mule', however, one has to visit the nearby Bolton Industrial Museum at the Tonge Moor Library, where there are also examples of Arkwright's Water Frame and Hargreaves' Spinning Jenny.

When the first spinning mill was erected in Bolton in 1780, the population was only 8,000 (one third of that of Manchester at that time). But in the great impetus which Bolton gave to the rapid expansion of the cotton-spinning industry, its population and its fortunes rose accordingly. In 1842, when the Lancashire cotton industry was in the throes of a grave depression, its population had risen to 50,000. An accurate observer of the cotton towns at this time, while noting the condition of the 'distressed operatives in Bolton', was yet full of praise for all that he saw in the mills of nearby Turton owned by the enlightened Henry Ashworth:

'The working rooms are lofty, spacious and well-ventilated, kept at an equable temperature, and scrupulously clean. There is nothing in sight, sound, or smell to offend the most fastidious taste. So much space is occupied by the machinery that crowding is physically impossible. I should be very well contented to have as large a proportion of room and air in my own study as a cotton spinner in any of the mills of Lancashire.'[14]

The same observer expressed this view of the mill-owner and his operatives:

'No nobleman ever took more pride in a large estate than a genuine Lancastrian does in a large business; he would rather have your admiration of his mill than of his mansion, and if you happen to be pleased by any of his peculiar mechanisms or contrivances his admiration is complete. In the same way, the operative is far more thankful for employment than for alms; if he could obtain the one, he would look upon the offer of the other as an insult. An instance of this feeling came under our notice in Bolton: an operative out of work solicited us to enter his house; it was for the purpose of showing us some water-colour paintings which he had made in this period of reluctant leisure.'[15]

It may be pertinent to add that ten years later the first Bolton Public Library was opened under the provisions of the Public Libraries Act of 1850—the second such institution in the whole country. Civic pride and industrial expansion seemed to march together in Bolton from the middle of the nineteenth century. In 1855, its magnificent Market Hall was opened, 'all classical dignity outside and engineering beauty within', as one Bolton historian has described it.[16] In 1873 the impressive new Town Hall was opened, which has now become the focal point of the attractive and ambitious modern Civic Centre. Clearly Bolton over the centuries has lived up to its civic motto, which is freely translated as 'Overcome all difficulties', though literally in its Borough Coat of Arms it represents 'On the moors', which Bolton geographically and in ancient name is.

Metropolitan Borough of Bury

In 1795 John Aikin described Bury as 'pleasantly situated about nine miles north of Manchester, with the Irwell running close on its west side, and the Roche about a mile's distance on the east'. He commented on the country surrounding it as 'greatly diversified with hills and vallies, in which many rivulets wind, of great service in working the numerous machines used in the thriving manufactures of these parts'.[17] Bury, then, was well set to play its part in the gradual transference of the production of textiles from the domestic to the factory system.

During the early Middle Ages, the manor of Bury was part of the extensive barony of the de Montbegon family, which was centred upon the important and ancient manor of Tottington. In 1230 this manor, somewhat reduced in size, passed into the honour of Clitheroe, which was owned by the de Lacys, until by marriage it became part of the Earldom and ultimately the Duchy of Lancaster.[18] At some point in the fourteenth century the manor of Bury passed into the Pilkington family but when Henry VII confiscated the estates of those Lancashire landowners who had the temerity to support Lambert Simnel's bid for the throne, he gave most of them, including the manor of Bury, to the rising House of Stanley to which it still belongs. During these swiftly changing times, when family fortunes depended upon the judicious support of the right party, a licence had been granted to Thomas Pilkington 'to build, fortify and castellate a mansion, within his Manor of Bury'. It stood in the district now known as Castelcroft, and when John Leland visited this region about 1540 he referred to 'Bury on Irwell' as a poor market, having a ruin of a castle by the parish church and commented that 'yarn is made thereabouts.' In the summer of 1974, some enterprising members of the Bury Archaeological Group undertook a 'dig' in the Castelcroft area. They uncovered the remains of an inner defensive wall of the old castle behind the White Lion Hotel in Bolton Street. The Group is applying to the Department of Environment for permission to have this discovery recognised as an ancient monument as part of the town's redevelopment scheme.[19]

Bury grew up round the castle and the parish church, with the Market Place as the only street of consequence. In the early eighteenth century it was described as 'a little market town' and even later as 'a dingy place of old dilapidated buildings'.[20] Yet it was during this period that John Kay, of Walmersley, near Bury, invented in 1733 his 'flying shuttle', a mechanical device which greatly increased the speed at which the weavers of cloth could work. It was this invention which led to the gradual disappearance of the old hand-loom and the adoption of the loom powered by water, in the supply of which the district of Bury was well-endowed by nature. There is in the centre of Bury a statue of John Kay, erected in 1903. It is there as a symbol of pride and respect on the part of all citizens of his native town today. The domination of the woollen industry in Bury until the early years of the nine-teenth century is indicated in a directory for 1816, which records that there were in the town thirty-five woollen manufacturers, fourteen cotton manufacturers, six calico printers and four bleachers.[21]

It was the advent of the Peel family into the district which marked a new era in the industrial and social development of the town. The beneficial results for Bury of the various enterprises of Sir Robert Peel (the elder), in partnership with William Yates, have been well described by a contemporary local historian:

'The town and neighbourhood of Bury have been highly ben-efited by the establishment of the very capital manufacturing and printing works belonging to the Company, of which that very respectable gentleman, Robert Peel, Esq., member of Parliament for Tamworth, is the head. The principal of these works are situated in the side of the Irwell, from which they have large reservoirs of water . . . The premises occupy a large portion of ground, and cottages have been built for the accom-modation of the workmen, which form streets, and give the appearance of a village.'

The firm of Peel, Yates and Peel had several mills spread over a wide area of Bury. The principal concerns were the Bury Ground Print Works with its bleaching ground, not far from the present-day centre of the town. The spinning mills, however, were a con-siderable distance from the print works. One of them, Burrs Mill, which produced calico yarn for the printing works, had a row of twenty back-to-back workers' cottages. The working conditions, the wages and the standard of living of those who occupied these cottages have been scrupulously described by the daughter of a cultured Manchester merchant, in a beautifully produced book.[22] The Peel family was largely responsible for the introduction and development of the printing of textiles, which by 1825 was an extensive industry in the region. At that time there were 120 dyers and 130 printers with works or offices in Manchester, eleven dyers and three printers in Rochdale. So successful was this regional industry that complaints came from their London rivals: 'How can persons of taste, fashion or opulence be expected to give five or six shillings a yard when their very servants can have an imitation for two or three shillings?'[23]—a grudging tribute to Sir Robert Peel and his associates. One can understand, also, how it came about that this eminent Bury mill-owner was the inspiring force behind the passing of the first Factory Act (1802), which set out to limit the employment of apprentices in the cotton mills to twelve hours per day. His contribution to the town's prosperity and position at this time has been eloquently described:

> 'In short, the extensiveness of the whole concern is such as to find constant employ for most of the inhabitants of Bury and its neighbourhood, of both sexes and all ages, and notwithstanding their great number, they have never wanted work in the most unfavourable times. The peculiar healthiness of the people employed may be imputed partly to the judicious and humane regulations put in practice by Mr Peel, and partly to the salubrity of the air and climate.'[24]

Bury in no way matched at this time in its civilised agencies the industrial benefactions of the Peel family. There were no recreation grounds, no municipal hospital, no efficient, general sewage scheme or drainage, no public library, no art gallery, no museum, no technical or art school, no municipal secondary school, no tramways or electricity works. Not until the Charter incorporating Bury as a Borough was granted in 1876, was the way opened up for sorely-needed municipal progress. Even then the provisions of the Public Libraries Act (1850) were not adopted until 1897, and an Art Gallery and Public Library opened in 1901. Today, Bury is the leading town in a large Metropolitan District. It is conscious of the many challenges and demands which such a status presents and is determined to meet them.

Metropolitan Borough of Rochdale

To understand the industrial character of Rochdale it is important to examine the coat-of-arms granted by the College of Heralds on the incorporation of the town as a borough by royal charter in 1856. The Crest contains a silver-coloured fleece while the centre of the shield itself is occupied by the woolpack, both signifying the predominance of the ancient woollen industry. On closer inspection, one discovers that the woolpack is encircled by two branches of a cotton plant, this time symbolic of the newer, invading cotton industry. This is highly significant because in the very year when the charter of incorporation was granted, there were in Rochdale about 138 cotton manufacturers, compared to 108 woollen manufacturers.[25] Although wool was about to take second place in the industrial history of the town, it continued, with engineering and other industries, to make its own important contribution, which explains why, during the cyclical cotton slumps, Rochdale was able to weather the storm more successfully than some of its neighbours deeply committed to the cotton industry.

Rochdale has visible claims to its ancient origins. In addition to a Roman silver bracelet and sixteen third-century coins, found in the district and which may be seen in the Rochdale Public Museum, there is the clear evidence of a Roman road at Blackstone Edge, beyond Littleborough 'over the rocks, peat and hummocks of the high moors'.[26] When the Romans departed from the region in the late fourth and early fifth centuries, their later successors evidently set about making clearings for habitation in the surrounding forests and woodland. The late Sir Ian Richmond, son of a much-respected Rochdale doctor, has described their activities in this way:

'It is to the Saxon that we owe the clearing of the woods and jungle . . . This expansion must have begun soon after the close of the seventh century; and to it belong names indicative of clearing . . . quite close to Rochdale, doubtless contributing to make it the centre of Saxon life which it had become at the time of Edward the Confessor.'[27]

He refers also to the Norse names indicative of their arrival and settlement in the valley of the Roche during the tenth and eleventh centuries. In the Domesday Survey it is recorded that a thane named Gamel had held the lordship or manor of *Recedham*, consisting of two hides, during the reign of Edward the Confessor, and that he continued to do so when the Survey was undertaken in 1086.

This is the beginning of the manor of Rochdale, which in the early Middle Ages came into the possession of the de Lacy family, lords of Clitheroe and Pontefract. As has already been noticed, many of the Lancashire estates passed into the hands of John of Gaunt, Duke of Lancaster, and through his son, Henry Bolingbroke, into the possession of the Crown. So it was with the manor of Rochdale, but not before it had been granted a royal charter in 1251 to hold a weekly market and an annual fair for three days in October. It may even, for a short time, have acquired the status of a seignorial borough, as reference is made in documents of the Manor Court of the early fourteenth century to burgesses, but no charter to this effect has been preserved. However, the Manor Court continued to function in Rochdale from this time, although with ever-declining powers, until 1928. Its Records give evidence of Rochdale as a trading centre which had already developed a sizeable woollen industry, together with the grinding of corn by hand in local corn mills as symbolised by the millrind in the crest of the coat-of-arms below the fleece. There are several types of hand-mills for grinding corn, which have been found in the Rochdale district, now on display in the Public Museum. This combination of domestic industry and farming remained in Rochdale until the late eighteenth century, although towards the end of this period there was much more putting out, with the materials remaining the possession of the merchants, and consequently less of the old, independent operations of the Rochdale farmer-weavers. For a time the development of machine spinning in the woollen trade led to a boom in hand-loom weaving which took place, as has already been noticed, in the rows of stone-built 'weavers cottages' which may still be found in Rochdale and in its neighbours of the Metropolitan District such as Wardle and Milnrow.

As the textile revolution developed during the nineteenth century and power by steam became more and more the rule rather than the exception, cotton became the great industry even in Rochdale, almost the last bastion of woollen manufacture in what is now the Metropolitan County. Gone were the days for Rochdale when 'the neighbourhood abounds in clothiers' and when 'every considerable house is manufacturing, and is supplied with a rivulet', as a local historian described the town in the late eighteenth century. Gone, too, the lordship of the manor which Sir John Byron acquired in 1638 and which his family retained until

Old Rochdale – fording the Roche

150

Lord Byron, sixth Baron of Rochdale, sold it to James Dearden in the year before his death in 1824 at Missolonghi.

The new Rochdale of the incorporated borough, the Liberal stronghold of social reform, was about to enter upon its distinctive career. It had been given a remarkable send-off by the determination of thirty-two Rochdale men, not all but mostly weavers and artisans, to found the Rochdale Society of Equitable Pioneers, by which they proposed to establish 'a store for the sale of provisions and clothing' and to form 'arrangements for the pecuniary benefit and the improvement of the social and domestic condition of its members', with the grand design 'that as soon as practicable this society shall proceed to arrange the powers of production, distribution, education and government, or in other words to establish a self-supporting home colony of united interests, or assist other societies in establishing such colonies.'[28] On the evening of 21 December 1844, they opened their shop at no. 31 Toad Lane with just small amounts of butter, sugar, flour and candles for sale. Thus began what is now the world-wide Co-operative Movement, whose members look upon 'The Stores', the little shop in Toad Lane, Rochdale, now a museum, as their Mecca. The first Mayor of Rochdale was Jacob Bright, son of the Quaker cotton-spinner and brother of John Bright who, with Richard Cobden, MP for Rochdale from 1859 until his death in 1865, and C. P. Villiers, formed the spearhead of, and provided the intellectual armoury for, the Anti-Corn Law League. Sir James Kay-Shuttleworth, whose work as a young doctor at the Ancoats Dispensary has already been noted, was born at Bamford, now in Rochdale, in 1804.

It may, perhaps, not be inappropriate at this point to refer to the first university tutorial class, a land-mark in adult education, to be held in this country. It took place in Rochdale in 1907, and its tutor was R. H. Tawney, then aged twenty-seven. Among its members was a young Rochdalian, A. P. Wadsworth, who had attended Rochdale Higher Grade Elementary School, which he left at the age of fourteen. After a sound and valuable apprenticeship with the much respected *Rochdale Observer*, Wadsworth was appointed as a reporter in 1917 to the *Manchester Guardian*, which brought him under the eye of the great C. P. Scott. On the death of W. P. Crozier in 1944, Wadsworth was appointed Editor of the *Manchester Guardian*—a remarkable achievement for an intellectually self-made man.[29] In this respect he was the counterpart of

'The Stores', 31 Toad Lane, Rochdale (1844)

those Rochdale yeomen weavers who, working themselves up from small beginnings, founded and established the new steam-powered factories of the early nineteenth century. Such was Henry Kelsall, who originally had a few hand-looms and jennies in a house near the parish church. He went on to lay the foundation of Kelsall and Kemp, one of the most famous woollen manufacturing firms in Britain. And there were others such as the Smiths, Fieldens, Royds and Walmsleys, self-made men industrially and commercially, who were the salt of the earth in their day.

During the past century there has gradually evolved in Rochdale an industrial pattern consisting of a most fortunate variety of mills and factories whose products are known throughout the world: John Bright and Brothers, Limited, one of the country's largest manufacturers in industrial textiles; Clover Croft and State (Spinners) Limited, a successful amalgamation of three well-known cotton-spinning mills; Dunlop Cotton Mills, one of the largest producers of yarn for motor-tyres in the world; T.B.A. Industrial Products Limited, a firm renowned for its products, including asbestos, plastics, glass fibre and transmission belting; Fothergill and Harvey, one of the world's leading manufacturers of synthetic fabrics and an outstanding example of an original cotton firm which has successfully adapted itself to the new industry of man-made fibres; Farrel Bridge Limited, producers of rubber washing machinery; Tweedales and Smalley, manufacturers of textile machinery; Whipp and Bourne Limited, electrical engineers and manufacturers of switchgear for ships all over the world.

Nor has the municipal authority lagged behind private enterprise. In 1904 the Rochdale County Borough Council resolved to create an entirely new Town Centre. To do so it undertook the gigantic task of covering the River Roche which flowed right through the centre of the town. It took the Council over twenty-two years to complete its task, but the result was that Rochdale may claim to have the largest and most attractive town centre in Lancashire. If one stands on the top of the 'Church Steps' (122 of them from ground level) close to the medieval Parish Church of St Chad and the graveyard which contains Tim Bobbin's last remains, one sees a medium-sized Lancashire manufacturing town nestling among the moors and hills which are never far away. To the left stretch the slopes of Broadfield Park, which loftily surveys the busy Town Centre. To the right below is the grand, old woollen mill of Kelsall and Kemp and directly in front, on the far side, the graceful neo-Georgian General Post Office, which the Rochdale Council typically insisted on having to its own design. Next to it are spacious Memorial Gardens, and to their left the late nineteenth-century Public Library, Museum and Art Gallery, buildings of local millstone grit. But the glory of it all is the beautiful Gothic Town Hall, opened in 1871, of which, it has been said, 'the citizens have every right to be proud.' So well is this civic jewel placed, that one almost has the impression that the new Town Centre was especially designed as a setting for it. While acknowledging that the centre of Rochdale 'is green and pleasant', Pevsner warns the visitor that 'a few steps away all is mean shopping streets without character or direction.'[30] However true that may have been at the time of his visit (although one recalls with personal pleasure the warm and friendly atmosphere of the place), the Rochdale Council, maintaining the progressive policy of its predecessors, adopted a few years ago an ambitious plan of redevelopment of the area surrounding the Town Centre, which will be described in a later chapter.

Metropolitan Borough of Oldham

If ever the Industrial Revolution placed a town firmly and squarely on the map of the world, that town is Oldham, which has been claimed as 'the greatest cotton spinning town in the world'.[31] Before its rapid rise to fame in the textile industry, it was little more than a hamlet, as compared to Rochdale, for example, which was a market town. In the thirteenth century, Oldham was a manor held from the Crown by a family named Oldham, whose seat was at Werneth Hall. It was this family which produced one of the greatest benefactors to education for Lancashire and the nation. It has been stated that 'while Hugh Oldham was probably born in Oldham, he spent the early part of his life and perhaps received some education later in Manchester (Ancoats) when his family had settled there.'[32] After his appointment in 1504 as Bishop of Exeter, he most fortunately turned his mind towards his native Lancashire, which ultimately resulted in the founding of the Free Grammar School of Manchester, whose feoffees were given 'full powers and authority to augment, increase, expound, and reform all the said acts, ordinances, articles, composition, and agreements,' because in the future 'many things may grow' which at the foundation 'were not possible to come to mind.' Many things have indeed grown for countless generations of south Lancashire boys with 'pregnant wit', so much so that, nearly four centuries later, one of Her Majesty's Commissioners, investigating the state of secondary education in his region of Lancashire, accorded the School in his report to the Bryce Commission 'a foremost and in some respects the foremost place among the great day schools of England'.[33] It is fervently to be hoped that Manchester Grammar School, nurtured under such fortunate conditions, both academically and geographically, will be restored to its direct-grant relationship with the central authority for, in this era of a mixed economy, there could be no sounder investment of public money than in the education of the youth of the Greater Manchester County, from which the School draws the majority of its boys. The benefits for the nation of such an inspired and truly democratic system are immeasurable. If Oldham produced this gentle Tudor prelate, it has indeed enriched the Metropolitan County of which it is now a constituent part.

In the seventeenth century there were in Oldham various thriving crafts and trades chiefly devoted to cloth-making and linen-making on a domestic basis. It was in the closing decades of the next century, however, that Oldham came into its own with machines driven by water-power. It has been stated that the first cotton mill was established in 1778; two years later there were six, three of them still working with horse-power. The first steam engine went into operation in 1794, and six years later there were seven mills using steam, with the population of Oldham at 10,000. The town was well placed for the production of steam power, as the supply of coal was plentiful in the district. As Dr Aikin noted: 'Coals are found in great plenty in the several townships (of the Oldham parish), which, besides supplying the neighbourhood, are sent in large quantities to Manchester',[34] so much so that 'the supply from the Duke of Bridgewater's pits at Worsley (by means of his canal) is less considerable, although a very useful addition for the poor.'

155

One of the largest sources of supply for Oldham lay in the neighbouring township of Royton where, it has been stated, 'coals are a considerable product in this township, more than half of it containing valuable beds of this mineral. They have been worked here about 100 years back.'[35] Equipped with such a generous supply of coal by nature, Oldham cotton-spinning mills multiplied rapidly; in 1831 there were 62 mills and a population of 32,000; in 1866 there were 120 mills and a population of 80,000; in 1888 the climax was reached with 265 mills and a population of 130,000.[36] The period of greatest building activity was in the 1870s, when the later mills, long, high and even, except for a short tower on one end, impressively dominated the town. It was a century of tremendous expansion which made Oldham 'one of the most important centres of the cotton and textile industries in England', as it has been proudly proclaimed.[37] But the pace was bound to slacken and because, on the whole, it was dependent upon cotton-spinning alone, the thousands of operatives, men, women and children, who manned the mills were bound to be at the mercy of the 'stop-go' caprices of the cotton trade—boom periods followed by depressions—in the latter of which those least able to bear the strain had to suffer poverty and unemployment. Although in the early years of this century efforts were made in Oldham to establish the industry on a sounder basis, by increasing wages and improving working conditions, little was done to provide cotton mill operatives with better homes or the amenities of life.

Fortunately, in recent years the industry has undergone a considerable transformation. It is now more compact and more economically managed. The proportion of local workers employed in the cotton industry has declined, but employment has been taken up in engineering and in newer light industries which have, since the Second World War, developed within the borough of Oldham. When Oldham celebrated, on 13 June 1949, the centenary of the granting of a charter for its incorporation as a municipal borough, it claimed to produce more than half of Lancashire's total annual output of a million pounds' weight of yarn, in which great enterprise firms such as the Belgrave Mills Co. Ltd., Coldhurst Spinning Co. Ltd. and James Greaves Ltd. 'carried the name of Oldham to the remotest parts of the globe.'[38] With them were firms of historic reputation such as Lees and Wrigley Ltd., which has been producing yarns for three centuries, and Thomas Mellodew & Co. Ltd., manufacturers of velvets and corduroys, whose first mill at

'Spindledom', Oldham (1939)

Moorside was established over 130 years ago. The manufacturing of textile machinery has similarly engaged great firms such as Platt Bros., the largest concern of its kind in the world; Dronsfield Bros. Ltd., which occupies the site where James Dronsfield 128 years ago started making handgrinding strickles in the attics of four cottages; William Bodden & Sons Ltd., founded in 1858, and S. Dodd & Sons Ltd., founded in 1865, both of which are still exporting the most modern textile machinery to all parts of the world. In other fields of manufacture, George Orme Ltd. began in 1856 the production of gas meters, and more recently have been engaged in producing measuring instruments and indicators for cotton machinery, while Joseph Nadin Ltd. were established in 1886 as thermal insulation engineers and sheet metal workers. Most renowned of all, Stotts of Oldham is a household name as manufacturer of catering equipment. With so great a diversity of manufacture and commerce within its area, the Metropolitan Borough of Oldham may well look forward to an assured and soundly based future.

Metropolitan Borough of Stockport

Stockport leads, after Manchester, the largest District in population of the Metropolitan County. In 1842 the town was described thus: 'Although situated in the county of Cheshire, it belongs commercially to Lancashire and it is still further identified with the palatinate by the feelings, the interests, and the spirit of its inhabitants.'[39] Indeed at this period the town was divided from east to west by the River Mersey (the original name, Mersam, means boundary), which at this point is formed by the confluence near the town centre of the Rivers Tame and Goyt. Historically it was a medieval town, whose lord, Robert de Stockport, had granted a charter in 1260 by which he bestowed 'an homestead and an acre of land to each of his burgesses, on the yearly payment of one shilling'.[40] Based upon the original charter for Salford, that for

Stockport had the advantage of Manchester in that its burgesses were given the right to elect a mayor and aldermen instead of a borough reeve, which gave Stockport a corporate constitution.[41] In the same year (1260) Robert de Stockport secured for the town the right to hold a weekly market and an annual fair which have ever since been held on the present site of the market place between the Parish Church and Castle Yard. The earliest reference to a castle in Stockport occurs in a medieval chronicle of 1172, which records that in the struggle between Henry II and his feudal barons, both in England and Normandy, this castle was involved. It was probably reduced to ruins about the time when Prince Rupert, 'this fierce thunderbolt' as a parliamentary general called him, on his victorious march through Cheshire stormed through Stockport on 25 May 1644 and swept on to relieve the siege of Lathom House. It is said that the site of the castle became a storage space for stallholders in the market.

At the beginning of the eighteenth century Stockport, with a population of some 2,000, was a picturesque market town with its parish church and spacious market-place, completely surrounded by rows of houses, situated on the summit of a hill with a steep descent towards the Mersey but easy of access on the other sides. In the town was a grammar school founded in 1487 by the Goldsmith's Company in London. The first mills for winding and throwing silk were erected at this time and those engaged in its production were looked upon as 'the principal people in the place'.[42] With the eventual decline of this industry, the machinery was applied to cotton spinning which, with the different branches of the cotton manufacture, became by the end of the eighteenth century the chief industry of the town. At this time, in addition to the large number of handloom weavers' cottages, such as a row called 'Seventeen Windows' which, until recently, may have been seen in Marple Road, Offerton, but, as with all the others, has now disappeared, there were twenty-three large cotton factories, four of them powered by steam engines.

One of the most remarkable men operating in the area was Samuel Oldknow. Before coming to Stockport he conducted a putting-out system at Roscoe Lowe in the local textile industry.[43] Taking advantage of Samuel Crompton's perfecting of his spinning mule in Bolton in 1779, which enabled the cottage spinner to produce yarns fine enough for making muslins, Oldknow by the early 1780s was employing in Stockport hundreds of domestic

Stockport Market Place in 1859

weavers as a wholesale merchant in the production of the first British muslins. Aikin refers to 'the people of Stockport' as 'so ingenious as to attempt muslins which were introduced about ten years since upon the invention of the machines called mules . . .'[44] Samuel Oldknow is best known, however, for his outstanding work at Mellor and Marple Bridge, into which area he moved about 1783. There he built, just on the Derbyshire side, one of the largest cotton-spinning mills in the region, which employed the majority of the young people in the neighbourhood. He was well in advance of his time in the treatment of his young apprentices, for whom he provided a school. An inspector of his mills reported: 'Any commendation of mine must fall short of Mr Oldknow's very meritorious conduct towards the apprentices under his care, whose comfort in every respect seems to be his study; they are all looking very well and extremely clean.'[45] His versatility was remarkable. He was not only a factory spinner and a former employer of domestic weavers; he was also an agricultural innovator, cutting osiers for the basket-making trade, oak barking for tanning leather and sheep breeding for hatters' wool. He had his own water power and coal mine and at Marple he developed lime kilns. He was active in the promotion of Turnpike Trusts and he took a leading part in the constructing of the Peak Forest Canal. The Metropolitan District of Stockport is not likely to produce again a man who mastered such a variety of trades as Samuel Oldknow.

Another important domestic industry in Stockport and some of its neighbouring towns was hat-making which, in the later eighteenth century, was described as 'a considerable branch of employment'.[46] The hatters worked at home in farms and cottages, combining this craft with work in their fields or smallholdings and selling their products locally. Until the middle of the eighteenth century the fashionable trade in fine hats was confined to London, with the Feltmakers' Company in control and laying down the regulations for the craft. With the decline of this Company in its ability to control and regulate the trade, Stockport and Manchester tended to become the centres for hatting, with more and more London houses content to have their work done here. In 1797, for example, Thomas Worsley, of Stockport, began to make hats on commission for the famous London House of Christy's. With the introduction of fur-forming machines from America in the 1860s, hatting entered the factory era, although domestic hatting continued for many years. As the industry grew, Stockport, with Denton and Hyde, became the great centres of the trade.[47] Today, with the almost constant use of the motor car for outdoor movement, the wearing of hats has declined, and most of the famous names of nineteenth-century hat-making have disappeared in amalgamations and reorganisations, such as two which operate in Stockport at present—the Associated British Hat Manufacturers Ltd. and the Hat and Felt Laboratories Ltd., both situated in Higher Hillgate.

The third great industry which has sustained Stockport and its neighbouring towns is engineering in a variety of forms. One of the earliest is Herbert Parkes and Nephew Ltd., a great civil engineering firm founded in 1848 and known as Waterloo Steelworks in Stockport. Fifty years later, another great firm was established in Hazel Grove, Mirrlees Blackstone Ltd., specialists in the production of diesel-engines. Over sixty years ago there was founded the firm of Oweco Ltd. in Cheadle Heath, internationally famous as Oil Well Engineers, and in 1927 the well-known Fairey Engineering Ltd. was founded, with important works in Heaton Chapel for the production of nuclear machinery and soft drinks machinery. In Heaton Mersey there is Acrow Engineers Ltd., which specialises in civil engineering. Probably the most famous of them all is the Simon Engineering Group of Companies, with its head office at Cheadle Heath. Founded in 1878 as Simon Carves Ltd., this group of companies, in its production of flour-milling machinery and turbine engines, has become one of the greatest engineering enterprises in the world and has brought much distinction to Stockport.

One of the most inspired acts of the former County Borough Council of Stockport was its decision in 1946 to accept on lease for a term of ninety-nine years the sole responsibility for the care and maintenance of Lyme Hall with its great park of 1,320 acres. This handsome hall, only five miles south of Stockport, had been occupied by the Legh family for over 600 years until 1946 when Richard Legh, the third Lord Newton, presented the house and its extensive grounds to the National Trust, leaving on permanent loan some of the pictures, tapestries and rare furniture which in themselves constitute a treasury of history. With its adjacent ornamental gardens, its orangery and greenhouses, and its long undulating vistas of moor and woodland, over which the famous red deer roam, Lyme is indeed the ideal place 'for the Health, Education and Delight of the People', as a stone plaque within the

Elizabethan porch of the North Entrance commemoratively records. That it lies within the care jointly of the Metropolitan Borough Council of Stockport and the Great Manchester Council is a matter both of good fortune and genuine congratulation.

Metropolitan Borough of Trafford

The Trafford family, from whom this Metropolitan District derives its name, is said to be able 'to trace its descent from ancestors as far back as the conquest'.[48] The earliest reference to the name locally may be found in Thomas Grelley's Charter of 1301, to which Sir Henry de Trafford was a signatory as a witness and as a freeholder. He held tenements in Ancoats and most of Chorlton-on-Medlock.[49] John Leland, describing his journey into Manchester in 1538, referred to 'a great bridge of timber called Crosford bridge ... and after that I touched within a good mile of Manchester by Mr Trafford's Park and Place.' This was the old Trafford Hall, which the family left some time between 1673 and 1703 and went on to settle in their later residence in Trafford Park itself,[50] where the family remained until the construction of the Manchester Ship Canal.

The Trafford family must have long been conscious of the value of their estates in this area. At the end of the eighteenth century John Trafford undertook the drainage and improvement of two large tracts of waste land called Chat Moss and Trafford Moss, the former being very near the road from Manchester to Warrington and the latter adjoining his Park. In view of the fact, also, that the comparatively new Bridgewater Canal passed through both these areas, it seemed to 'render the improvement of these lands particularly eligible', as Aikin rightly surmised in 1795.[51] Neither he nor John Trafford could have foreseen that within thirty years Chat Moss was to become for George Stephenson his greatest challenge in the constructing of the railroad for the pioneering

Liverpool and Manchester Railway. Nor could either have possibly foreseen that a century later, Trafford Park would become a vital factor in the negotiations over land for the constructing of the Ship Canal. Most fascinating of all was the manner in which the purchase of the Chat Moss Estate from the agents of Sir Humphrey de Trafford in 1893 by the Manchester Corporation, on behalf of its Cleansing Committee, ultimately brought to a head in a signal form one of the city's greatest problems, that of sewage disposal. During the greater part of the nineteenth century, Manchester was one of the more backward local authorities in dealing with this problem, yet so serious had the lack of adequate and effective provision for the disposal of sewage become towards the end of the century that it compelled Manchester, in conjunction with Salford and Stretford, to become a pioneer in this field. Eventually, due to the research undertaken by Sir Henry Roscoe, one of the great protagonists of Owens College for many years and the real founder of its Chemistry Department, on the biological oxidation of sewage and similar recommendations put forward by two research scientists of the Manchester Davyhulme Sewage Works in a paper presented to the Society of Chemical Industry in 1914, the subsequent discovery of the activated sludge process made the sewage treatment plant at Davyhulme one of the most advanced in the world, and a mecca for scientists concerned with this subject from many other countries.[52]

This Metropolitan District, then, has been most appropriately named, as was also the main centre of its administration—Stretford. It has been recorded that the origin of its name is derived from its situation on the River Mersey at the point where the road ('Streta') from Manchester to Chester crossed the river at the 'ford' where Crosford Bridge now stands. It is also claimed that the neighbouring village of Flixton derived its name from 'Fleecetown', as the presence of the old Bishop Blaize Inn (Bishop Blaize was the patron saint of wool-combers) indicated an involvement in the woollen trade.[53] Stretford, itself, while never within the barony or manor of medieval Manchester, was, in conjunction with the manor of Trafford, one of the thirty historical townships of the ancient parish of Manchester.[54] The real development of Stretford began in the mid-eighteenth century with the construction of the Duke of Bridgewater's Canal, first from Worsley to Stretford and eastwards to Castlefield, Manchester, and then westwards from Stretford to Runcorn-gap. Thus Stretford is situated at what is picturesquely called Water's Meeting, where the Duke's original canal from the coal-mines of Worsley meets the main canal from Castlefield to Preston Brook, near Runcorn. With the opening of the Liverpool and Manchester Railway on 15 September 1830 and, within twenty years, the Manchester, South Junction and Altrincham line, the strategic position of Stretford in regard to industrial and commercial transport was further enhanced.

But what undoubtedly made Stretford was the completion in 1894 of the Manchester Ship Canal, with its large terminal docks in close proximity to Trafford Park. Here was a wooded estate of 1,200 acres of level meadow land, bordered on the south and east by the Bridgewater Canal, on the north and west by the new Ship Canal, and in its immediate vicinity the Liverpool and Manchester Railway. The potentialities almost spoke for themselves: the Bridgewater Canal provided the link with the inland canal system of the country; the presence of the railway opened up the possibilities of a network intersecting the estate and connecting it with the Manchester Docks and all the main line railways of Great Britain; most important of all, the Ship Canal enabled ocean-going ships to ply between Manchester and the principal ports of the world. Yet when Marshall Stevens, who became the first General Manager of the Manchester Ship Canal Company, formed the Trafford Park Estates Company in 1896 for the purpose of purchasing the Park and developing it, he and his colleagues in the Estates Company intended to preserve the rural characteristics of much of the Park. Thus farmlands were leased, Trafford Hall was converted into a residential hotel and a club-house for golf, the lake was let for fishing and boating, plans for a race-course were drawn up and the public were admitted to the Park on a small charge for their recreation and pleasure. But the Company had a more serious purpose in mind for certain portions of the land, and set about a policy of attracting industry to the Park. Realising that roads and railways would have to be provided if they wished to succeed in this policy, they proceeded not only to lay down tracks for passenger and goods railway trains but also, within a space of twenty-five years, came to operate horse-drawn buses and tram-cars—gas, steam and electric—and motor-omnibuses.[55] During this period 'Trafford Park', as it is known, gradually developed as one of the most remarkable examples of industrial planning in the world. With wharf-space alongside the Ship Canal of 2,500 feet, with over 200 factories on its estate employing some 50,000, with its extensive rail, road and canal communications, this great industrial estate today stands as one of the largest engineering centres in the world and the home of some of the most renowned firms in British commerce. In support of this working population, as large as some former county boroughs, Trafford Park Dwellings Limited have built 700 houses and shops, together with churches, two schools, a public library, public baths and a child welfare clinic. Correspondingly, Stretford itself, originally a local government district in 1871 under the Local Government Board, raised to Urban District status in 1894, became a Municipal Borough in 1933 with a population of 60,000.

To celebrate this promotion in the sphere of local government, Stretford opened in this year its new Town Hall, with its high central tower as a landmark, and described by Nikolaus Pevsner as 'large, symmetrical, of brick, with vaguely Adamish detail'.[56] One of Stretford's most distinguished citizens was John Rylands, the Manchester merchant, who lived at Longford Hall from 1857 until his death in 1888. It was here that Rylands kept his fine library of books and manuscripts in theology and literature, from the sharing of which with his friends he derived much satisfaction. He was a generous benefactor to the town, endowing it with a Public Hall in 1878 and with a free Public Library in 1883. Wishing to help those who had not the sight to read, Thomas Henshaw, an earlier benefactor, by his will in 1810 left £20,000 towards the establishment and support of a Blind Asylum. The school was opened in Old Trafford in 1844 and today provides education for blind boys and girls from northern England. It is planned to build a new school in Harrogate, but the headquarters of Henshaw's Society For The Blind are to remain in Stretford.

Almost by accident of location, it is probably in the sphere of sport that both the historical name of the new Metropolitan District and the ancient name of its administrative centre have found fame. Wherever Association Football is played and the fortunes of its famous clubs are followed, the ground where Manchester United has its headquarters will be known—'Old Trafford'. Likewise, wherever throughout the Commonwealth the noble art of cricket is played and loved, there is a phrase familiar to them all—'bowling from the Stretford end'.

Metropolitan Borough of Tameside

At the time of printing, the College of
Arms has not yet approved a coat of
arms for Tameside.

The river valley has always attracted the angler and the producer
of cloth: for the one it offers the prospect of fish to be caught, for
the other the means of harnessing water-power to his machinery.
So it was until the beginning of the nineteenth century with the
valley of the River Tame. According to Aikin in 1795, 'This river
abounds with trout. It is also of the highest utility to the machinery
of the woollen and cotton factories of the neighbourhood; it being
reckoned that within the space of ten miles from Ashton there are
near 100 mills upon this stream and its tributary branches.'[57]

It would appear also that, for about two months in the summer,
the inhabitants of Ashton were 'obliged to fetch their soft water in
carts from the Tame'. It is most appropriate, then, that this new
Metropolitan District should be named Tameside. Forming, as it
did, the eastern boundary of the original medieval manor of
Manchester, it now passes through three modern Metropolitan
Districts. It rises in the quiet and unspoilt countryside near
Saddleworth on the fringe of the Pennines, where fishing is still
available over long stretches in the Metropolitan District of
Oldham. It then proceeds through its own District and ultimately
joins the River Goyt to form the River Mersey in the District of
Stockport. But the condition of its own District where it passes
through Stalybridge, Ashton and Dukinfield is very different from
what it was less than two centuries ago:

'The valley becomes heavily industrial in character, and the
river, now badly polluted, is overshadowed by tall warehouses
and mills which rise directly out of the water. Many of the old
industrial buildings and the grounds which surround them are
only partly used, most are unsightly, and the canals in the area
are over-grown with weeds and cluttered with rubbish. Not
until the river has passed through a wide area below Dukinfield,

given over to the disposal of society's refuse and effluent, does it flow out into open and wooded country in South Hyde and reflect the unspoilt beauty which once belonged to the whole of the valley.'[58]

In 1964 Dukinfield Borough Council convened a meeting of neighbouring local authorities with a view to formulating a policy, on a basis of 'community identity', by which this background of gross neglect could be eliminated and the valley of Tame made a region worthy of human habitation. An outline study was undertaken by the local planning authorities and broad principles of action were decided upon and published in 1968. It was at this point that the Civic Trust for the North West offered to act as planning and landscape consultants and to lead a committee drawn from the ten participating local authorities, the Lancashire and Cheshire County Councils and the appropriate statutory bodies. In this way the Tame Valley Improvement Scheme was born, with the blessing and full support of the Civic Trust for the North-West, which was thereby admirably fulfilling the declared object for which the Civic Trust was formed in 1957, 'to improve the appearance of town and country'.[59] What is highly significant about this joint enterprise is the fact that ten neighbouring local authorities came together to embark upon a policy of collective action 'to create a linear park in the valley (of the Tame) for the use of their townspeople and as a major recreational resource within the Manchester metropolis' ten years before the Greater Manchester County came into being. Even more significant is the fact that nine of these former local authorities (Stockport County Borough was the tenth) came to constitute the Tameside Metropolitan District of the new County. It is a clear example of 'coming events casting their shadows before', in the desirable sense.

There are today in this Metropolitan District five Civic Societies which are very conscious of their responsibilities towards the Tame Valley Improvement Scheme. They have excellent relations with their District Council; their representatives hold quarterly meetings with the Planning Officer who, in turn, issues relevant information fortnightly to each of these Societies. Their involvement in the progress and control of development in their District was amply demonstrated at the Annual Convention in October 1974 of the Civic Trust for the North-West, at which was shown a film, originally prepared by the Tameside Civic Societies for presenta-

168

tion to the members and officers of their Metropolitan Borough Council. It was an impressive performance, clearly indicating the valuable and sustained contribution which these voluntary societies are making towards improving the appearance and recreational opportunities of the Tame Valley. It was entirely appropriate that, following the showing of the film, the Chief Executive of Tameside summarised the achievements of the Civic Societies in co-operation with his colleagues and members of the Metropolitan District Council. One was moved to recall the words of the psalmist who sang of those who 'going through the vale of misery use it for a well: and the pools are filled with water. They will go from strength to strength.' May this be so with Tameside.

This, then, is the setting for the ten Districts which constitute the Greater Manchester County.

Chapter 10

'The centre of the web'

If there is one factor more than any other which has moulded Manchester and its neighbouring towns and villages into a cohesive unit, it is transport. It has already been seen that, long before the Industrial Revolution, industry was firmly established in the Manchester region and that, with its arrival, Manchester became the centre of a pattern of industrial settlements located on the foothills of the Pennines. It has been seen, also, that the system of transport by packhorse, cart and waggon, even with the advent of the turnpike roads, had proved inadequate by the mid-eighteenth century for the growing demands of industry. Thus Manchester pioneered water transport in the form of the artificial canal and by 1830 had become one of the termini of the first regular rail passenger service in the world, leading in a remarkably short space of time to a network of canals and railway lines which linked the metropolis to its neighbouring towns and, in particular, to the arc of cotton towns on the western slopes of the Pennines.

Yet so transient and capricious were the advantages of these new modes of transport that when, in the late 1870s and early 1880s, Manchester found itself facing alarming symptoms of local economic stagnation due to the world-wide 'Great Depression' of that time, its leading citizens realised that cheaper transport costs were vital to its survival as one of the commercial capitals of the world. One such citizen has written: 'I remember well the state of things in the late 70's and the early 80's when trades were being transferred from Manchester and there were ten thousand empty houses to mark a steady migration to other centres.'[1] Another noted: 'Walk through what used to be our busiest districts, such as Ancoats, and we find many shops closed and half of the workshops and mills empty ... Large employers of labour have gone where taxes are light and land and labour cheap.'[2]

There were two immediate and related reasons for this depressing state of affairs: firstly, Liverpool dominated the Mersey, and its Docks Board, in its own interest, was levying what Manchester men considered to be grossly excessive charges for its services in organising the import trade in raw cotton; and secondly, the railway companies serving the cotton towns were taking advantage of their quasi-monopolistic position to charge high rates on goods traffic. The traders of the Manchester region had become increasingly aware that they were working with a mill-stone round their necks, which was exemplified by the fact that Oldham spinners could buy cotton in Bremen or Le Havre, pay shipping freights to Hull and railway charges from Hull to Oldham, and still save one farthing a pound weight on the price they would have paid for the same cotton at Liverpool. As Manchester's life-blood depended primarily on the cheap transport of cotton and cotton goods in and out of its neighbouring towns, what was urgently needed was a waterway from Manchester to the sea, wide and deep enough to carry ocean-going ships—a ship canal which, in effect, would be 'an arm of the sea'.

This bold idea soon took hold of men not only in Manchester but in the civic and mercantile circles of the neighbouring towns. Perhaps they remembered that in 1841 a vessel had arrived in Manchester from Dublin, conveying a cargo of potatoes along the waterway provided by the venerable Mersey and Irwell Navigation Company. This ship discharged its cargo at the Old Quay Company's Wharf, after which it proceeded to take on a cargo of coals from a colliery at Pendleton as its consignment for the return voyage to Dublin. The first practical step taken towards the goal was on 27 June 1882 when Daniel Adamson, son of a long line of Northumbrian yeoman-farmers, who had set up his own boiler-making business at Dukinfield, called a meeting at his house, The Towers, in Didsbury, Manchester, to which he invited thirteen representatives of large Lancashire towns and fifty-five leading merchants and manufacturers, 'to consider the practicability of constructing a tidal waterway to Manchester and to take such action thereon as may be determined'. Among his guests were the Mayors of Manchester, Salford, Ashton, Stockport, Rochdale and Stalybridge, three Aldermen of Salford, two from Oldham and one from Dukinfield—a clear indication of Adamson's regional approach to the vast enterprise, as these dignitaries represented eight out of what are now the ten Metropolitan Districts of the Greater Manchester County. Adamson must have been in a confident and jovial mood at this meeting, for he declared, 'If the Suez Canal, situated in a barbarous country . . . could be carried out, there ought to be no engineering difficulties to stand in the way as far as the Mersey is concerned.' Not to be outdone, the Mayor of Salford, in moving that a Committee be appointed to enquire into the best means of carrying out the project, expressed his belief that 'there would not be a grander sight under the canopy of Heaven than the docks at Manchester crowded with shipping from all parts of the world.'[3]

The supreme confidence of these stalwarts of the Manchester region was based upon something more than Victorian self-righteousness; they had the solid fact before them, expounded at this meeting, that four-fifths of the export trade of Liverpool passed through Manchester. Despite this, the supporters of the Ship Canal project needed all the confidence in their cause that they could muster during the next three years, for they found themselves up against not only violent and protracted opposition from Liverpool and local railway vested interests but, also, 'the powerful antagonism of the merchant aristocracy of Manchester many of whom were, it seems, committed to the support of steamship lines sailing from Liverpool'.[4] Even the local Press poured cautious ridicule upon the feasibility and outcome of the project: 'Real salt water could not come to Manchester', reported the *Manchester Guardian*, and it wondered whether 'we should not have a repetition of the Amsterdam Canals with their smells.' One of the crucial factors in the fight for Parliamentary sanction for the construction of the canal was whether the Manchester City Council would agree to committing itself to contribute from its rates to the financing of the scheme. At its meeting in October 1882, the Council's General Purposes Committee passed this important resolution: 'That the question of widening and improving the rivers Irwell and Mersey and so making them navigable as a ship canal be referred to the Parliamentary Sub-Committee, and that they be instructed to consider whether the administration thereof should be invested in a public trust instead of private individuals.' It is interesting to note that the seconder of this resolution tentatively suggested that 'in view of a tidal navigation there should be one great and extended Manchester that would embrace Salford and the surrounding districts',[5] while, two months later, the Parliamentary Sub-Committee responded by proposing to the City Council that 'Manchester and other municipal bodies and local authorities . . . should be authorised to contribute to the cost of the undertaking, and to take part in supervising the execution of the works and also in the general management of the canal.'[6] Here is a clear example of one of the many historical antecedents, albeit an important one then and now, of the Greater Manchester County. Jacob Bright, first Mayor of Rochdale in 1856 and an MP for Manchester from

1867 to 1874, speaking at a crowded Town Meeting at the end of 1882, eloquently described the day 'when the smoke of big steamers would mingle with the smoke of their tall chimneys, when thousands of homes would again be prosperous and this great community might occupy a yet greater place in the position of the world.'[7]

When the Ship Canal Bill received the Royal Assent on 6 August 1885, there were great rejoicings among all classes throughout what is now the Metropolitan County. Returning from London, Daniel Adamson was met at Stockport by a brass band and, on being escorted home to Didsbury by a large crowd, passed under triumphal arches and was presented with an address of congratulation by the Secretary of the Trades Council on behalf of the working classes of the region. In Eccles, Oldham, Stockport and other towns of the region, cannons were fired, church bells rang out and bands paraded the streets. Before the promoters could embark upon the construction of what the *Liverpool Daily Post* derisively described as 'this gigantic ditch', it was necessary to raise £8,000,000 and to purchase the property of the Bridgewater Navigation Company which included the rights of the Mersey and Irwell Navigation Company. This purchase was effected by the presentation of a cheque for £1,710,000, the largest cheque ever drawn up to that time. The great waterway itself took six years to build and required the regular employment of 16,000 navvies, whose labour of months was more than once swept away by floods and storms in a single night.

Throughout the long period of the construction of the canal, which ultimately involved for the Company an outlay of £15 million, the Manchester City Council loyally supported the great enterprise, unanimously voting two large sums amounting to £5,000,000 for its ultimate completion. This is an outstanding example of a large municipal authority showing courage and foresight in financially committing itself to a private venture which had to contend with powerful opposition from various competitive interests. The settlement finally reached by the Ship Canal Company with the Manchester City Council in 1904 'was a compromise between the conceptions of those who planned the Canal as a private enterprise and those who urged that it should be taken up by the Corporation as a public trust.'[8] The Company remained a private undertaking, with the Corporation now funding about half the capital. But there is more to it than that: the composition of the Board of Directors of the Company was almost equally divided between the representatives of the shareholders and those of the Manchester Corporation—a combination of municipal and private interests unique at that time in Britain. Today, although the Corporation has holdings worth about £10 million in the Company, out of a total investment of £22 million, the Directors nominated by the City Council outnumber the other Directors by eleven to seven.

The Manchester Ship Canal was opened on 1 January 1894, when the first ocean-going ships sailed into the Terminal Docks in Salford. It was a day which marked the beginning of a new epoch in the commercial and industrial life of Manchester and its neighbouring towns, made all the more remarkable by the fact that the completion of the Canal coincided with the end of the 'Great Depression'. Thus the fulfilment of Daniel Adamson's dream stood ready to give the whole region of Manchester the advantage of the general increase in British overseas trade at a time when rates of interest and prices of raw materials were low. Within two years of its opening, the Ship Canal was being used by thirty-five regular shipping lines with resident agents in Manchester, while its services provided direct communication with 140 of the principal ports of the world. By 1910 Manchester had become the fourth port in the United Kingdom in terms of the value of traffic handled.

The Port of Manchester, owned and managed by the Manchester Ship Canal Company, is in effect an elongated harbour, stretching from Eastham to Manchester, a distance of 35½ miles. When the Canal was originally constructed, it contained a number of small ports which had previously carried on a good deal of independent trade. The Canal, with its greater depth of water, has brought a greatly increased trade to these ports. At Eastham, where ships enter the Canal from the Mersey estuary itself, the great Queen Elizabeth II Dock was opened in 1956. It is the largest of its kind in the country, has its own entrance lock and is capable of accommodating four large oil-tankers at one time. At Ellesmere Port, some three miles from the Eastham entrance locks, the canal frontage has been developed and fully provided with docks, with large paper mills and a wharf available for ocean-going vessels. It is also the transhipment point for the Midlands and Potteries. Two miles along the Canal lies Stanlow where, with two great oil docks at their disposal, most of the leading oil companies have established themselves, so that Manchester has

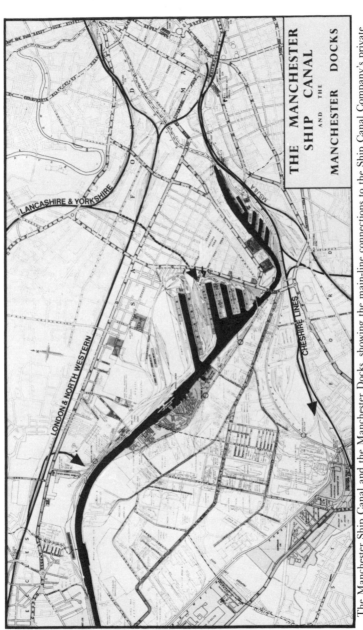

The Manchester Ship Canal and the Manchester Docks, showing the main-line connections to the Ship Canal Company's private railway system

become one of the leading oil ports in the country. Just over twenty miles farther along the Canal, a ship would pass the large Coaling Basin at Partington, the Swing Bridge at Barton, one of the wonders of the engineering world, the great industrial estate of Trafford Park and would finally enter the Terminal Docks which today are spread over three Metropolitan Boroughs of the Greater Manchester County—Salford, Trafford (at Stretford) and Manchester. It is here that the main line railways connect with the Ship Canal Company's elaborate and up-to-date dock system so that there is direct communication between every ship's berth and every railway station not only in the Greater Manchester County but in the whole kingdom. Some 5,000 cargo ships use the equipment and services of the Port of Manchester each year, including tankers of up to 30,000 tons deadweight. It has been well said that

'What the Manchester Ship Canal cost can be reckoned to a halfpenny. How much it has enriched the vast community it serves cannot be measured within millions. It has brought all the advantages of deep water transport to a large inland area. It has attracted to its vicinity a great variety of industries. Unquestionably it has played a leading part in the development of one of the world's greatest industrial regions.'[9]

It is significant that the Canal's unifying influence, especially during the testing years of the struggle for Parliamentary sanction, was such as to prompt a distinguished member of the Manchester City Council to suggest that 'a communion of interests may present a golden opportunity for amalgamation with Salford', a sentiment echoed by a Salford alderman at a Council meeting on 6 December 1882 when, during an important debate on 'the projected Ship Canal', he expressed the view that 'there is also a side issue looming in the distance ... it is the question of the amalgamation of the City of Manchester with the Borough of Salford. Our borough is an integral part of the greatest manufacturing and commercial centre of England.'[10] It is in this respect, as promoting 'a communion of interests' between Manchester and its neighbouring towns, that the construction of the Manchester Ship Canal may be seen as historically one of the most powerful factors in the creating of the Greater Manchester County. The historian of the Canal has claimed that 'no other event or enterprise can compare with it in its far-reaching results so far as Manchester and indeed South Lancashire as a whole are concerned', and for him the story of the Canal 'contains all the elements of a romance.'[11] Further emphasis is added to its regional character when it is realised that, although it carries the name of the Manchester Ship Canal, there is only one point at which it impinges on the city boundary. This is at No. 1 Pomona Dock, so named because the dock was built in Hulme on the site of Pomona Gardens, one of those pleasure-gardens of the nineteenth century where Mancunians and visitors alike sought refreshment and relaxation in the 'Magic Bridge, Gymnasium, Flying Swings, Bowling Green, Rifle Shooting Gallery, Boats on the Irwell, Beautiful Flower Beds, Romantic Walks and Extensive Pasture Grounds', which were advertised by the proprietors of the Gardens as 'affording enjoyment to every class of the community'.[12] It may be that their successors, the Directors of the great waterway, deem it equally desirable to provide 'Trips down the Canal' for the delectation of the great community which gains so much from its presence.

Ten years after the opening of the Manchester Ship Canal, the son of a Manchester doctor was working as third engineer on board the S.S. Inchanga, plying between England and South Africa. He spent much of his off-duty time watching the flight of an albatross, for the sight of this huge bird floating in the air and almost effortlessly keeping pace with a ship driven by powerful engines both fascinated him and incited his naturally inventive mind: if those wings could support and propel a body of that size and weight, could not wings designed in proportion maintain a man in flight? From that point there was no turning back for Alliott Verdon Roe. In midsummer 1908, Roe flew his biplane, which he had built at his brother's stables at Putney, a distance of sixty yards at a height of three feet over the race-course at Brooklands. A year later he flew his first triplane 900 feet at an average height of ten feet over Hackney marshes—the first Englishman to fly over British soil in his own plane powered by a British engine. Six days later, Louis Blériot flew across the English Channel. Flying was now an accomplished fact and Roe joined with another brother in Manchester to establish A. V. Roe and Company Ltd. (it was this firm which produced the Lancaster bomber described by Air Chief Marshal Sir Arthur Harris as 'the greatest single factor in winning the Second World War').

In order to encourage this new form of transport, the enterprising *Daily Mail* offered early in 1910 a prize of £10,000 for the first airman to fly from London to Manchester. Accepting the challenge, a Frenchman named Louis Paulhan set off from Hendon on the afternoon of 26 April 1910 in a plane described by the *Manchester Guardian* as 'not unlike some new-fashioned garden tent'. Just under three hours later, he landed at Lichfield, stayed the night there, and set off at 4 o'clock next morning for Burnage (Manchester). At that point young John Alcock arrived on his bicycle at Farmer Bracegirdle's land just by Burnage railway station to await his hero. At 5.10 a.m. he spotted, with thousands of others with him by now, a tiny object in the sky flying towards them over Alderley Edge 'with astonishing speed'. Paulhan circled above them and landed his flimsy plane on the clover field, where John was one of the first to reach him. This first flight from London to Manchester had been accomplished in four hours nineteen minutes flying time. Nine years later, John Alcock met A. Whitten-Brown at the Metropolitan-Vickers factory in Trafford Park. They resolved together to be the first to fly non-stop across the Atlantic. On 14 June 1919 the two men set off from Newfoundland in a Vickers Vimy aircraft and after 'a terrible trip' of almost 2,000 miles across the Atlantic in sixteen hours twelve minutes, during which 'sleet and ice chewed bits out of our faces', these two intrepid fliers sighted the west coast of Ireland and nosedived their plane into an Irish bog at Clifden. Among the many congratulations was a telegram from the Lord Mayor of their home town, saying, 'Manchester is proud of the high and historic achievement of two of her sons.'

This civic pride in the pioneering of air travel was no mere passing mood so far as Manchester was concerned. In 1928 its City Council was advised by a committee of its own members that 'in the interests of the trade and commerce of the city, the Corporation should reserve or acquire a site in or near Manchester for the purpose of an aerodrome.'[13] No sooner said than done, for early next year the City Council formed its Aerodrome Special Committee for the purpose of conducting its own municipal aerodrome at Rackhouse, Wythenshawe—the first in Great Britain. A year later a more permanent aerodrome was opened at Barton, near Eccles, close to the Manchester Ship Canal. It was even suggested that the city should buy and operate its own planes. Owing to the rapid development of speedier and heavier aircraft during the 1930s, Barton was found to be unsuitable for the ambitions of the Airport Committee. This gave rise to much argument

Paulhan, on the second leg of his flight, heading for Manchester at daybreak on 27 April 1910

in the circles of the Corporation, but a determined Airport Committee persuaded the City Council in 1938 to purchase 400 acres of land owned by three farmers at Ringway in Cheshire, half a mile outside the city boundary—a decision passed by a majority of one vote! The first aircraft to use Ringway in 1938 was a K.L.M. DC-2 from Amsterdam, which opened the Airport to immediate international operation. During the Second World War Ringway was not requisitioned by the Government (a major factor in its subsequent development) but was used intensively for war purposes, including the training of the early airborne forces. At the conclusion of the war, the Airport was re-opened for civil use and the first international service was inaugurated in June 1946 by Air France. Three years later, the Minister of Civil Aviation announced that he proposed to exercise his powers under the Civil Aviation Act (1946) to take over and manage Ringway Airport, but the Manchester City Council insisted on retaining it, regarding itself as perfectly capable of managing and developing its own Airport. Agreement was reached early in 1953, when the Government announced that the City Council would be allowed to retain its Airport and be responsible for its operation. That Manchester has fulfilled its desired responsibility with distinction and success may be judged from its traffic statistics for the period 1947 to 1970:[14]

Period	Aircraft Movements	Total Passengers Handled	Freight in Metric Tons
Jan/Dec 1947	7,682	33,915	149
Jan/Dec 1954	29,080	265,513	6,468
Jan/Dec 1962	40,225	1,079,239	14,886
Jan/Dec 1970	55,487	1,927,436	45,756

When the Duke of Edinburgh opened the new Manchester Airport on 22 October 1962, he described it as 'the gateway to the world from the industrial heart of Britain'. It was in that year that the Airport for the first time handled over one million passengers. It must have been a proud day for those pioneers of the original

Airport Committee, some of whom were still there as the custodians of its future. But what a day for Louis Paulhan! He, too, had been invited to the ceremony and naturally he compared his fifty-eight minutes flight from Paris to Manchester in a luxurious Caravelle with his fabric-covered plane of fifty-two years earlier. 'Today,' he said, 'I enjoyed champagne and smoked salmon, but on my first flight I did not take any food with me. I had so much fuel on board that even a packet of sandwiches might have made the plane too heavy for take-off.' Ten years later the total number of passengers per annum was over two-and-a-half millions, and already it is anticipated that by 1982 there will be passenger traffic of five millions. To meet this growing challenge of air travel, the Manchester City Council approved in 1969 plans for the further development of the passenger terminal facilities and for the provision of the more sophisticated services which would be necessary to accommodate the new generation of high-capacity aircraft. All this involved:

(i) doubling the capacity of the Control Tower Administration Block

(ii) building an additional pier with associated aprons and taxiways

(iii) erecting a 13-level car park building to accommodate 2,500 cars

(iv) converting the existing customs hall into an extension of the concourse

(v) enlarging the international departure and transit lounge.[15]

The foundation stone of these Terminal Extensions was laid in April 1971 by Alderman Tom Regan, the last surviving member of the original Airport Committee. On 25 March 1974 the Lord Mayor of Manchester opened the first phase of the extensions listed above. Later phases provide for a new cargo village built to accommodate all cargo aircraft, an additional multi-storey car park with bus and coach stations at ground floor level, and a second main runway.

Altogether, Manchester Airport, the largest municipal airport in the United Kingdom, promises to bear comparison with any international airport in the world. The story of its outstanding growth, which may well take its place, similar to that of the Manchester Ship Canal, among the greatest commercial enterprises of this region, would surely have stirred the hearts of Alliott Verdon Roe, Sir John Alcock and Sir Arthur Whitten-Brown. As the prosperity of an industrial and commercial region relies heavily upon the speed with which its exports can reach the markets of the world, and equally upon the means by which it can attract overseas and domestic business interests to its markets, Manchester International Airport, as it is now rightly named, has an increasingly vital rôle to play in the economic growth of the Greater Manchester County. Boundless opportunities for holiday travel to all parts of the world are also available to all living in and well beyond this region. It would not seem to be inappropriate that this great enterprise is now managed by the City Council and the Greater Manchester Council jointly through the Manchester International Airport Authority.

The development of passenger transport by road does not seem to have the same dramatic quality as is evident in that of travelling across the seas or through the air. Yet it has its own nostalgic attraction: for many the era of the stage coach has an aura of romance and adventure on the highway; for others, the final day of 'the last tram' was the magnet, as when Manchester's official last tram, No. 1007, entered Birchfields Road Depot on 10 January 1949 to be greeted by a large crowd of sympathisers.[16] Although the services provided by the stage-coach companies were mainly for long distances—for example, the coaches from London, York, Liverpool and Birmingham were timed to arrive each day at 4 o'clock at the Royal Hotel, Manchester (where now Lewis's store stands)—there were before 1800 daily coach services linking all the main towns in Lancashire with one another. With the passing in 1832 of the Stage Coach Act, which allowed passengers to be picked up or set down at any point on the route, the local services were greatly facilitated, although in the main the fare was high, such as the five shilling cost of the journey from Manchester to Rochdale. At this time, most people lived within walking distance of their work, while those who could afford to do so had their own carriages, although it has been said that in Manchester 'it was not until 1758 that any person actually in business set up a carriage.' In 1810 the first hackney carriages began to operate from St Ann's Square, plying for hire within an area of four miles around Manchester. It was shortly after this that John Greenwood, the keeper of the toll-bar at Pendleton, realising that the days when merchants and others resided in the centre of Manchester were rapidly passing, decided in 1824 to inaugurate a 'sixpenny omnibus' service from Pendleton to Market Street, Manchester. Although Greenwood's first omnibuses were said to be little more than boxes on wheels, their popularity encouraged him to extend and augment his services so that by 1850 he and his son, John, had sixty-four omnibuses operating services in the Manchester area. These two virtually held a monopoly of local transport until 1852, when a Mr McEwen put into service a double-decker omnibus drawn by three horses abreast, with accommodation for seventeen passengers inside and twenty-five 'on top', at a fare of threepence.

A great incentive in the demand for public transport arose out of the opening of the Art Treasures Exhibition in May 1857 at Old Trafford. Throughout its six months' season, John Greenwood (his father had died in 1851) operated a four-minute service from which he gained considerable revenue. When, in 1860, an American, George Francis Train, laid down the first tramway in Great Britain at Birkenhead with the object of providing a smoother and easier form of transport, he used a 'step-rail', that is, one which protruded above the surface of the roadway. Due to this danger to other vehicles, Train's early experiments delayed the adoption of this form of urban transport. John Greenwood, however, experimented in Salford with another type of tramway in which the rails or plating were laid flush with the road surface. This tramway seems to have had a chequered career and was finally dismantled in 1872 by workmen of the Salford Corporation. Meanwhile, John Greenwood concentrated upon the Manchester Carriage Company, which he had helped to found in 1865 in order to operate horse-bus services throughout the Greater Manchester area.

In 1870 Parliament had passed the Tramways Act, which gave local authorities the power to construct their own tramways. Thus, the Manchester City Council, while it constructed its own tram routes, leased the provision and operation of the tramcars to the Manchester Carriage and Tramways Company until 1901. By the mid-1880s, however, other forms of traction were being considered by Manchester and some of its neighbouring cotton towns, as a result of which the Manchester, Bury, Rochdale and Oldham Steam Tramway Company was formed. But the steam-tram did not seem to catch on with the local authorities which, by the end of the century, were more attracted to the new type of electric tramcar. On 6 June 1901, the 'First Tram Day' was celebrated in

Manchester, when a procession of six electric tramcars, heavily decorated with potted palms and loaded with local dignitaries, left Albert Square to the delight of an admiring throng. By the end of the first decade of the new century every major street in the city had tram-lines, and their tracks were extended into the neighbouring boroughs. During this period Salford embarked upon its electric tramway system, which was soon linked up with Eccles, Swinton and Pendlebury, Prestwich and Whitefield. By the 1920s the tramway system had reached its peak. Not only were the streets of Manchester thronged with the city's own tramcars, but cars from eight other tramway operators ran into its centre: the small green and cream trams of the Stalybridge, Hyde, Mossley and Dukinfield (S.H.M.D.) Joint Board; the white and dark-blue cars of Ashton-under-Lyne; the neat bright red and white trams of Stockport; the sedate maroon and ivory cars of Oldham; the plum and primrose liveried cars of Rochdale; and the red and cream trams of Bury, Salford and the South Lancashire Tramways Company. Altogether they covered 300 miles of routes, a tramway network probably unequalled in the country, with Manchester at the centre.[17]

Here was indeed an acceptable and reasonably cheap mode of transport, linking Manchester with its neighbouring manufacturing towns, which together came to form the inner structure of the Greater Manchester County. By the 1930s, however, the tramcar found itself having to contend with an ever-increasing volume of motor traffic—a precursor of the greatly intensified problem of how to reconcile the requirements of private motor car traffic with the necessary facilities for public transport, a problem which is at present greatly occupying the minds of public officials and private citizens alike. A further threat by the internal combustion engine to the supremacy of the electric tramcar came in the early 1930s, when the motor bus began to replace tramcars on certain routes and eventually came to outnumber them as old tramcars were withdrawn. It was intended that the whole of the tramway system in Salford would be replaced by motor bus services by 1940, but the outbreak of the Second World War gave the tramway system a new lease of life. Overhead wires were re-erected and routes already closed were re-opened. With the restoration of peace in 1945, headlamp masks and window blackouts were removed from the tramcar, but its days were now numbered. It had served the community and had been an accepted component of the street-

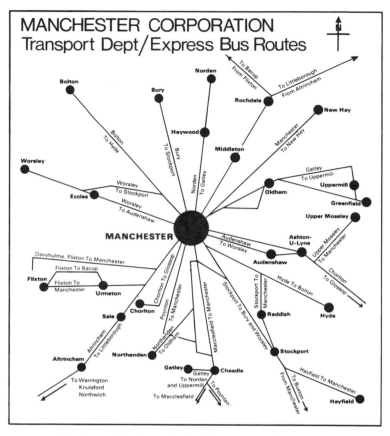

The Express Bus Routes in the Manchester region in 1930

More than forty years before they were absorbed by the SELNEC Passenger Transport Executive, ten transport authorities in the region were providing a comprehensive network of express bus services, in addition to many jointly-operated tram routes. This diagram, issued by Manchester Corporation and its neighbours in 1930, shows some of the twenty-seven inter-town links which resulted from the most extensive co-ordination scheme of its kind in the country.

scene in the towns of the Greater Manchester region for more than fifty years. There are, fortunately, enthusiasts in this region who, as members of the Manchester Transport Museum Society, have a scheme to establish a working tramway in a Manchester park as a visual reminder of the great tramway age. They take their honourable place with those who sponsor the veteran car rallies, those who are striving to restore the canals for recreation and pleasure, and those who plan to retain at least some of the monarchs of the railway age—all part of the colourful pageantry of transport.[18]

As early as 1910, a Manchester City councillor declared: 'The problem which we have at the present time is how to adapt the resources of modern civilisation to an environment which has been produced by an old civilisation. The fact is that we have an old centre through which we are trying to drive our modern tramcars and we find that it is impossible to do it.'[19] Nearly sixty years later, the City Planning Officer for Manchester, concerning himself and others with the planning of the Central Area of the city, wrote:

'Any City Centre Plan has to represent a reasonable balance between the three variable factors of accessibility, environment and economy . . . Indeed it may be said that the whole future of cities depends on being able to provide a sufficiently high degree of accessibility to ensure that they can function efficiently and conveniently whilst creating an environment of quality to make them centres of attraction. The essential relationship between land use and the planning of the whole transportation system, public and private, is now being increasingly realised and accepted.'[20]

It needs to be for, during the years 1931 to 1938, the number of private motor vehicles in use in the United Kingdom rose by 66 per cent, and between 1938 and 1958 they more than doubled. During these years almost 100,000 persons crowded daily into the central square mile of the city of Manchester by train, bus, tram and car between 8 am and 9 am to work in its warehouses, banks, exchanges, shops, offices and factories or to pass through the city to adjoining industrial areas. These metropolitan sub-groups, as they may be identified, such as Salford and Stretford, Stockport, Bolton, Bury, Rochdale, Oldham, Ashton, Altrincham and Wigan, had themselves to contend with a local traffic problem in that, during the peak hour, they together aggregated about 14,250 vehicles in one direction, which number has steadily increased during the past twenty years. When one considers also the journeys undertaken for shopping and entertainments both to the city centre of Manchester and to the centres of these sub-groups, one realises that this dynamic region has, for at least the past forty years, been building up a traffic problem which is metropolitan in its nature and is only possible of solution by being dealt with by one metropolitan authority.[21]

By the Transport Act of 1968 the Minister of Transport was able to set up in the following year the SELNEC (South East Lancashire and North East Cheshire) Passenger Transport Authority. Its purpose was to secure, through its Executive, the provision of a completely integrated and efficient system of passenger transport to meet the needs of its area. It was this comparatively new organisation for road and rail transport which the Greater Manchester Council took over on 1 April 1974, as the largest single unit in the United Kingdom after London Transport. Through the Council's Transportation Committee, the Greater Manchester Passenger Transport Executive is responsible for the provision of bus and rail services for the whole of Greater Manchester. To fulfil this task the Executive at present has almost 3,000 vehicles under its control.[22] Thus the Greater Manchester Council is now ultimately responsible for the strategic planning and all policy decisions relating to public transport and highways in the County. It is evident that this Council realises that an attractive and efficient public transport system is an essential part of any plan for its metropolitan region. As a considerable number of those employed in the centre of Manchester travel by bus, it is important that this form of urban transport should be efficient, reasonable in its schedule of fares and as comfortable as possible for its customers. Yet it has been stated that 'it is difficult to escape the conclusion that buses will always suffer due to the competition for road space with other transport.'[23]

On the other hand, the railway system, with its separate reserved tracks, offers speed, comfort and safety to balance against the door-to-door advantage of private transport. As the rail system at present carries about 25 per cent of those who work in the centre of Manchester, the position of the three main stations—Victoria, Piccadilly and Oxford Road—in relation to the main centre of the city, is of paramount concern. This is why the SELNEC Report on the future of public transport for Greater Manchester placed considerable emphasis on, and appeared to show a good deal of pride in, what is called the 'Picc-Vic Tunnel'. This was to be an underground rail line linking Victoria Station and Piccadilly Station and connecting with the electric rail system at both these stations. Its purpose was to open up fifty miles of fast, 'no change' rail travel from Bolton, Bury, Radcliffe and Prestwich in the North to Stockport, Cheadle Hulme, Wilmslow and Alderley Edge in the South. It was intended that this 'Picc-Vic' line would be available to the public in 1978, but it looks as if we shall have to wait rather longer for this ambitious innovation.

The most difficult problem for the Greater Manchester Council is how to reconcile the requirements of public transport for the benefit of the whole community with the civic rights of the private motorist. On the one hand, the bus, as the most flexible form of public transport and as 'an all-purpose vehicle catering for a complete cross-section of the travelling public's needs', finds itself at a disadvantage both in its use of the road and in its uneconomic fares. On the other hand, the private car, usually carrying one or two persons and taking up, especially on major roads, a disproportionate amount of space in comparison with a bus carrying a large number of passengers, tends to aggravate the traffic congestion, especially at peak hours, to the detriment of the bus services. And with the constantly increasing number of private cars on the roads, the problem is likely to become even more intractable. The SEL-NEC *Plan for the Future* in 1973 suggested that 'there is an important place for the private car, with its special advantages, in the work, leisure and cultural activities of the population . . . But we suggest that the car's future is not on the roads of a major conurbation in the morning and evening peak periods.'[24] It may be that one solution to this problem of the claims of public transport vis-à-vis those of the private car may be found to a certain degree in the demarcating of separate bus lanes along short, strategic lengths of heavily-used main roads. It may be, too, that the proposed railway innovations and the rail/bus services will considerably ease the problems of public road transport. Above all, one hopes that whatever plans are adopted for the standard of service in public transport within the Greater Manchester County, the environment of town and country will be enhanced and not disfigured.

The tasks, present and future, facing Greater Manchester have been described as 'the biggest urban district transport programme since the railways were built'.[25] This long-term plan contains proposals which will take at least thirty years to implement, and in itself symbolises the immense and complicated tasks before the Greater Manchester Council if it is to keep open its lines of communication by sea, air and road.

Chapter 11

'Such great achievements . . .' (1963-74)

Manchester, with the industrial towns of its region, would seem to present a contrast in reputation. On the one hand, these towns in their heyday brought great material wealth and civilised benefits to Britain. On the other, they have come to represent for many observers the epitome of ugliness and even squalor in their appearance and environment. Ten years ago, a government interdepartmental study-group set up to investigate the problems of the north-west region, while acknowledging that Manchester throughout the nineteenth century 'could then claim with some justice to be the centre of gravity of industrial Britain', although 'the First World War marked the end of this long period of buoyant self-confidence', felt impelled to point out that: 'The tracts of derelict industrial land which blight many of the towns, the drab, huddled shopping centres, the ugly obtrusive factories and mills, above all the streets and streets of old, mean and dilapidated houses—these are constant reminders that the character of the region was forged during the heyday of the industrial revolution.'[1] An even more trenchant example of this contrast occurs in an article on Manchester written by a well-known modern historian who was born in Lancashire. While claiming that 'Manchester is the only English city that can look London in the face, not merely as a regional capital, but as a rival version of how men should live in a community', he considers that 'Manchester is irredeemably ugly . . . quite as ugly as people say.'[2]

It seems to be generally agreed that until about 1960 Manchester and its regional neighbours had become crystallised in their Victorian setting and remained essentially as the Victorians built them. An architect of note, who patently loved the city, accepted that 'the vast majority of Manchester buildings are nearly all the products of the Victorian age.'[3] But were they irredeemably ugly? Evidently the mid-Victorian editor of a reputable architectural journal did not think so: 'Manchester is a more interesting city to walk over than London. One can scarcely walk about Manchester without coming across frequent examples of the *grand* in architecture. There has been nothing to equal it since the buildings of Venice.'[4] While admitting that only a Victorian could have made such an improbable statement, one has to say that there is a certain substance in his claim. The newly-built ware-houses in Portland Street and Princess Street, designed in the palazzo style, seem to epitomise the vigour and self-confidence of the mid-Victorian Manchester merchant. 'Structures fit for kings', was how George Bradshaw described them in 1857.[5] Fortunately, Watts Warehouse, built in 1851 and described a century later as 'the most grandiose, the most pretentious, the most opulent ware-house in Manchester',[6] still stands in Portland Street as a gran-diloquent reminder of the great age of the palatial warehouse.

One of the beneficial effects of the Clean Air legislation has been to encourage the custodians of civic buildings and the more public-spirited men of commerce to reveal, by a modern process of clean-ing, the original colour and architectural features of their build-ings, which had been for a century enshrouded in grime and soot. Thus the craftsmanship and wealth of detail, combined with the warm tones of finely worked stone, are there for all to see in buildings such as the Town Hall and its modern Extension, the Central Library, the Free Trade Hall, the Cathedral, the Victoria University, the John Rylands Library and various commercial buildings. Particularly pleasing is the revelation of the classical proportions of the Portico Library, which stands in Mosley Street as a symbol of the style of living which the doctors, scientists and merchants who lived in its vicinity cultivated during the early decades of the nineteenth century. This was not an area ugly to look upon and there were others like it, such as that of St Ann's Square, with its pleasant rows of streets and Georgian houses of red brick and stone, while the Square itself was bordered with trees, and, a little further south, that of St John Street, which still retains its domestic dignity. But such areas as these were the exception rather than the rule in early nineteenth-century Manchester. For the great majority of the working class, living conditions were appalling in the squalid courts or mean streets. Dr James Kay and others have described them vividly enough for all to understand how degraded human dignity had become. And Friedrich Engels, as all know, was quick enough to take up these politically conven-ient descriptions as if they were all still applicable in 1844. That they were not, in many instances, was due to the wholehearted manner in which the members of the first Manchester Borough Council applied their energies and talents to the urgent tasks of reforming the housing and sanitary conditions of the working classes. So successful were they, with the help of powers granted by

Parliament,[7] that after 1844 back-to-back houses ceased to be built in Manchester, and by 1851 the Council had reconditioned over thirty-five per cent of all the dwellings in the Borough. These were achievements of which those pioneers of the early Manchester Borough Council had every reason to be proud.

Have their successors, elevated since 1853 to the status of City Councillors, attained proportionately such great achievements in this sphere? When they met in full Council, preparatory to the commencement of business, they pledged to their City their 'time and strength and thought to speed the day of her coming beauty and righteousness'—words evocative enough for the toughest of consciences. In the face of the problems which have confronted them since the middle of the nineteenth century, they have certainly needed all the time, strength and thought which they could summon for the fulfilment of so worthy an aim. It has been said that 'the city of Manchester is the outstanding example of a city that has never been planned.'[8] Its extensions into the townships of its intermediate ring in 1885 and 1890, nearly fifty years after the incorporation of the original Borough, and in 1904 into those of its outer ring embracing Withington, Didsbury, Chorlton-cum-Hardy and Burnage, resulted in a long, unwieldy area, almost completely covered with buildings in the centre, and with practically all its open spaces in the intermediate and outer rings. But it was in the inner ring of Manchester that the depressing results of the speculative builder of private enterprise, hastily seizing the land round about the newly-built mills and factories, were most manifest. Here was street after street of those meanly-built terraced houses which prompted Lord Shaftesbury, presiding at the opening meeting of the Social Science Congress in Manchester in 1866, to declare:

'The master evil which nullifies every effort for the benefit of the working people . . . is the domiciliary condition of many thousands of our people. There are hundreds where there should be tens, and thousands where there should be hundreds. The overcrowding is frightful; it disgusts every physical and moral sense, and the more so when we see it as a growing, not a declining, evil.'[9]

Despite the adoption of by-laws by the City Council, designed to control overcrowding and to established standards of cleanliness, 'the master evil' continued to dominate the inner zone. In 1886 Manchester's Medical Officer of Health reported to the City Council:

'The old houses are rotten from age and neglect. The new houses often commence where the old houses leave off and are rotten from the first. It is quite certain that the working classes are largely housed in dwellings which would be unsuitable even if they were not overcrowded . . . Nothing stronger could be said in describing the effect of overcrowding than it is conducive to the spread of epidemic and contagious diseases.'[10]

This Victorian setting of slum property, which characterised the inner ring encircling the commercial centre of the city, was the inheritance of rapid industrial expansion, with an equally rapid growth of population, from the mid-nineteenth century. Even as late as 1962, the City Surveyor felt compelled to announce that 'a new look for the City has been long overdue. Its thousands of outworn dwellings have been allowed to exist too long and have become a reproach to its citizens and a blot on its name.'[11] It is this aspect of Manchester, described as 'still essentially as the Victorians built it', which has placed upon the metropolis the stigma of ugliness. In a sense, it gives the impression of being all-pervading which is both unfortunate and inaccurate. For when a visitor, either by road or rail, crossed the city boundary intent upon entering its centre, he would be bound to pass through this inner ring of Victorian inheritance. Equally, on departing from the centre of the city, whichever road he took—north, south, east or west—he would pass through an almost continuously built-up area until he arrived at the next town, such as:

to the north:	Rochdale Road to Middleton
to the north-east:	Oldham Road to Failsworth and Oldham
to the east:	Ashton Old Road to Ashton,
	Hyde Road to Hyde
to the south-east:	Stockport Road to Stockport
to the south:	Oxford Road leading to Cheadle
to the south-west:	Chester Road to Stretford
to the west:	Liverpool Road to Salford and Eccles
to the north-west:	Bolton Road to Pendleton and Bolton,
	Bury New Road to Whitefield and Bury.

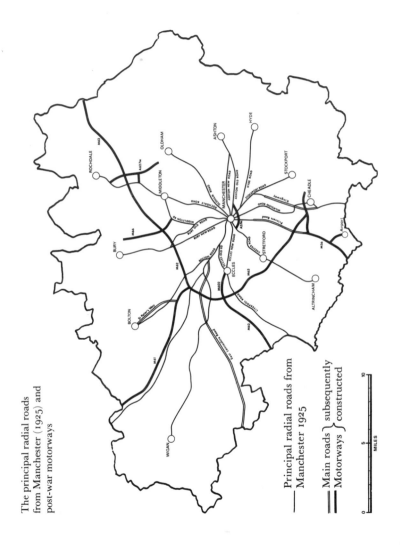

The principal radial roads
from Manchester (1925) and
post-war motorways

Principal radial roads from
Manchester 1925

Main roads } subsequently
Motorways } constructed

0   5   10
MILES

If the visitor were perceptive enough, he would realise that these towns (and others in their vicinity) had become, by the very nature of their historical ties with Manchester, so closely linked with the metropolis as to constitute a unit of regional administration. Indeed, the very names of the majority of the roads constitute a pattern of communication which in itself predicts the structure of the new County, unlike the anonymous modern motorways which tend to link the surrounding towns rather than radiate from Manchester. If he thought along those lines, he would have anticipated, possibly unwittingly, all that has led up to that part of the Local Government Act of 1972 which has established the Greater Manchester County. But he would hardly know that these roads, radiating like spokes of a wheel from the city centre, would eventually lead him to all the Districts of the Metropolitan County, which themselves bore ample evidence of the Victorian legacy of slum property.

The provision of housing both in Manchester and in its neighbouring towns was, until almost the end of the nineteenth century, the sole responsibility of private enterprise. Despite the persistent attempts of the municipal authorities to overcome the problems of bad housing and overcrowding by a well-intentioned policy of reconditioning of slum property, despite the efforts of a few enlightened social reformers to provide housing for the working class in large blocks of flats ranging from two to five storeys,[12] despite even the first experiment by the Manchester Corporation at building its own Council housing estate at Blackley in 1904, the seemingly intractable problem of a comprehensive housing policy remained. In the midst of the First World War, a highly respected Manchester alderman, on receiving the Freedom of the City, warned his fellow-citizens that

'Housing is a question that vitally concerns the health of the people . . . It will be your duty to see whether you can carry out some scheme of housing that will meet the necessities of the poorest of our working classes . . . Whether it raised our rates or not, we shall have to do our best to alter the state of things in connection with the housing of this city.'[13]

When the war ended, the Lloyd George appeal for 'homes fit for heroes', supported by the promise of strong financial aid from the Government, induced the Manchester City Council to set up in

1919 its own Housing Committee which, during the next six years, strove hard to provide working class houses of a reasonable standard. Although numerically the results were disappointing (less than 5,000 houses were built), the experiment proved that, given the necessary freedom of action, the Corporation was capable of building houses for its citizens at least as competently as private enterprise.

It was just at this time that a new problem arose which threatened to jeopardise the housing programme of the Committee and was to cause considerable concern to the City Council for many years to come—the shortage of land for new housing within its own boundaries. This factor had, by 1936, already raised the price of land within the city to about £400 an acre. Fortunately at this time the opportunity came to the Corporation of purchasing the Wythenshawe estate of about 2,500 acres from the Tatton family at £80 an acre. Plans were made for founding and developing a satellite garden town to house eventually 100,000 people, living in both municipal and private enterprise houses. The long and bitter struggle from 1926 to 1931 for the incorporation of the whole Wythenshawe area of over 5,000 acres arose out of factors which did not obtain in the earlier extensions of the city boundary. Manchester wanted the incorporation; the inhabitants of the three Cheshire townships of Northenden, Northen Etchells and Baguley, which made up Wythenshawe, did not.[14] Manchester was a large urban area governed by a City Council; Wythenshawe was almost completely rural and governed by rural district councils under which 7,000 residents were content to abide. Manchester was in industrial Lancashire; Wythenshawe was in agricultural Cheshire. Superficially, but not identically, one finds in this contest with Manchester almost the same factors which motivated the residents of Wilmslow and Poynton successfully to oppose in 1971 their inclusion in the proposed Greater Manchester County. But in the late 1920s the primary factor of drainage and efficient sewage disposal, which had made necessary the earlier extensions, ultimately won the day for Manchester in the Parliamentary struggle for recognition of its Wythenshawe scheme. In 1930 Wythenshawe came into the city, and also into the county of Lancashire.

It is pertinent to observe that probably the first official joint enterprise of Manchester and its neighbouring towns concerned itself with the river system of the Wythenshawe area. During the latter half of the nineteenth century the increasing industrial pollution of the river Mersey and its convenience as a depository for untreated sewage not only made fishing from its banks unprofitable but also moved some neighbouring local authorities to join together in 1892 for the common purpose of preventing the further pollution of the Mersey and Irwell. This Joint Committee was financed and administered by the following authorities: Manchester, Salford, Stockport, Oldham, Rochdale, Bury, Bolton and the counties of Lancashire and Cheshire. The Committee employed a clerk, a chief inspector and four sub-inspectors, and engaged as its chemical adviser the distinguished Sir Henry Roscoe.[15] The Committee met frequently, and pursued energetically the purposes for which it had been formed. It is significant that, apart from the two counties, the local authorities which formed this Committee today constitute seven of the ten Metropolitan Districts of Greater Manchester County.

If a visitor, flying into Manchester Airport today, elects to travel into the city by the Airport bus, he will find himself speeding effortlessly along a modern motorway (M56) until he reaches the old inner ring. There he will see the old township of Moss Side, in process of urban renewal, and a little later the massive redevelopment of Hulme, where acre upon acre of mid-Victorian slum dwellings have been demolished to make way for 'the building of a new city within the old', as the former City Planning Officer once graphically described this phoenix-like process. When the visitor reaches his destination at the central bus station in Chorlton Street, he will see around him many new commercial buildings where once stood the great warehouses and Georgian dwellings of the Manchester merchants who conducted their business with the manufacturers of the neighbouring cotton towns now in the Greater Manchester County. If, however, this visitor had flown into Manchester Airport three or four years ago, he would not have been able to speed along a new motorway but in return, in having to travel through the satellite town of Wythenshawe, he would have had the exhilarating experience of seeing for himself Manchester's outstanding achievement in municipal housing reform. There he would see homes set in pleasant and spacious surroundings, with gardens and many of the amenities of modern society for health of body, mind and spirit. He would doubtless realise that these are not the provisions of a beneficent charity, but civic recognition of the natural rights of every citizen of a civilised community, in which human dignity expects no less. This is what Wythenshawe really means.

When Manchester celebrated in 1938 the first centenary of its incorporation as a municipal borough, a leading citizen, whose family played a prominent rôle in the creation of Wythenshawe, wrote of the problems to be solved in the next hundred years: 'Chief among these is the problem of town planning. Manchester today, like our other great industrial cities, is a disgrace to civilisation. She has grown up mean, unplanned and so dirty and unattractive as hardly to be fit for human habitation.'[16] Yet, mingled with such astringent observations as these, her affection for the city of her adoption was clearly expressed: 'With all her faults—and the worst are those that leap to the eye—I am so passionately convinced that there is no other city in the country that is her equal, that to suggest that she needs whitewashing—except literally!—would seem a sheer impertinence.'[17] What concerned her most of all was that there should be 'a bold re-design of the face of Manchester'. Encouraged by 'the achievements of the past' and with 'the much greater scientific and administrative knowledge of today', she predicted that 'Manchester should, long before the bi-centenary is reached, be a model city both in appearance and in the quality of her citizens.' In all this, her final conviction was that 'we need a far-reaching regional plan for the future of the greater Manchester, one with courage and imagination.'

Is the City today, not so far distant from the half-way mark to the bi-centenary of its incorporation, measuring up to her aspirations 'for the future of the greater Manchester', which she visualised as embracing all the neighbouring towns of the region? That she would have rejoiced in the statutory creation of the Greater Manchester County in 1972 and in the subsequent official recognition of its reality on 1 April 1974 goes without saying. That she would equally have rejoiced today in Manchester's premier place as 'the home of smoke abatement', in the early reforms of which she took a particular pride, may be evidenced from her full account of the measures taken by the municipality, in advance of national legislation on the subject, since 1844.[18] As for the 'literal whitewashing', she must have been very gratified to see for herself, in the evening of her long life, the most pleasing results of the expert cleaning of the exterior of many public and commercial buildings both in Manchester and in the neighbouring towns of the region. Yet the crucial test, from the point of view of her high and exacting standards, would lie in the sphere of housing and town planning about which she wrote in 1938, 'there is still much to be done before every citizen is housed either in a separate cottage with a garden, or in a flat with green belts near at hand for gardens and allotments and playing fields.'[19]

Even before the outbreak of the Second World War, the housing problem had long been regarded by the local authorities of the region as having first priority in the apportionment of their resources. It was recognised then that the policy of building walk-up flats of three to four storeys, however much they represented a considerable improvement in living conditions over the slums they replaced, was not the ideal housing solution for all types of people. At the end of the war, the housing problems for these local authorities were more pressing than ever. The actual cost of building houses had increased dramatically, while in the inner city areas of Manchester land had risen to the price of £8,000 an acre. To solve the immediate problems of post-war housing needs, a short-term policy of building temporary pre-fabricated bungalows sited on small plots of land and on the fringes of some of the larger parks was adopted to avoid holding up the long-term solution to the formidable housing problem. By the mid-1950s the real extent of the housing problem in Manchester, for example, was clearly evident; it was estimated that at least one third of the city's dwellings were unfit for human habitation. A five-year programme of clearance was adopted but progress was painfully slow during what has been described as 'the great non-planning era' in Britain.[20] By the early 1960s the growing wave of property development had reached the North, with the result that the increasing pressure upon the local authorities for planning approval by eager and ambitious developers stung the municipalities into action. In 1964 Manchester set up its own separate Planning Department with an enlightened and forward-looking City Planning Officer in charge of it. He knew well the truth of what a prominent authority on housing in Manchester declared thirty years earlier: 'Re-housing carried out in connexion with individual slum clearance schemes here and there, unrelated to any general scheme, will not bring about the improvements needed in the whole area; there must be a comprehensive replanning scheme.'[21]

One of the major problems of housing reform facing the municipal planners during the post-war era has been the overall shortage of land with the consequent high cost of land available. This particularly applied to the inner areas of a city like Manchester, and it was this factor which prompted the City Council to seek land for housing development outside its boundaries. In this way overspill areas were established around the perimeter of Manchester at Wilmslow, Sale, Partington, Hattersley, Langley (Middleton), Whitefield, Heywood, Gamesley and Chadderton. Collectively these areas contain at least 20 per cent of Manchester's total housing stock.[22]

This factor of land value also encouraged architects to solve the density problem during the 1950s and early 1960s by designing high-rise flats to such an extent that they became an architectural vogue, in that they seemed to meet the economic and technological requirements of the day. In support of this view, a well-known editor of the *Architectural Review* claimed in 1969 that high blocks 'are built on industrial systems which—given the speed at which they are needed—is as it should be, though whether flats in the tenth or twentieth floor are what people want, or indeed what it is socially justifiable to give them, is another matter.'[23] It certainly is, for what most people need is a home on a human scale, and this is especially so for families with young children. The problems of high-rise living are now well documented, and among architects responsible for them there is a growing movement of recantation. Richard Seifert, the best known British tower-block architect, has himself recently described high-rise flats as 'socially evil' and confesses to having 'now capitulated to the human benefit of designing low-rise buildings, certainly not more than five storeys high.'[24] For Manchester this recantation is not stringent enough for, since 1970, it has adopted the policy of building low-rise flats no higher than four storeys, as may be seen in the great re-development scheme in Hulme, one of the most extensive of its kind in the country.

The period of great achievements for Manchester and the neighbouring towns which now constitute the Metropolitan County, not only in the vital re-development of housing but also in the enhancing of the quality of environment in a variety of forms, is the decade from 1963 onwards. This is the period when the real attack was made on the obsolete housing which has given the region such a bad name since the great population build-up in the years of the Industrial Revolution. In 1963 over 80,000 homes, about one-third of the total housing stock of the City of Manchester, were scheduled as potentially unfit. By 1974, so thoroughly had the clearance of this property been undertaken that it was evident that the process would be completed by the following year. The extent of this achievement was not only recognised in its early stages by the Ministry of Housing and Local Government as 'outstanding' and 'commanding admiration',[25] but was also acknowledged in a remarkable way by the fact that those responsible were asked by some members of the public to preserve one or two streets 'as a reminder of Coronation Street'.[26]

The complementary process of urban renewal has gone on steadily on the basis of comprehensive redevelopment of complete sectors designed to accommodate self-contained communities such as one would find in a conventional town. It is intended that a sector, to be comparatively complete, would require its own shopping facilities, schools, libraries, swimming pools, health centres, social services offices, community centres, churches, public houses, parks, play spaces and car-parking spaces. Equally important are the provisions planned to enable the residents of the sector or new town to live in conditions of maximum safety, where freedom from the nuisance of moving vehicles is achieved by the creation of a system of pedestrian footpaths entirely separate from vehicular routes, while at the same time access to an efficient public transport service is ensured.[27] Initially, four sectors forming a semicircle around the city centre—Hulme, Bradford/Beswick, Longsight and Harpurhey—have been chosen for renewal. The first to be tackled along these lines was Hulme, where over 400 acres of obsolescent housing have been cleared. The new Hulme will have a population of almost 15,000 (as against 28,000 in the old), with some 5,000 new dwellings and all the complementary requirements of such a community, such as the excellent new District Library, which for some time eloquently represented the new order amidst the rubble of the old. In contrast to the serious decline nationally of 54 per cent in the number of private houses being started in the autumn months of 1974 as compared to the same period of 1973—and this in a country where almost five million people still have to use a lavatory in the yard or garden— the number of council houses started in the autumn of 1974 increased by 24 per cent as against the same period of 1973, while completion of council houses in 1974 increased by 31 per cent as compared to 1973. This means in effect that in the Greater Manchester County the number of new council houses started (i.e. the laying of foundations) in 1974 exceeded the number of obsolescent houses pulled down in that year. It is greatly to be hoped that this positive trend will continue to be maintained in a period of national economic stringency.[28]

At the core of this radical process of renovation lies the City Centre, the renewal of which concerns not only Manchester itself but the whole of the Metropolitan County, of which it is the very hub. The proposals for the reformation of this Central Area were submitted to the City Council in the form of a draft report in December 1967. They are fascinating to read and it is particularly encouraging to know that so many intending developers and their professional advisers have recognised 'the need for a comprehensive approach and the wisdom of taking a longer term view of both their own and the City's interests',[29] for it is only in this way, with public and private interests working together as a team, that the objectives of a vast enterprise, as set out in this report, can be fully realised. A fundamental factor in the constructing of the report was the recognition that 'the Central Area of Manchester serves an area much larger than the City itself', and 'in this regional context' needs to provide 'more attractive and efficient shopping, commercial, social and higher education facilities', for 'whilst the City's population will continue to fall for a time, the total population of the City Region will move in an upward direction.'[30] While the plans for the renewal of the City Centre are rightly practical, in the professional sense, one is conscious of a mind of vision and idealism at work, in the human sense. Thus:

'It is not sufficient just to provide good accessibility and the right location for regional facilities; prosperity is related to the continuance and development of the Central Area as a centre of attraction at a time when higher standards of surroundings for living and working are not only appreciated but are beginning to be taken for granted. Landscaping and open space, good civic design and fine buildings, freedom to walk about in safety, all that is meant by the word "amenity" are becoming increasingly recognised as essential ingredients to the success and survival of a metropolitan centre . . .'.

And again:'The aim is to harness the forces of change to produce a Central Area that is efficient in human and functional terms but which also has variety of character' for 'Manchester has a very recognisable character and there are precious traditions which should be carried through and developed as a fine new City grows.'[31]

An excellent example of identifying the traditional with the new is the proposal to construct a riverside frontage to the Irwell where it flows below the West Front of the Cathedral and in the vicinity of Chetham's Hospital, the latter being an outstanding example of this process. Founded in 1653 by the will of Humphrey Chetham for the maintenance and education of '40 boys of honest, industrious and painful parents, not of wandering or idle beggars or rogues', this venerable, yet ever-young institution was reorganised in 1969 on a co-educational basis as Chetham's Hospital School of Music. Entry to the school is by audition only, with the object of evaluating the child's musical potential even though he is bound to undertake a full grammar school course of academic subjects, on the ground that it would be wrong to deprive a young musician of a sound general education. It is not surprising that this unique character of Chetham's has attracted the attention not only of many local education authorities in Britain (some 83 per cent of the School's pupils are there on municipal grants) but even internationally as far afield as Vienna, the musical capital of Europe. In this respect it is good to know that as many as 100 pupils (about one-third of the total number at present at the School) come from and are supported by the Metropolitan Borough Councils of the Greater Manchester County while, at the same time, the County Recreation and Arts Committee has sponsored a series of concerts given by the School in the various Boroughs. This is indeed a splendid example of participation in one of those 'precious traditions' which belong not just to the County but to every Borough within it—all the more precious in that it relates to an historic building which is situated at the very heart of the City's origin.[82]

One detects the same spirit at work in the imaginative proposal to landscape the section of the Rochdale Canal which runs through the Central Area linking the Ashton Canal system at the Dale Street Basin to the Bridgewater system at Castlefield. In June 1967, the author was a privileged member of the crew of a private cabin cruiser whose owner, determined to demonstrate that this rarely used stretch of the Rochdale Canal was navigable, set off at noon from moorings at the Castlefield Basin. It was a memorable journey, involving a view along the canal of the red-coloured tower of the Refuge Assurance Company's building, as the cruiser passed under City Road and proceeded towards Oxford Street, which temporarily transformed Manchester into Bruges or Amsterdam. It was also a hazardous journey, necessitating perilous passages through faulty and much-neglected locks and the frequent removal of floating and concealed debris. It took *Borderland* five-and-a-half hours to reach Dale Street Basin—a distance of just over one mile. Today, with this last stretch of the Rochdale Canal restored for public use, the way is open for the canal enthusiast to travel right round the famous Cheshire Ring, enabling him to enjoy in comparative comfort almost a hundred miles of waterways which span the whole life of the Canal Era. That small stretch of the Rochdale Canal and its continuation north of the City Centre is well worth the Greater Manchester Council's consideration for landscaping and recreation.[33]

Among the significant proposals of the City Centre Map there is the concept of the retention of groups of buildings or of areas of distinctive scale and character. This follows the provision of the Civic Amenities Act of 1967, which placed on local planning authorities the duties of identifying those parts of their areas which are of special architectural or historic interest, and of designating them as 'conservation areas'.[34] Examples of these are St John Street, the lower part of King Street and St Ann's Square. The last-named lends itself particularly well to such a designation as the historic remnant of the medieval Acresfield, with evocative street-names such as Ridgefield and Dolefield in the vicinity and with the beautiful St Ann's Church and the impressive Royal Exchange dominating the Square at either end. Here the purpose is to free the conservation area from all but essential traffic, to pave and landscape the surface making it substantially pedestrian, and to exploit to the full the natural advantages of the Square as a safe and attractive open space.[35] There is no doubt that this timely Act has provided legislative protection not only to the planners of the City Centre but also to the District Councils of Greater Manchester, who are enjoined, once a conservation area has been designated by them, 'to take action to preserve or enhance its character and appearance'.

Fortunately, at a time when fears may naturally be expressed as to the desirability and efficacy of large administrative structures such as a Metropolitan County, the opportunity afforded by the founding of the Civic Trust in 1957 to establish Civic or Amenity Societies 'at the grass roots', as it were, is greatly to be welcomed. Their general purpose can hardly be better defined than in the words of the late President Kennedy: 'Only when the citizens of a community have participated in selecting the goals which will shape their environment, can they be expected to support the actions necessary to accomplish those goals.' By September 1974 there were forty Civic Amenity Societies already established in the Greater Manchester County. They are to be found in each of the ten Districts as follows: Manchester (7), Salford (2), Wigan (4), Bolton (1), Bury (3), Rochdale (4), Oldham (5), Trafford (4), Stockport (5), Tameside (5). It would appear that Bolton and District Civic Trust covers in itself the entire Metropolitan District. All these Societies are registered with the Civic Trust For The North West, which was formed in 1961, and is 'dedicated to the promotion of high standards of planning and architecture and the creation of a better environment'. There are about 130 Societies registered with this Trust, which periodically invites its members to support and participate in an intensive campaign, as it did in 1967 when it launched 'Operation Spring-clean' in an 'all-out effort to clean up the face of the region and dispel its tarnished Coronation Street image', in which it is claimed that 'an estimated 65,000 people were involved'.[36] It is interesting to observe that by New Year's Day 1972 twenty conservation areas had been designated by the local planning authorities of what is now the Greater Manchester County, five of which were contained within the City of Manchester. Compared to what many other counties and county boroughs had achieved in this sphere (there were seventeen in the City of Liverpool and fifty in the West Riding of Yorkshire), this is not a record of enterprise on the part of the seventy former local authorities which now constitute the new county. Although a further twenty-one conservation areas have been designated since that date, there is little doubt that this is a sphere in which the forty Civic and Amenity Societies, in co-operation with the District Councils of the new County, could well take the initiative.

It has been well said that those owners of commercial buildings in the city centre who have responded to the lead given by local public bodies in the cleaning of the exterior of their buildings have, in so doing, presented 'a reminder of the quality of design and the robustness of construction of the Victorian era that has remained for so long unappreciated'.[38] Such a determination to conserve what is good and of value must have warmed the hearts of the members of the Manchester Victorian Society. Founded early in 1966 with the wholehearted support of that great national protagonist of the best of Victorian architecture and design, Dr Nikolaus Pevsner, this Society has, with a large measure of success, directed all its resources and energies towards 'protecting all that is of architectural value from 1837 to 1914' in Manchester and its neighbouring towns. In a fascinating article on the cost of conserving Manchester's city centre,[39] Robert Waterhouse selects two of Victorian Manchester's outstanding buildings, the Mechanics' Institute in Princess Street, and Watts Warehouse in Portland Street, both built about 1854. It has recently been announced that the former, where the first Trades Union Congress took place in 1868, is seriously being considered by the City Council for conversion into a national library and museum of labour and industrial history. This is indeed historically imaginative and could well be of national significance.

One of the most pleasing results of the cleaning of Victorian buildings in Manchester is the transformation which has been effected in the Oxford Road buildings of the University, which were inaugurated as the new Owens College on 7 October 1873 at 'an impressive ceremony in the mid-Victorian style'.[40] What they built, and what has been added in the course of time to complete the quadrangle, still imparts in its ornamental Victorian Gothic an intimate atmosphere and dignity amidst all its surrounding modernity, which are the very essence of what is desirable for study, research and meditation. At that inaugural ceremony, Thomas Ashton, a leading industrialist of the region and one of the foremost protagonists of the movement for the extension of Owens College in new buildings in Oxford Road, evidently 'looked ahead by announcing that the building was only a part of the grand scheme',[41] and this was when, for the first time, Owens College reached just over 1,000 students in attendance in the last session at Quay Street (1872–73). Just over a century later, the Vice-Chancellor announced at the annual meeting of the University Court that between 1963 and 1974 the number of full-time students increased from 6,470 to 9,700, a rise of about 50 per cent.[42] Further, when the University held an Open Day on Saturday, 19 May 1973, as part of its celebration of the centenary of the inaugurating of the new buildings in Oxford Road, over 25,000 members of the public participated in this historic event.[43]

It is interesting to note that this recent decade, when the growth in the number of students attending the University increased most rapidly, is the very period when so much was achieved in laying

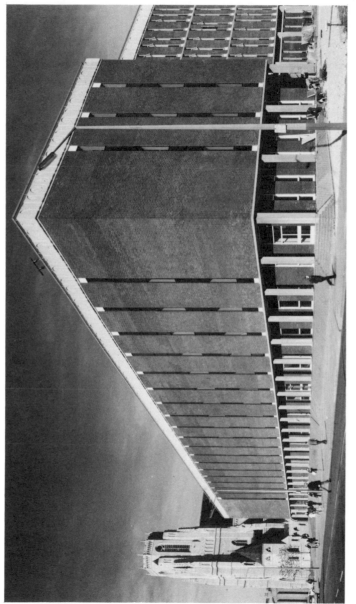

Manchester Education Precinct – the new University Medical School

the foundations for the improvement of the quality of environment in many spheres, in regard both to Manchester and to the neighbouring towns which now constitute the Greater Manchester County. It is the period, also, when at its beginning (1963) the Joint Committee representing the Manchester City Council, the University, its Institute of Science and Technology and the United Manchester Hospitals, appointed its two Planning Consultants, who were instructed to prepare an overall plan for the development of the Manchester Education Precinct. One of the main principles upon which these two architects based their plans for this great enterprise was that 'there should be integration with City development.' They saw their task as 'a comprehensive activity and never more so than in the case of this vital and important example of urban renewal in a great City', in which 'the social, physical and economic needs of the City of Manchester and of its University are essentially complementary. To improve one automatically improves the other.'[44] These views are echoed in the draft report for the City Centre Map, published in the same year:

'The Plan is essentially for a "City University" and the close relationship between the area of the City Centre and the Precinct both physically and as regards activities is recognised and exploited ... The planning proposals for the area and for the adjoining areas of the City Centre are designed to permit the maximum use of educational, recreational, cultural and entertainment facilities by both students and a wide section of the public.'[45]

Eight years later, when many of the new institutions planned for the Precinct are already functioning, both students and citizens of the Greater Manchester County are presented with a remarkable variety of artistic and musical productions at the University Theatre, the Royal Northern College of Music, the Polytechnic and in the beautiful Renold Hall of UMIST in surroundings both graceful and comfortable. By 1984, when it is possible that the Precinct will have been fully developed, it is estimated that there will be a total day population of about 40,000, of which about 25,000 will be students. One can only hope that the Planning Consultants will have successfully solved the almost bewildering variety of problems involved in so complex a development— transport, parking of vehicles, safety of pedestrians, catering facilities, library accommodation and elimination of noise—all this so as to make the Precinct 'a good place in which to study, to live and to work'. The challenge is there, for: 'The opportunities that exist are perhaps unequalled in any city in Europe; here there can be created a fine group of buildings and inter-related spaces worthy of a great educational centre in a great city. There could also emerge a relationship between town and gown which could be unique in its scope and influence.'[46]

What of the University itself in this great complex of institutions for the advancement of computer-science, for the supplying of television and radio programmes, for the education of students for teaching in the schools and of those who wish to enter industry or commerce, for those who seek the means of spiritual insight and for those who desire to dedicate themselves to the study of music and art? The University is ready to accept a planning figure of 14,000 full-time students by 1981, provided certain conditions relating to academic buildings and to residential and administrative accommodation can be met and, most important of all, 'if sufficient students come forward of the necessary quality and appropriate balance of disciplines . . .'[47] In a very wise 'Letter to a fresher at the University of Manchester',[48] Professor Brian Chapman discusses some of the problems which today face both the novitiate and the more senior members of the University. While admitting that Manchester has never had the physical infrastructure of the Oxford and Cambridge colleges to rely upon, and that she is not a federal university like London, she is by the nature of things 'very large but unitary'. Both her ethos and her problems arise from the fact that, in company with some other great Manchester institutions such as the Hallé, the *Guardian*, and the Literary and Philosophical Society, the University has not only international and national rôles to fulfil, but also 'acts as regional godmother to a variety of institutions of higher education . . .' One detects here an intuitive allegiance to the ancestral preference given by the terms of John Owens' will to children of parents resident in Manchester or South Lancashire.

This continuing relationship of the University to its region is demonstrated in the statistics of full-time students for the session 1972–3. Under the heading 'Home Residence of Students', the following details are given of those students whose homes were in the former county boroughs which now by name constitute eight of the ten Districts of the Greater Manchester County:

Home Residence	Number of Students
Bolton	103
Bury	49
Manchester	983
Oldham	54
Rochdale	44
Salford	88
Wigan	37
Stockport	172

This means that almost one student in six of those registered at Manchester University for that session came from what is now the Metropolitan County, but on the criterion of merit, not of geographical preference. It is interesting to note, also, that the total of regional students (1440) nearly equalled in that session the total of Commonwealth and foreign students (1735).[49] Professor Chapman considers that the long-term answer to many of the questions which he poses lies in the Education Precinct—'that great Manchester vision of the future'. But he brings his fresher back to earth by reminding him 'of that part of the Manchester tradition which the University has learnt from her city', which consists of 'neighbourliness, nonconformity, dedication, imagination and hard work. They all sound very old-fashioned virtues. Perhaps there is some hidden point behind the official title—The Victoria University of Manchester.'

Perhaps, too, this is the answer to the question as to what place those venerable buildings in Oxford Road have in the new Precinct, which is impressive in its size but seems generally to be bereft of beauty and pleasing ornamentation. The primary function of the University still remains as it was defined over forty years ago by one of the greatest of its professors: 'I should describe a university as an association or corporation of scholars and teachers engaged in acquiring, communicating, or advancing knowledge, pursuing in a liberal spirit the various sciences which are a preparation for the professions or higher occupations of life.'[50] In these words, Samuel Alexander was not expounding a vision of an ideal university, but was interpreting what he felt to be the trend of Manchester's experiment in the making of a university, what was in fact inherent in the original idea of its founder but now expanding into a larger life. This is traditionally what those original buildings of the new Owens College in Oxford Road stand for, both academically and in their architectural significance. One would like to think that the Greater Manchester Council, in its developing association with Manchester University, will become more and more involved in this intrinsically regional tradition.

Probably the most salutary and significant achievement of the decade from 1963 in the region now known as the Greater Manchester County lies in the sphere of smoke abatement or what is now more positively described as Clean Air Reform. Although this is only one aspect of the great problem of pollution, which has been defined as 'the introduction by man of waste matter or surplus energy into the environment, directly or indirectly causing damage to persons other than himself', reform in this particular sphere has both a visual and physical impact, especially upon a region which is heavily industrialised and has a high population density, factors which to those engaged in the promotion of such a reform make the new county 'particularly interesting from a pollution standpoint'.[51] Nature has not been kind to Manchester in helping her to get rid of smoke. As the pivot of 'the first industrial society' and lying in a hollow, the city has tended to receive the smoke blowing from its neighbouring towns, which may explain why it early sought powers to deal with this particular problem of air pollution. It was recognised as early as 1800 that industrial smoke could be greatly diminished. The Commissioners of Police, appointed under the Manchester and Salford Police Act of 1792 and at that time the effective local authority, received from its Nuisance Committee in 1800 a report which stated that 'the increase of steam engines as well as smoke issuing from chimnies used for stoves, foundries, dressers, dye houses and bakehouses has become a great nuisance to the town unless so constructed as to burn the smoke arising from them which might be done at a moderate expense.'[52] But it was the first Borough Council which, pursuing its policy of obtaining local powers through Parliament, succeeded in securing an anti-smoke clause in the Manchester Police Act of 1844, which required that every furnace used for the purposes of trade or manufacture should be so constructed as to consume its own smoke. A few years later, the Town Clerk for Manchester pointed out that 'in the opinion of practical and scientific men the law ought to apply to the making of smoke and not to the construction of the furnace.'[53] Indeed, Joseph Heron was so far in advance of his time that he referred to smoke from house-fires and proposed that this form of pollution could not be prevented except by the use of coke. Twenty years later his views were incorporated into national legislation when the Sanitary Act of 1866 decreed that 'any chimney sending forth black smoke in such a quantity as to be a nuisance shall be deemed to be a nuisance liable to be dealt with summarily'; it is significant, however, that this did not apply to 'the chimney of a private dwelling-house'.

As so often has been the case in matters of reform, especially where human health is concerned, both locally and nationally, it has been the patient insistence of voluntary societies which has eventually compelled authority to legislate for reform. Thus from 1856 onward the Manchester and Salford Sanitary Association concerned itself with the smoke nuisance and at frequent intervals presented memorials to the City Council; in 1891 the Noxious Vapours Abatement Association sent a severely-worded address to the City Council, complaining that only a very small proportion of offenders was summoned before the magistrates, and equally strongly urging 'the increased use of gas as one of the most feasible methods of lessening the present excessive pollution of the air by coal smoke'; in 1909 the Smoke Abatement League of Great Britain was formed, with its headquarters in Manchester, and twenty years later amalgamated with the Coal Smoke Abatement Society (originally founded in London) to form the National Smoke Abatement Society, based in Manchester. It was this society which suggested to the Manchester City Council in 1938 the establishment of a smokeless zone in the city which, owing to the intervention of the Second World War, did not come into operation until 1 May 1952. The City Council was able to effect this because Manchester was the first local authority in this country to obtain powers, under the Manchester Corporation Act of 1946, to establish 'smokeless zones'. Ten further smokeless zones were established under the local powers before the Clean Air Act of 1956, promoted 'to make provision for abating the pollution of the air', came into operation, to be followed twelve years later by another Clean Air Act which made further provision for the long and hard-fought fight against air-pollution.[54] Since 1959 the winter daily averages for smoke have been reduced by 80·2 per cent and for sulphur dioxide by 62·9 per cent. This is the first time, since measurements began to be taken, that the target for smoke-abatement has been overtaken. At a time when just over three-quarters of the total area of the city and over 61 per cent of the total premises are subject to smoke control orders, there is every prospect that, when the last order is made in mid-1976, the Clean Air programme for the City of Manchester will be completed in time. When that day arrives there will justifiably be cause for rejoicing, both in the City Council and among the officials and technicians who have worked with so much enthusiasm for its attainment. But none more than they know how much more there is to be achieved in the controlling of the whole realm of urban pollution.[55]

It was not only among voluntary societies vis-à-vis the Manchester City Council that the problem of air-pollution caused grave concern. In 1924 some fifty-six local authorities of the Regional Town Planning Area (there were between eighty and ninety local authorities in this consortium) formed the Manchester and District Regional Smoke Abatement Committee with the object of acting in an advisory capacity for the attainment of clean air in the region. This eventually became the Manchester and District Regional Clean Air Council, for which the Health Department of the Manchester Corporation provided secretarial services for a number of years. From 1 April 1974 this Council, in company with two similar organisations, has been superseded by the Greater Manchester Council for Clean Air and Noise Control. It is composed of the ten District Councils within the Greater Manchester County and such other local authorities as have a geographical association with the region. The functions of the Council include acting as an advisory body for improving the control and reduction of air pollution and noise.[56] The offical map showing the progress made in the Greater Manchester Metropolitan Area in smoke control at the time when this Council was formed indicates clearly those Districts in which much has been done and those in which much remains to be done. Speedy and effective action by the authorities responsible for the latter Districts is a matter of serious concern for the new Council, because smoke does not as a rule stay where it has been emitted.

This determined and sustained attack upon the image of grime and obsolescence has already effected a transformation, especially during the decade since 1963, in the quality of the environment. Clean air legislation has not only made possible the cleaning of buildings and a new outlook for the city centre of Manchester, it

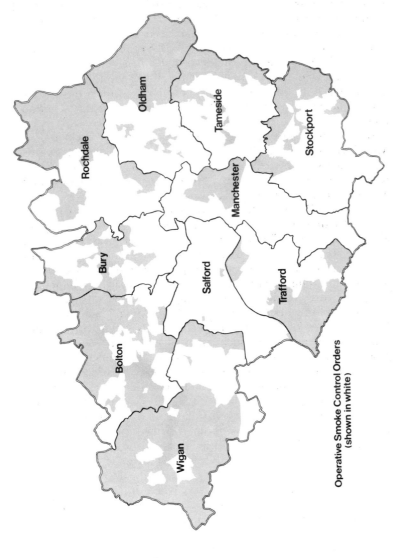

Progress in Smoke Control in the Greater Manchester Area (1975)

Operative Smoke Control Orders
(shown in white)

has also revolutionised conditions in the neighbouring manufacturing towns situated in the north of the region. Whereas before this decade there was an increasing tendency towards a thinning-out of population in such towns as Bolton, Oldham and Rochdale, while there was at the same time a gradual increase in building and population in the south of the region, there has been during this decade, as, a result of clean air and improved accessibility, a rejuvenation of the former cotton towns, to the entire benefit of the Greater Manchester County. Further, the improved accessibility of these towns has undoubtedly been facilitated by the construction during this decade of new motorways. These modern highways, although national by designation, have provided a regional network of immense value to the towns of the Greater Manchester County and, at the same time, have opened up excellent communications with many areas of Britain. Within Manchester itself there is a highway (in more senses than one) which, although not a motorway, carries the regulations of a national motorway. Officially opened on 5 May 1967, its function was to divert east–west through-traffic from the centre of the city. It has the historically appropriate name of 'Mancunian Way', which arose out of a competition among Manchester schoolchildren, sponsored by the City Council.

A municipal enterprise which developed strong regional potentialities was that concerned with the supply of pure water. When Manchester was accorded the status of a City in 1851, its Council had already bought up the Manchester and Salford Waterworks Company, a private venture, and had introduced the supply of water into the town from its first reservoirs in the Longdendale valley. Just over twenty years later the Manchester City Council, realising that the supply from its Derbyshire reservoirs was insufficient for the needs of a rapidly increasing population, embarked upon the great Thirlmere project, which prepared the way in 1929 for its second waterworks scheme in the Lake District at Haweswater. By the mid-1950s the Manchester Waterworks Committee was supplying water to an area of well over 100 square miles and a population of $1\frac{1}{4}$ million. Today the same municipal organisation, but now known as the Manchester Water Supply Unit of the North West Water Authority, still supplies this vital necessity from its highly developed waterworks resources to twenty former local authorities now within the Greater Manchester County. They are the following:

Salford	Urmston
Eccles	Worsley
Prestwich	Altrincham
Stretford	Hyde
Swinton and Pendlebury	Sale
Atherton	Stockport
Denton	Bowdon
Droylsden	Hale
Irlam	Longdendale
Tyldesley	Bucklow

Bolton and Ashton-in-Makerfield are supplied with water in bulk directly from the Manchester reservoirs for the villages in their surrounding districts. In this way the former Manchester Waterworks Committee now serves the new County as a direct result of its far-sighted investment in the great schemes in Derbyshire and the Lake District.

The City of **Salford**, which heads this list, has had to contend, in its efforts to secure the rehabilitation of the city, with two factors: the proximity of Manchester, which contributes to many of its planning difficulties and the built-up and congested nature of the city, as it has practically no virgin land within its boundaries and no opportunity for expansion beyond them. Its post-war Council has, as a result, concentrated its efforts in two main directions: to sort out existing conditions so as to give some coherence to the chaotic state to which much of the city had been reduced and to produce a satisfactory basis upon which to build a new and revitalised city. To these complicated tasks the leaders of this 'classic industrial town'[57] have brought courage and enterprise. By 1972 the Corporation had built over 5,300 new homes, including bungalows, houses, maisonettes and flats ranging from four to twelve storeys. During that year Corporation policy tended to change from high-rise flats to houses, although private developers continued to prefer the former. Linked with the process of slum clearance and redevelopment in the centre of the city is a comprehensive scheme for the improvement of the major roads, in joint consultation with Manchester and the Greater Manchester

The University of Salford

County. As part of this scheme the City Council has taken the opportunity of redesigning the shopping area by creating a large shopping precinct on modern lines which will provide the nucleus for a civic centre which hitherto Salford has lacked. One of the most exciting events during this decade was when, in April 1967, the Salford Royal College of Advanced Technology was granted full University status. Beginning as the Royal Technical Institute in 1896, the new University of Salford, with strong science and technical faculties balanced by a rapidly expanding activity in the Arts and Social Sciences, has already developed into a regional and national institution of considerable importance, with over 3,600 full-time undergraduate and postgraduate students.[58] But Salford wisely keeps its eye on the sources from which fundamentally its wealth is derived. The City Council has established the 'Salford City Industrial and Commercial Development Council', whose objects are to promote the industrial and commercial development of the city so as to maintain a high level of investment and employment for manufacturing, exporting and local services. It is the declared objective of the Salford City Council to 'upgrade and enhance the environment of the City for the benefit and quiet enjoyment of its citizens and visitors.'[59] In so doing, it will contribute greatly to the future of the District which it serves and to the new County of which it is so distinguished a part.

As with the two cities, so also with the former county boroughs and boroughs of Greater Manchester has the policy of renewal of the environment been actively pursued during this remarkable decade from 1963.

Wigan, situated on the western edge of the Metropolitan County, is somewhat different in type from the other towns. With the decline of its two principal industries, coal and cotton, Wigan has had to face up to many of the ravages created by the industrial revolution, such as appalling housing conditions, high unemployment, poor environment with vast amounts of derelict land and widespread pollution of the air and water courses, lack of open spaces and facilities for recreation and poor internal communications by public transport. In each of these spheres the County Borough Council has shown enterprise and foresight: many new industries have been encouraged to establish themselves within its boundaries with a consequent decrease in unemployment; large schemes have been undertaken, such as the area of Scholes close to the town centre, to replace nineteenth-century slum dwellings with well-planned and attractive modern houses and flats; a start has been made on reclaiming derelict land to provide amenity open spaces and facilities for organised and informal recreation. Most encouraging of all are the facilities which have been opened up for the enjoyment of the Arts in a converted art gallery and museum and a flourishing 'Little Theatre'—both at the core of the 'new' Wigan. Much has been achieved, much remains to be done, and in this respect the Greater Manchester Council will be expected to play a prominent rôle.

Bolton considers itself 'a town worth looking at, worth getting to know and worth preserving'.[60] It claims that, for leisure pursuits and entertainment, its citizens 'can almost always find what they want "on their own doorstep" and journeys to Manchester are undertaken simply for a change of scene and not as a necessity.'[61] There may be justification for this claim, for the County Borough Council was one of the first in the country to provide its own civic entertainment programme, well before local authorities were given statutory powers in 1948 to spend up to a 6d rate on entertainment. In order to tackle the problems of reorganisation of the cotton industry, the Town Council sensibly joined forces with the Chamber of Commerce, Chamber of Trade and the United Trades Council, with the result that many of the redundant cotton mills were converted to operate a great variety of new industries with the consequent beneficial effects on local employment. In the problem of housing considerable progress has been made during the past decade in the replacement of Victorian blocks of houses by a mixture of traditional and industrialised building, to which have been added many attractive private housing developments. But the glory of post-war Bolton lies in its Town Centre Redevelopment Plan. With its impressive Town Hall as the focal point, the new Civic Centre provides a covered Mall and a capacious Precinct, free from all traffic and enhanced by attractive large flower-beds, for a surrounding population of over a quarter of a million people. In June 1975 this Precinct received a Civic Trust Heritage Year Award, as did also the Wallsuches Bleachworks at Horwich, originally founded in 1777 and now most successfully restored and adapted by the company's own maintenance department for use as an engineering works. With its well-equipped new central library, its modern Octagon Theatre and its

Bolton's capacious Precinct, part of the new Civic Centre opened in June 1973

fifty separate societies and clubs devoted to cultural and social activities, Bolton stands in its own right as a civic community and, as such, has much to contribute to the new County.

Bury, which is situated on the northern edge of the Greater Manchester County, prides itself on its 'attractive blend of town-and-country life'. At the same time, it was described at the last official census (1971) as 'the fastest-growing town in all Lancashire', while more recently the national Press has nick-named it the 'Booming Borough'. Bury clearly has a reputation to maintain. While the town centre and market have been renewed and social welfare and educational facilities are being established to cater for this rapid growth in population, the post-war Town Council has inherited an unfortunate legacy of sub-standard environment and derelict land and buildings. New developments in general improvement areas, the establishment of further smokeless zones and the reclamation of derelict land, especially in the Irwell valley, are being adopted to combat these handicaps. During the past decade some 14,000 new houses have been built by the former County Borough Council and plans are being prepared for further development. The new Metropolitan Borough clearly intends to co-operate wholeheartedly with the Greater Manchester Council in the fulfilment of its schemes and its first Mayor was right to remind his fellow-citizens that 'the new era of local government presents us with a tremendous challenge', in which 'every member of the new community has a part to play.'[62]

The **Rochdale** Town Centre, whose original grand design has already been described in an earlier chapter, still seems to hold the centre of the stage in the present pageantry of the town's life. A visit there soon reveals the comprehensive character of the ambitious development scheme already in active progress. The new police headquarters and Crown Offices have already been built, while provision for a new market and shopping precinct, magistrates' courts, municipal offices, bus station, a new museum, and a social centre incorporating a theatre, public hall and library has already been planned. The Parish Church, the Town Hall and the Post Office have been cleaned, each revealing anew the distinctive attributes of its architectural style. But the most challenging feature of the busy scene lies in the seven massive fifteen-storey blocks of modern flats which almost defiantly tower over the quiet setting of the Memorial Gardens to outstare the elegant beauty of the Gothic

Town Hall. Whether one approves of these monarchs of a new age, which seem to thrust into the sky like gigantic fingers, is a matter of personal taste. Nikolaus Pevsner considers them 'well and crisply designed', and 'as an earnest of intention they must be respected.'[63] On a less dramatic scale, Rochdale regards its general policy of housing as 'already well developed' and places as one of its priorities 'the provision of suitable accommodation for the aged and handicapped'. In the sphere of smoke control, the Borough had by the end of 1972 covered 61 per cent of its acreage and 68 per cent of the total premises. It confidently expects that by 1977 the whole Metropolitan Borough will be smoke controlled. A democratic feature of the new Borough's administration is the setting up of Community Councils in comparatively small areas of the District, with the object of enabling local people to make their views known to the Borough Council. There are already well-established community groups in many parts of the District. Rochdale, centrally situated in the new Borough, is proudly conscious of its Metropolitan responsibilities and is equally determined to play its full part in the plans for the future of the Greater Manchester County. It has a distinguished reforming tradition to uphold.

Oldham is sensibly and acutely conscious of the many problems which it has inherited from the extremely rapid growth of the town during the latter half of the last century. It is aware, for example, that its physical fabric is in need of extensive renewal, despite much new development in recent years, and that its self-confessed 'poor image' has been a disadvantage when competing with other towns for new employment. While unemployment is not particularly high in the town, there is a lack of diversity in the opportunities for work. Wages in the Borough are on average lower than elsewhere in the Manchester area, partly because it has not so far been possible to attract the better-paid jobs. Yet the Town Council has for the past decade been actively engaged in redeveloping its housing (which it regards as the first priority), its community facilities and public buildings, especially its provisions for education, and, most sensitive of all, the appearance of the town. These municipal efforts have been much commended by one discerning observer: 'In the last few years Oldham and its Borough Architect have shown themselves uncommonly enterprising in new buildings and large development schemes. They deserve high praise.'[64]

So also does the Borough's Director of Libraries, Art Galleries and Museums, who has evidently caught the imagination of its citizens, young and old, by engaging their civic pride in the promotion of a Local Interest Centre which has considerable potentialities. Adjacent to the Central Library, this new Centre in Greaves Street is amply accommodated in the former Friends Meeting House, built in 1867. The ground floor and basement contain a local history museum in which 'there is something for children of all ages to appreciate—whether it be the youngster marvelling at the curious fashions of days gone by, or the older visitor succumbing to a bout of nostalgia.' With his interest aroused, the visitor is invited (almost lured) upstairs to the Local Studies Library, where he will find a variety of reference books, maps and photographs into which he may delve for further information on what he had seen downstairs. In this way the museum and library are intended to complement each other in a specific field of interest. But they do more than that: by the attractiveness of its display and the clarity of its presentation, this two-fold Local Interest Centre positively encourages the older visitor 'to summon up remembrance of things past' and the younger to wonder at the ways in which his forefathers lived in their home town of Oldham.[65]

Oldham justifiably looks to the new County for 'special treatment to help us overcome the problems of large-scale obsolescence and essential renewal of houses, factories and community facilities'.[66] But there is evidently at least one Victorian virtue which the town has retained; in reviewing what has to be done, the new Borough Council warns its citizens: 'To pay for all this, we need a prosperous Oldham.' For them the maxim of Samuel Smiles still holds good.

Stockport has an air of optimism and confidence both in its civic atmosphere and in reports of itself, such as: 'With direct links to the national motorway system, with the main Inter-City railway line between Manchester and the south running through its centre, with excellent local rail services and with Manchester airport on its doorstep, Stockport is a town with a great deal to offer.'[67] It certainly has, if one is to judge from its progress during the post-war years. Here one detects almost an *embarras de richesses* in a variety of spheres; in its population it expects an increase of 20,000 during the next twelve to fifteen years; in housing redevelopment it undoubtedly has an enviable record, especially in its 'neighbourhood units' at Brinnington (1950) and Offerton (1966), where the services for a complete community have been provided; in opportunities for jobs, which have been increasing both in the town itself and in neighbouring Manchester; in industry, in which the demand for land by both local and outside firms exceeds the amount available in the Borough; in commercial and local services, offices have mushroomed in the town centre and it looks as if further growth in office building is bound to come; for shoppers there is a fine town-centre Precinct, which increasingly attracts visitors from a wide area around Stockport. This popularity is placing such a heavy strain upon car-parking accommodation that the Borough Council is considering whether to inaugurate a public transport system to relieve congestion in the town-centre. Although its immediate environment needs serious attention, Stockport is fortunate in having the Cheshire and Peak District countryside near at hand and the Tame Valley project in which to participate. All in all, although Stockport is facing 'one of the most challenging eras in its history', it does so in the confidence that 'it is now planning for the future ... a future within Greater Manchester.'

Trafford and **Tameside** are in a rather different category from their fellow-Districts in the new County. While in the latter there is either a city or a former county borough around which to assemble, the two former Districts are made up of municipal boroughs and urban districts, with a consequent tendency for their administrative offices to be dispersed over the District. In Trafford the general headquarters is at Stretford, whose boundary with Manchester is almost imperceptible. But Stretford has been steadily making its own plans for redevelopment in recent years. With a major problem of slum-clearance on its hands, it has pursued a progressive housing policy, especially in the provision of small blocks of flats and bungalows for the elderly. In 1969 the Borough Council opened to the public the first phase of the Stretford Arndale Shopping Centre—an ambitious project undertaken jointly by Stretford Council and Town and City-Arndale Properties Limited. As a concept this Centre was ahead of its time and marks the beginning of a new era for Stretford. At the other end of the District, Altrincham, with its neighbours Bowdon and Hale, constitutes the stockbroker belt with its well-appointed dwellings situated in an area of sylvan opulence. With its northern neighbour, Altrincham has been the scene of much office development, for which there have been until recently plenty of takers. Tameside includes several distinctive communities, each with its own particular needs and hopes for the future. Yet, as a District, it has a distinctive unity, which is exemplified by the Tame Valley project. Its general headquarters are at Ashton-under-Lyne, which claims to be the natural weekly shopping centre for about 150,000 people, for whom there is a thriving market-ground operating five days a week. Ashton, in company with its neighbouring former boroughs and urban districts, has resolutely tackled its serious problems of urban renewal, reflected in its smoke control programme which was designed for completion throughout Tameside by 1976. Both Trafford and Tameside look to the new County to recognise their special needs in view of the neglect they have suffered in the past due to the remoteness of the old county authorities and a general shortage of resources. One hopes that they do not look in vain.

The great achievements carried out during the decade from 1963 not only by Manchester but also by the Councils of the neighbouring towns have already contributed significantly to ridding the region of the grey image which has in the past so adversely prejudiced its true potential. So heartened and determined have all the District Councils become as a direct result of what their immediate predecessors have already achieved that it may perhaps be no exaggeration to say that they themselves aspire to enter into 'the high moments of his history when man has answered the beauty of nature with the beauty of his cities.'[68] This is what is meant by 'quality of environment' at its highest level.

This is also historically and appropriately the time to greet the emergence of the Greater Manchester County.

Chapter 12

Emergence of the Greater Manchester County

When was the term 'Greater Manchester' first used? A few months before the outbreak of the First World War, a Manchester City Councillor read a paper to the Institution of Municipal and County Engineers entitled, 'Greater Manchester: The Future Municipal Government of Large Cities'. In it he declared that

> 'After many years of careful investigation, inquiry and subsequent observation, the only conclusion I can arrive at in connection with the future local government of large cities is that . . . it becomes desirable, wherever future extensions are probable, to constitute one Central Council for the whole area to deal with certain functions and District Councils to deal with all strictly local matters which in the public interest and convenience are better dealt with locally.'[1]

The Councillor was clearly basing his views upon the experiences of London in municipal administration, following the setting-up of the London County Council in 1889 and, ten years later, the creation of the Metropolitan Borough Councils. What he had in mind was 'the Manchester known in commerce' and not merely 'municipal Manchester', for he anticipated that the former 'may ultimately govern an area more extensive, though not as populous, as the present administrative County of London.' He postulated two schemes of extension open to Manchester: the first would include Salford and Eccles and the more immediate, surrounding townships; the second he visualised as much more comprehensive, in that 'Greater Manchester would be coterminous with what I designate "the Manchester of Commerce", which would bring under our Central Council a substantial part of South-East Lancashire and part of Cheshire, comprising all municipal boroughs and minor authorities within a radius of eight or nine miles of Manchester.' For him the criterion was that 'the people of this larger area are one community, with common interests' and he even welcomed 'the recent introduction of motor vehicles for the transport of the productions of these towns to the centre of Manchester' as 'tending in the direction of permanently establishing common interests'. No doubt it did in those early days of motor transport, a situation viewed somewhat wistfully today by the officials of Greater Manchester Transport.

It was the Housing Act of 1919, following the virtual cessation of the building and reconditioning of houses during the war years, which made possible the first joint planning experiment by the local authorities of the region. In the early 1920s the new suburbia of the municipal housing estates, pierced by motor roads for the new buses and cars, had begun, and it was to meet this social revolution that the Manchester and District Joint Town Planning Advisory Committee was formed in 1921. Comprising representatives of ninety-six local authorities, this Joint Committee saw its ultimate aim as no less than 'to prepare an advisory plan in broad outline which will facilitate the progressive development of every part of this important Region, so that the most may be made of its vast resources, the enterprise of its citizens, and to bring about the best possible conditions of life.' Five years later, it produced its plan in a substantial *Report*,[2] which collated valuable information on the municipal services, recognised the inevitability of residential growth and forecast an expansion of industry which did not in fact take place. As it regarded the area under survey as too vast and the number of local authorities within it as too many, it recommended the dividing of the region into nine Group Sub-Committee Areas, so as to enable an individual local authority to place its own proposals before other local authorities within its own particular Group. Although this Committee was only advisory and could do little more than line its walls with maps while the outward trek continued unabated, it encouraged local government to raise its sights from the ephemeral problems of servicing local communities to the more distant horizons of planning the future life of a region on a co-ordinated and comprehensive basis.

In the mid-1930s a well-known evening newspaper brought to the fore in practical terms the issue of regional unity. With typical journalistic flair, it presented in striking headlines the clarion call:

'GREATER MANCHESTER'
THE RATEPAYERS' SALVATION!

The issue arose out of the paper's claim that 'increasing demands for the exploration of the possibilities of a greater merger of public services throughout Manchester and the surrounding municipalities are being advanced by civic leaders in Manchester and Salford.'[3] More immediately, it centred upon the municipal supply of gas; while Salford was faced with the problem of modernising its gas undertakings, in which service it had already accumulated a huge financial deficit, Manchester's superior gasworks at Partington, in which over £1,000,000 had already been spent, was in grave danger, due to industry's diminishing demands, of becoming a 'white elephant'. Commenting on this unfortunate situation for both cities, a Manchester Alderman loftily declared: 'It is not within the province of Manchester to interfere with the internal arrangements of Salford, but Salford might ponder well ere it spends another £89,000.' It was left to a former Mayor of Salford, however, to place the issue in its right perspective when he told the evening paper that he looked forward to the day when 'there would be a merging of the essential services of Manchester, Salford, and the surrounding districts constituting a Greater Manchester'.

It would appear that about this time there was an unofficial organisation called 'The Manchester Development Committee'. It existed, by its own profession, 'for the purpose of assisting those who seek information on the industrial and commercial aspects of Greater Manchester' and offered its services 'to carry out investigations for business interests who contemplate establishing themselves in the area'. It received a modest grant of £50 from the Manchester Chamber of Commerce.

The pace of proposals, official and unofficial, for the reform of local government perceptibly quickened during the decade immediately following the close of the Second World War. Out of a plethora of proposals during this period there were four substantial recommendations involving Lancashire. First, the Local Government Boundary Commission (1945–1949) recommended five new two-tier counties, one of which roughly corresponded with what was later labelled SELNEC. Second, Lancashire County Council proposed for itself in 1947 a division of its area into three new counties, in effect a three Ridings solution. Third, a sub-committee involving twenty-six Lancashire local authorities suggested the setting up of a regional body to be called the Manchester County Council, which would be indirectly elected by its constituent local authorities, while the members of the authorities themselves would be directly elected. The proposal met with sharp opposition, especially from those who feared that the method of indirect representation would permit the county boroughs, and Manchester in particular, to exercise a dominating influence upon the county council. And fourth, as the Census of 1951 officially recognised South-East Lancashire as a conurbation for the first time, the whole subject was taken up in a *Report* which had important implications for the region.[4] After pointing out that the six conurbations together accounted for two-fifths of the population of England and Wales, the *Report* devoted a chapter to the strong potentialities of South-East Lancashire, regarding the Manchester area as 'the centre both of the conurbation and of the North Western Standard Region'. This variety of proposals during the first post-war decade culminated in the Local Government Act of 1958, which made provision for a complete review by a new Commission of the local governments of each of five conurbations defined as Special Review Areas, of which South-East Lancashire was one. The spirit of independence soon made itself felt among the county boroughs of South-East Lancashire, for the mayors of Bolton, Bury, Oldham and Rochdale announced their opposition to any idea of a Greater Manchester, while Stockport was prepared to fight to be left alone. Among the smaller towns, proposals for amalgamation were revived to suggest the formation of new county boroughs on the principle that this was their best way of securing their independence.

One of the major factors which was tending to bedevil the many problems involved in the reform of local government at this time was the increasing use of the official term 'conurbation'. What was it exactly and what forces and influences, both material and human, merited its acceptance as a definition of an organic region? It has been suggested that the word was first coined about 1911, when the population of England's five main conurbations (Greater London, South-East Lancashire, West Midlands, West Yorkshire and Merseyside) nearly doubled in forty years.[5] Fortunately, two authoritative studies of this important subject, both published in 1959, have helped considerably to clear the air.[6] Although Mr T. W. Freeman regards 'conurbation' as a word of extreme ugliness, he considers that it is 'not jargon'. According to him the word was inspired by a contemplation of Lancashire: '. . . here,' wrote Sir Patrick Geddes in 1915, 'far more than Lancashire realises, is growing up another Greater London as it were—a city-region of which Liverpool is the sea-port and Manchester the market, now with its canal port also; while Oldham and many other factory towns, more accurately called "factory districts", are the workshops.' Speaking of its towns, he concludes: 'Constellations we cannot call them; conglomeration is, alas, nearer the mark, but it may sound inappropriate, what of "Conurbations"?'[7] The concept was carried a stage further by C. B. Fawcett in 1932 when, in his study of the 1931 census of population he defined a conurbation as 'an area occupied by a continuous series of dwellings, factories and other buildings . . . which are not separated from each other by rural land, though in many cases in this country such an urban area includes enclosures of rural land which is still in agricultural occupation.'[8]

Dr L. P. Green, however, while considering that this definition over-emphasises the physical pattern of bricks and mortar, regards its basic weakness as being originally conceived at a time when the incidence of motor transport on the growth of great cities and their regions was not considerable, whereas he sees the use of modern motor transport as 'fast becoming the decisive factor in the evolution of the great city'. He prefers the term 'metropolitan' in the sense of implying, in relation to its region, a great political and governmental centre, or a commercial and industrial giant, or a cultural capital, preferably all three attributes, but at least two. He prefers, also, the word 'region' in preference to 'area', in that it 'belongs to a family of concepts the nature of which is generally recognised', although not in itself absolute, 'for what we find depends very much on what we are looking for.' For him a metropolitan region cannot be 'an amorphous, soulless mass of houses, factories and business premises, or a mere communications network'; it is essentially 'a dynamic, complex society of people who have cultural as well as economic needs, who constantly reorganise and adapt their society to its changing environment, and who thus develop resilient regional characteristics', one of which is that, as they must get to work, they depend a great deal on technological invention. Indeed, it may well be that the extent of the metropolitan region is determined primarily by the journey to work.

It can hardly be doubted that in this context Manchester fulfils all three requirements as the metropolitan centre of a great, organic region. Politically it has long been considered that, in a General Election, 'the party which wins Lancashire wins the country', and in this sphere Manchester has always played a crucial part. As a governmental centre, the city has at least two major functions: it is the regional headquarters for the nationalised services such as health, hospital, gas and electricity in addition to those of the National Coal Board and the British Transport

Commission; it contains also the regional offices of seventeen Ministries and Departments of central government. In industry and commerce Manchester has for over two centuries been regarded as 'one of the capitals of Europe'. While its citizens would be the first to acknowledge its incalculable debt to what the Census of 1951 described as 'the crescent of industrial towns' of the region, they in their turn equally recognise the city as the metropolitan hub comprising the central business district and industrial core, a 'sine qua non', so far as Dr Green is concerned, for a genuine metropolitan region. As a cultural capital for the region and even beyond it, the reputation of Manchester speaks for itself as much today as ever it did. Indeed, what has emerged from a study of the region is its important contribution to the cultural aspect of metropolitan life. If, then, the hub and the inner metropolitan zone of close and intimate daily contact with it have been established, what is to be the periphery or outer zone which in effect constitutes the boundary of the entire region? This was the question which became one of the major problems to occupy two Commissions and two successive Governments during the next fourteen years, at the end of which the Local Government Bill finally became law in 1972.

The Local Government Commission for England was set up in 1958 and was instructed by Parliament to review in particular the five conurbations which were at that time defined as Special Review Areas, of which South-East Lancashire was one. Basing its proposals for this area upon the two-tier structure plan as operated by the Greater London authority and on the strength of journey-to-work ties in the Metropolitan region, the Commission recommended the creation of a continuous county stretching from Whitworth to Alderley Edge and from Westhoughton to Stalybridge. While the county authority would be responsible for planning, highways and traffic, housing, police, fire, ambulances and civil defence, the second tier would consist of nine boroughs based on the existing major towns of Manchester, Salford, Bolton, Bury, Rochdale, Oldham, Stockport, Stretford and Ashton-under-Lyne—remarkably close, apart from the exclusion of Wigan, to the ultimate division of the Metropolitan County into Districts. The proposals of this Commission are of interest also as the closest approach to the Greater London authority seen in any provincial conurbation. In the event, the recommendations of this Commission were not officially adopted, and in 1966 a Royal

Commission on Local Government in England, under the chairmanship of Sir John Maud (later Lord Redcliffe-Maud) was appointed by the Home Secretary. Its terms of reference were 'to make recommendations for authorities and boundaries, and for functions and their division, having regard to the size and character of areas in which these can be most effectively exercised and the need to sustain a viable system of local democracy'.

After three years of investigation and deliberation the Commission found itself unanimously of the opinion that 'local government in England needs a new structure and a new map due to the present unprecedented process of change in the way people live, work, move, shop and enjoy themselves.' Among the many factors which contributed to this anachronistic nature of local government were two which are particularly relevant: first, that 'many local authorities are too small in size and revenue and in consequence too short of highly qualified manpower and technical equipment to be able to do their work as well as it should and could be done'; secondly, 'failure to recognise the interdependence of town and country is the most fatal defect in the present structure —a local government structure which does not recognise this interdependence does not correspond with the realities of life.' In a striking passage, the Commission pointed the way along which the reform of local government could be most effectively secured to meet the requirements of present-day society: 'England needs a pattern of local authorities with clear responsibilities, big enough in area, population and resources to provide first-class services and determined to ensure that all their citizens have a reasonably convenient point of access where they can get answers to their questions and advice on how to get whatever help they need.' And the means of effecting this reform?: 'We were convinced by our surveys that the conditions necessary for a unitary authority (i.e. one-tier) exist everywhere except in three extensive and heavily urbanised areas for which we decided that the term "metropolitan" was the best description.'[9]

It became, then, the object of the Commission to reform the number of local government areas into which England was at that time divided—namely, forty-five counties and seventy-nine boroughs, each exercising independent jurisdiction, with 1,086 dependent county district councils—so as to 'fit the pattern of life and work in modern England'. To effect this, the Commission proposed that England should be divided into sixty-one new local government areas, in fifty-eight of which a single authority should be responsible for all services and the remaining three should be metropolitan areas around Birmingham, Manchester and Liverpool, each operating on a two-tier basis. It was from the latter group that the 'Selnec Metropolitan Area' emerged.[10] It was so-called because the Area was intended in the main to embrace South-East Lancashire and North-East Cheshire, in addition to which parts of North-West Derbyshire and of the West Riding of Yorkshire were to be incorporated. The Commission confessed that 'the choice even of a label of convenience for this metropolitan area is difficult', and recommended that its official name 'should in due course be locally determined.' This area contained an estimated population of 3,232,000 and consisted of just over 1,000 square miles.

The Commission felt strongly that this large area should be administered as a whole on a two-tier County and District basis because of its pressing problems of land-use planning and major development and the urgent necessity for a re-modelling of its communications system. To the District Councils it proposed the allocation of the provision of education, the personal social services, house-building and house-management. Its division of the Area into nine Districts followed on the whole the nominations of the major county boroughs, with the interesting inclusion of Warrington, mainly because of its new town development at Risley as an overspill housing area for Manchester. The inclusion in this metropolitan area of towns such as Macclesfield and Knutsford was based upon their employment links and private housing development, while those in the mid-Cheshire saltfield, such as Northwich and Winsford, were considered to have 'more to do with Manchester and the conurbation centred on it than with Merseyside or Chester'. But the most remarkable grouping of towns was that designated as the Manchester Metropolitan District, with a population of practically a million, far in excess of the other Districts. The Commission considered that 'the present boundary between Manchester and Salford county boroughs does not correspond to any physical, economic or social realities', and that 'the two places are completely joined in one continuous built-up area.' Perhaps they are, but what Salfordian would admit to so heinous an assumption? He would be more likely to accept that 'Manchester, Salford, Stretford and Urmston form, in effect, the core of the Selnec conurbation', if not, as the other eight Districts might well have feared, a dominating rôle in the Metropolitan Area. The Royal Commission concluded its *Report* in 1969 with the unanimous conviction that 'if the present local government system is drastically reformed . . . and the grip of central government relaxed, England can become a more efficient, democratic and humane society.'

In February 1970 the Labour Government issued a White Paper on the reform of local government in England, indicating that it accepted the main recommendations and all the boundary proposals made in the Maud *Report*, but it transferred the provision of education from the Districts to the County. Great pressure, however, was brought to bear upon the Government to reduce the size of the Selnec Metropolitan Area so as to enable Cheshire, as a unitary county, to retain the maximum area under its authority and the consequent maximum sources of revenue. The victory of the Conservative Party at the general election in the summer of 1970 turned out to have a marked effect upon this problem and upon the ultimate boundaries and composition of the Greater Manchester County. Initially it appeared that only Northwich, Knutsford and Macclesfield would be retained by Cheshire, but later the residents of Alderley Edge, Wilmslow and Poynton succeeded in persuading a reluctant Government to allow them to remain within the county of Cheshire. Similarly Glossop, although a major overspill area of Manchester, and its neighbouring districts were retained by Derbyshire, but Saddleworth was transferred from the West Riding of Yorkshire to the new Metropolitan County. Thus when the Local Government Bill, submitted to the Commons in November 1971, finally became law in the following year the new County had been deprived of a third of the acreage as proposed for it in the Maud *Report* and with it more than half a million people. In all this legislative tug-of-war procedure, exacerbated in many instances by local pride and prejudice, the new Government had to act quickly in order to fulfil its promise to achieve the long-awaited reorganisation of local government in England—the first comprehensive local government reform of this century.

One of its major problems was the recognition that 'there will always be conflicts between those who argue for large-scale organisation on grounds of efficiency and those, on the other hand, who argue for control by a body close to the people for whom the service is designed.' Accepting that it 'obviously must seek efficiency', the Government decided that 'where the arguments are evenly balanced its judgment will be given in favour of responsibility being exercised at the more local level', as it evidently felt strongly that 'above all else, a genuine local democracy implies that decisions should be taken—and should be seen to be taken—as locally as possible.'[11] It was for this reason that the Government resolved that the provision of education, personal social services and libraries should be the responsibility of the Metropolitan District Councils. Equally, as it regarded the provision of housing as a service which 'should be operated as close to the citizen as possible', it decided that this should be 'primarily the responsibility of the district councils', while the metropolitan county itself 'will need powers to deal with those housing problems that transcend the boundaries of the districts.' Elsewhere, outside the metropolitan areas, all these services 'must be the undivided responsibility of the county authorities.' It was within these non-metropolitan authorities, also, that the Government seemed anxious to give every encouragement to the existing rural parishes: 'The general character of parishes should remain unchanged; they should remain bodies with powers rather than duties and as much a part of the social as the governmental scene.'[12]

While the Government, then, was rightly concerned to identify the citizen as closely as possible with these more personal services, it realised the necessity of 'having units of population sufficiently large to provide a base for their effective organisation and a high quality of service.' In this respect, it accepted the recommendation of the Maud Commission that such a unit should have a population 'in the range of around 250,000 to not much more than 1,000,000 appropriate both for the effective provision of the personal services and for their democratic control.' When one realises that in 1971 there were no more than twelve cities and towns in England, outside London, which had a population of at least 250,000,[13] it becomes clear that something more than the unit of a city or town was generally required for the purposes of effective local government throughout the country. At the same time no one structure could be suitable equally for the densely and the sparsely populated areas. Complicating the issue further was the recognition that, in addition to the 'personal' services appropriate to such authorities, there were 'environmental' services such as planning, transportation, police, fire-service and major development which, by their very nature, require the control of a larger authority. It

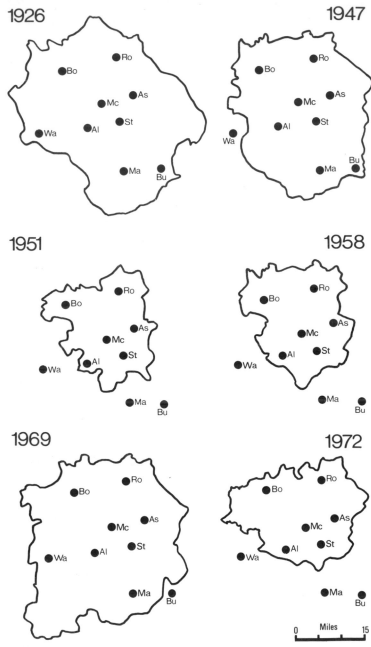

The Changing Spatial Concept of Greater Manchester
(as shown in a series of maps 1926–1972)

1926   Manchester and District Joint Town Planning
        Advisory Committee

1947   Local Government Boundary Commission

1951   Census Report: South East Lancashire
        Conurbation

1958   Local Government Commission

1969   Royal Commission on Local Government in
        England

1972   Greater Manchester Metropolitan County

The location of some of the principal towns is shown on all the maps by these abbreviations:

Al = Altrincham

As = Ashton-u-Lyne

Bo = Bolton

Bu = Buxton

Ma = Macclesfield

Mc = Central Manchester

Ro = Rochdale

St   = Stockport

Wa = Warrington

was these factors, strongly supported by the conclusions of the Maud Commission, which influenced the Government to accept the concept of the 'metropolitan' pattern as suitable 'where a county is divisible into districts all of which are populous and compact', that is, that each district would have a population of at least 250,000. Outside these metropolitan counties, the control of both the 'environmental' and 'personal services' would lie with the newly-constructed unitary counties. While being 'in no sense a continuation of the existing county authorities' it was nevertheless hoped that, where possible, existing county boundaries would be retained 'in order to keep the maximum existing loyalties and to minimise the administrative problems'. In addition to the metropolitan and other counties the Government, again following the recommendation of the Maud Commission, accepted the view that 'there are functions of both central and local government which need to be considered in a regional or provincial context.' It was felt that there would be problems in the formulation of the broad economic and land-use strategy, which could only be solved in the context of a very large area for which purpose it was decided to set up provincial councils. It was for this reason that the *Strategic Plan for the North West* was commissioned in 1971 by the Government, the report upon which was completed in July 1973.

It may be seen, then, that the Local Government Bill, introduced in 1971 by the Government's White Paper, was designed to establish an entirely new comprehensive system of local government for the whole of England and Wales, except that already applying to Greater London. Its general structure was based upon the concept of a limited number of two-tier metropolitan counties with the rest of the country divided into new counties, unitary in character but in no sense merely a continuation of the former county authorities. While the metropolitan counties were to be divided into districts, each substantial in population and directly responsible for 'personal' services, the unitary counties, binding together all the urban and rural areas contained within their boundaries, were directly responsible for 'environmental' and 'personal' services, with a qualified recognition of rural parish councils with strictly limited powers. While the Maud Commission recommended the creation of three metropolitan counties, the Government decided to increase this number to six: West Midlands, Merseyside, Selnec (still so called), West Yorkshire, South Yorkshire, and the Tyne and Wear area. On 29 November 1972 the Local Government Bill became an Act of Parliament. On this day the Greater Manchester Metropolitan County came into being—the only one to be named after its metropolis.

The new County covers an area of almost 500 square miles, with a population of over 2·7 million, greater than that of Wales and more than twice that of Cheshire. In this respect, it is the third largest metropolitan county, following Greater London and the West Midlands county centred in Birmingham. It contains some seventy former local authorities, including eight all-purpose county boroughs and sixteen municipal boroughs, which is an eloquent illustration of its urban strength and municipal experience. While not as large, either in area or population, as the Selnec county proposed by the Maud Commission, or as the earlier suggested conurbations already studied, this Greater Manchester County has an industrial, commercial and cultural wealth of historical lineage comparable to that of any metropolitan region in Europe. It has been said that one free man is worth more than ten pressed men and so it is with the constituent members of this new County. No tears need be shed on account of those former local authorities which, although neighbours as envisaged by the Maud Commission, were in so great a hurry in 1971 to scramble out of the proposed new metropolitan county. Greater Manchester today, as it has ultimately emerged, has an organic and cohesive unity, with excellent lines of communication, which will stand it in good stead in its future development for the well-being of its citizens.

In compliance with the basic principle that a metropolitan county should be divisible into districts all of which are populous and compact, the Greater Manchester County contains ten constituent Districts which have already been described individually in their historical evolution and in their relationship to the metropolis. As shown on the endpapers of this book, the Districts are as follows:

A WIGAN   Including Wigan, Leigh, Atherton, Ashton-in-Makerfield, Golborne, Standish, Aspull, Orrell, Billinge, Ince, Hindley, Abram, Tyldesley and parts of Wigan Rural District

A	**WIGAN**	Estimated population—301,000 Councillors elected to G.M.C.—13; to District Council—72
B	**BOLTON**	Including Bolton, Kearsley, Little Lever, Farnworth, Horwich, part of Turton, Blackrod, Westhoughton Estimated population—258,000 Councillors elected to G.M.C.—10; to District Council—69
C	**BURY**	Including Bury, part of Ramsbottom, Tottington, Radcliffe, Whitefield and Prestwich Estimated population—200,000 Councillors elected to G.M.C.—6; to District Council—48
D	**ROCHDALE**	Including Rochdale, Heywood, Wardle, Littleborough, Milnrow and Middleton Estimated population—200,000 Councillors elected to G.M.C.—7; to District Council—60
E	**SALFORD**	Including Salford, Swinton, Worsley, Eccles, Irlam Estimated population—318,000 Councillors elected to G.M.C.—13; to District Council—66
F	**MANCHESTER**	Including parish of Ringway Estimated population—590,000 Councillors elected to G.M.C.—20; to District Council—99
G	**OLDHAM**	Including Oldham, Lees, Saddleworth, Crompton, Royton, Chadderton and Failsworth Estimated population—230,000 Councillors elected to G.M.C.—9; to District Council—57

H TRAFFORD Including Sale, Stretford, Urmston, Altrincham, Hale, Bowdon and part of Bucklow
Estimated population—230,000
Councillors elected to G.M.C.—8; to District Council—63

J STOCKPORT Including Stockport, Cheadle, Hazel Grove, Marple, Bredbury
Estimated population—350,000
Councillors elected to G.M.C.—11; to District Council—60

K TAMESIDE Including Ashton-u-Lyne, Droylsden, Audenshaw, Denton, Hyde, Dukinfield, Stalybridge, Mossley and Longdendale
Estimated population—246,000
Councillors elected to G.M.C.—10; to District Council—54

It will be noticed that each Metropolitan District has an estimated population of at least 200,000, while some have considerably larger populations. The District Councils range in size from that of Manchester with almost 100 members to that of Bury with just under half that number. While Manchester and Salford each retain the title of City Council, the other eight Districts have Metropolitan Borough Councils. All of these Councils are directly responsible for the provision of the following services within their Districts:

1. **Housing**—including housing management, inspection, improvement grants and advice.
2. **Education**—including school services, further education and youth employment services.
3. **Libraries**—including all ancillary services.
4. **Personal–Social Services**—including residential day-care and services for the community and the family.
5. **Engineering and Public Services**—including building maintenance of all non-housing property, capital works, highways, refuse collection.
6. **Clean Air**—including air pollution and control of noise.
7. **Sewerage**—local servicing of sewers and drains.

8. **Environmental Health**—including food hygiene, meat inspection, offices and shops control, improvement of houses, slum clearance.

The Greater Manchester Council is made up of 106 members elected directly to the Council by the inhabitants of the ten Metropolitan Districts. In company with the other five new metropolitan counties, the Council is responsible for comprehensive planning, transportation and major development for the whole county. Within the broad survey of these terms, its functions may be stated more specifically as:

1. **Passenger Transport**—The SELNEC Passenger Transport Authority, originally established in 1969, was taken over by the Council on 1 April 1974 in order to co-ordinate bus and rail services within the new county. The Council has overall responsibility for the strategic planning and all policy decisions in transportation planning covering public transport and highways.
2. **Police**—Stated to be the largest provincial Police Force in the country, it patrols fourteen territorial divisions, each with a Chief Superintendent responsible for all local police matters. Although the Police Service is completely identified with the Council, it is not controlled by it other than for finance.
3. **Fire Service**—Retaining its locally-based service but now combined with the advantage of a large organisation, this important service operates in five Divisions, each responsible for two Districts.
4. **Consumer Protection**—Operating through advice centres in each District, the Council's Consumer Services Department provides advice and assistance on all aspects of consumer services and goods governed by statutory legislation. The Department also co-operates with the Citizen's Advice Bureaux and local Information Offices.
5. **Refuse Disposal**—By means of a co-ordinated programme, the Council intends through up-to-date disposal methods ultimately to eliminate the 'eyesores' scattered over the landscape of the county.
6. **Housing**—In this sphere the Council has reserved powers to provide overspill needs at the request of District Councils or central government.

7. **Planning**—In this sphere, in which the Council is expected to co-operate both with the District Councils and the Provincial Councils, the County Structure Plan and the Strategic Plan for the North West are in process of completion. As they are very important functions for the future of the County, they will be treated in their own right in the next chapter.

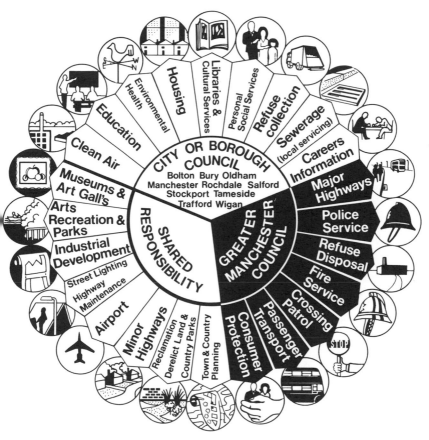

How services and responsibilities are shared between the County Council and the District Councils

Certain responsibilities and powers are held jointly by both the County Council and the District Councils. They are:

1. **Museums and Art Galleries**—This joint service of these important institutions, in which the whole region is undoubtedly rich, can be of incalculable value. Policy regarding exhibitions, purchases and development is to be formulated by mutual discussion and agreement between the County and District Councils and institutions concerned. If the special exhibition of 'European and Russian Master Drawings' from the renowned State Hermitage Museum of Leningrad, held at the University of Manchester's Whitworth Art Gallery under the auspices of the British Council and the Greater Manchester Council during the autumn of 1974, is a foretaste of what is to come, then the citizens of the County, and even those outside it, are indeed fortunate.

2. **Parks and Recreation**—This joint service provides for a variety of forms of physical activity and out-of-doors occupations, including open spaces, allotments, smallholdings, swimming baths, physical training and other recreational pursuits.

3. **Town and Country Planning**—These are essentially shared responsibilities which come within the scope of the County Structure Plan and the related Local Plans.

4. **Highways**—Included in this sphere are traffic control, road safety, lighting of highways, bridges, footpaths and bridleways.

Embracing the Greater Manchester County and its Districts there are two provincial councils responsible for two vital services which are deemed to require a wider regional basis. They are:

1. The North West Water Authority, which has taken over control of twenty-four water-supply undertakings, sewage disposal and river pollution, is now responsible for all aspects of the water cycle ranging from conserving rainwater to the treatment and disposal of sewage. In the actual supply of water there will be no change so far as the County is concerned.

2. The North Western Regional Health Authority, which is one of fourteen regional organisations through which the reconstructed National Health Service operates. It is divided into eleven Area Health Authorities, ten of which are coterminous with and are situated in the Metropolitan Districts of Greater Manchester. These A.H.A.'s, as they are called, are responsible

for the health centres, health visiting and home nursing, school health, vaccination and family planning. The medical practitioners and officers of this new Authority are inheritors of a great tradition founded by men such as Charles White, Thomas Percival, John Ferriar and James Kay and continued by eminent physicians and surgeons to the present day. They inherit, also, great hospitals throughout the County and the services of the distinguished Medical School of Manchester University, now housed in a marvellously equipped new building which, with its neighbouring teaching hospitals, is regarded as one of the world's major medical centres, all of incalculable benefit to the citizens of the Greater Manchester County.

In all this escalating of responsibility and authority, ranging from the District Councils to the Provincial Councils, it is good to know of Stockport Metropolitan Borough's initiative and enterprise in planning and creating local community involvement. Beginning with six Community Councils made up of representatives of local organisations, the new Borough was divided into three main areas and these in turn were sub-divided into eight areas, each of which is served by an area committee of council members. In thus providing opportunities for public participation in local government affairs, Stockport regards itself as 'probably better equipped than any other district in Greater Manchester to be receptive and responsive to public opinion in drawing up plans for its future'.[14] However this may be, and one suspects that some at least of the other District Councils (Rochdale, for example) are pursuing policies of similar intent, it is the spirit inspiring these policies which is the very essence of local democracy. If such policies become a real part of the Districts' corporate life and if a genuine co-operation with the County Council in its wider responsibilities for the whole community is effectively achieved, then the Greater Manchester County may indeed look forward to the challenge of the future with confidence.

Chapter 13

The County Structure Plan and the Strategic Plan for the North-West

On 12 April 1973 the members of the first County Council for Greater Manchester were elected District by District on a quota basis. They are 106 in number and they remain in office as councillors for the new County until 1977, when all of them are due to submit themselves for re-election if they wish to remain as councillors for a further four years. On 10 May 1973 the members of the Councils of the new Metropolitan Districts were elected. After an initial period of adjustment, a District councillor will remain in office for three years before submitting himself for re-election. It has already been noticed that, during the course of that year, Manchester and Salford were granted the right of retaining the title of 'City' with the result that the Council of each is known as 'City Council'. In like manner, each of the remaining eight Districts is controlled by a Metropolitan Borough Council. It may be observed that there is now a growing tendency to drop the term 'Metropolitan' not only for the City and Borough Councils but also for the County Council. All these Councils came into their own when their members officially took office on 1 April 1974, when the old councils ceased to exist. Thus Greater Manchester, as a county in its own right, became a reality. On that historic day there was little ado, only the knowledge that there was much to do.

In no sphere are the interdependence and the interlocking of interests between the County and its constituent Districts more evident than in the County Structure Plan. As early as January 1972 a Joint Working Party, representing those local planning authorities likely to be concerned with the future development of the proposed Greater Manchester County, was set up to undertake the preparation of a Structure Plan. It conceived the 'structure' of the area under study as meaning the social, economic and physical systems of the area so far as they are conducive to planning control or influence. In effect it refers to the important factors in any analysis of this nature such as the distribution of population, its activities and the corresponding relationships between them, the patterns of land use and their development, the communication networks and the utility service systems. The Structure Plan itself is seen as a new type of plan which sets out the long-term policy objective for these matters on an area-wide level. In practical terms, the working party judged that the county authority responsible for structure planning in the Greater Manchester Area would have to deal with the following main issues:

Population and Housing

While the population level of the Area has remained relatively stable during the past twenty years (circa 2·7 million) this overall total conceals certain internal differences such as the decreasing population of the older inner areas through redevelopment and the increasing population of the outer areas due to the availability of land for residential development. A Structure Plan must therefore concern itself with future housing policies because of people's aspirations for better living conditions, with the consequent implications for future land needs.

Social Facilities

Owing to the great diversity of groups in the social structure of the area, each with its different needs, it is a crucial function of the Structure Plan to recognise the nature, distribution and varying needs of different groups when proposals are being formulated, especially concerning areas of social stress due to housing shortages and the problems of immigrants.

Employment

Changes in the industrial structure over the last decade give cause for concern in that they reflect the decline in employment between 1961 and 1970 by 9 per cent in this Area as compared to a decline of only 3 per cent in the North West Region and a growth of 1·5 per cent nationally. Despite these changes, local specialisation and the concentration of linked groups of industries in particular parts of the Area are still characteristic and may well pose problems in those parts with an over-dependence on declining industries. A Structure Plan will need to investigate the possibilities of introducing or expanding nationally 'growing' industries and of making available retraining facilities in new skills. However much one may aspire to 'better living environments' and a more acceptable 'quality of life', greatly desirable as these are, it is the profitable use of natural wealth and human talent which is the prerequisite of civilised progress. Upon this all else in any Structure Plan, however well conceived, depends.

External Relationships

As it is not only desirable to live 'in love and charity with your neighbours' but also an axiom of common sense to do so, those who are formulating the Structure Plan for Greater Manchester will need to take into account Structure Plans for adjoining areas such as Merseyside, Lancashire, Cheshire, Derbyshire and West Yorkshire. It is in this respect that the Strategic Plan for the North-West, which covers the greater part of these areas, has a direct bearing upon the Plan for Greater Manchester and, as such, will be treated later in this chapter. In a wider sphere geographically, the retention by Britain of her membership of the European Economic Community is an issue of considerable importance to this area. It has been suggested that 'prospects for office development could be quite favourable bearing in mind that Manchester is the largest provincial office centre, has excellent air services and is the administrative centre of the country's largest industrial region.'[1] On the other hand, it is in this European perspective that the general poor state of the Area's industrial stock, with its considerable proportion of old, outworn properties, gives cause for concern. One hesitates to conjecture what Richard Cobden, with his international ideals, would have thought of this state of affairs.

Leisure and Recreation

A recent survey on leisure activities in the North-West revealed that full or half-day visits to the countryside are more popular than participation in sport. As the majority of trips from the Greater Manchester Area are to the countryside and not to the coast, the desirability of increasing investment in Country Parks becomes more feasible, especially when it is known that not more than 2 per cent of the adult population engage in individual games or physical activities. As it has been clearly indicated that 'the main bread-and-butter business of seeing that the general community have the right opportunities, in the right places, and in the right variety, is now seen to be the inescapable duty of those who are elected to serve the general needs of the local community',[2] it is right and proper that ample provision for the leisure needs of the community should be seen to be the 'shared responsibility' of the County and District Councils.

Shopping Patterns

The present pattern of shopping in the Area would appear to be four-tier: the regional centre at the heart of Manchester in its highly specialised rôle; centres based upon the main towns; subsidiary centres concerned with less specialised and more local needs; neighbourhood sub-centres and corner shops. This traditional pattern is now undergoing a process of change: the introduction of new shopping precincts into the suburbs and fringe centres influencing the more affluent to take their custom away from the older centres; the decline of the independent trader in face of the more competitive hypermarkets and multiple stores which are tending to monopolise the high-rental sites of the shopping precincts; the large-scale redevelopment of the Manchester central area aimed at reinforcing its highly specialised rôle. The scope for contraction and modernisation of shopping facilities in the Greater Manchester area is still substantial and will require careful planning.

Health and Education Services

With the reorganisation of the National Health Service on 1 April 1974, the hospital and specialised services, local authority health services and family practitioner services within the Greater Manchester Area were all merged into a single Service under the aegis of the North Western Regional Health Authority, notice of which has already been taken in the previous chapter. It is fortunate for the Area that the former Manchester Regional Hospital Board was so well advanced in the formulation of its plans over the last ten years for the future provision of hospital facilities throughout the North West. In the sphere of higher education the distribution of educational establishments is uneven between the Metropolitan Districts owing to the heavy bias towards Manchester and its new Education Precinct. This is understandable, but the Area should certainly count its blessings in having in its midst a richly endowed Precinct which eventually will become the largest of its kind in Europe. It is fortunate, too, in its possession of the new Salford University, founded in good time before the present economic recession and ready for further expansion when the time is ripe. If, as has been proposed, national financial stringency compels students to seek higher education within their own region, those living in the Greater Manchester Area will indeed be fortunate, however undesirable such a restrictive policy would be both for the students and the educational institutions of the Area.

Communications

The recently constructed network of national and regional motorways has brought at least two major benefits in communications to the Area: it has brought quicker and easier access for the peripheral towns both between themselves and in relation to the central core of Manchester; it has facilitated access to the ports and to other regions of the country. In these respects some areas have become more accessible and more attractive than others, making imperative further requirements for new channels of communication. This interaction between land use and physical communications is fundamental to planning the future structure of the Area. In the crucial 'journey to work' patterns, while Manchester itself has a dominant rôle, the peripheral towns also have their part to play. With the continuing improvements in communications (the telephone, telex and computer terminals) such towns will become increasingly attractive to developers. It is already well known that Stretford, Sale and Altrincham are in this position for promoters of new office development. Such a tendency could produce a decline in the present centralised structure in favour of a more dispersed form with many modes performing different functions. This has considerable implications for the central core of the Area.

Future Land Needs

Trends already noted certainly reveal a general demand in the Area for more space. This means that the suitability of land for future development will constitute a major concern of the Structure Plan. In general, the south, south-east and south-west parts of the Area are more attractive for development than the northern parts. The latter, on the other hand, lend themselves to the creation of Country Parks, the reclamation of river valleys and an enlightened use of the canals, about all of which more will be said shortly. The fullest possible use of derelict land, the renewal of outworn, older areas and a re-examination of the boundaries of the Green Belt could well make an important contribution to future land needs.

Aspects of Environment

It seems generally to be agreed that it is in the plans for the improvement of the physical environment of the Greater

Manchester Area that the enhancing of the quality of life can most effectively be achieved. This is to be seen in a variety of aspects: the problems of town and city centres with their physically and functionally obsolescent buildings, unsatisfactory lay-outs, congestion and lack of safety; the need for a high quality of environment for residential areas; the desirability of creating conservation areas for the preservation of special architectural and visual qualities; the protection of areas adjacent to major highways from physical intrusion and noise; the curbing of atmospheric pollution from industrial and domestic sources and of river pollution now in the care of the Regional Water Authority. Most serious of all are the unsightly areas of derelict land, particularly evident in former coal-mining districts and abandoned sidings of former railway stations, and the stock of old outworn properties of industrial buildings, relics of that 'foul drain' through which 'the greatest stream of human industry' flowed out 'to fertilise the whole world',[3] concerning which, it may be suggested, one need not, historically-speaking, feel ashamed. What is needed is a firm resolve to renew the environment of the past so as to make Greater Manchester a fairer place in which to live and work. That is fundamentally what the County Structure Plan is intended to do.

If the contemplation of these ten main spheres of operation for structure planning in the Greater Manchester County is to be more than a pipe-dream of cherished hope and aspirations, it is important that the proposals they contain are realistic in terms of the finances they involve and the resources available in both the public and private sectors. There will be many competing claims, and difficult choices will have to be made in order to assess priorities for expenditure. In a very real sense, success will breed success: the greater the improvement in communications, access to new land sites, availability of skilled labour and good housing facilities and, above all, a more attractive environment, the larger will be the flow into the Area of industrial investment and economic commitment. It is primarily in these factors that the future of the new County will be decided.

One of the striking features in the preparation of a Structure Plan and in its ultimate submission for approval to the Secretary of State for the Environment lies in the provision statutorily required both for public participation and examination in public.[4] There appear to be three stages at which public participation is to take place:

The Three Sisters at Ashton-in-Makerfield before and after reclamation

(i) On the publication by the County Council of the Reports of Survey which set out what the present situation is, how it is expected to change, what the current problems are, and what commitments already exist.

(ii) Early in 1976 when the views arising out of the public consultation on the Reports of Survey have been collated into Alternative Strategies for Greater Manchester.

(iii) When the Draft Plan is published later in 1976, allowing time for public comment before the Final Plan is decided upon and submitted to the Secretary for the Environment at the end of 1976.

The primary purpose of the examination in public, which follows the submission of the Final Plan, is to enable the Secretary of State to have the information and arguments he needs, in addition to the public objections and representations already made on it, to enable him to reach a decision on the Plan. The conducting of this public examination is governed by the Code of Practice[5] which sets out the procedure by which the small panel, consisting of an independent chairman and two other members, is to operate. The intention here is to enable the Secretary of State to concentrate upon controversial matters relating to the proposed Plan so that he can arrive at a decision on a structure plan in as short a time from its submission as is reasonably possible.

The Greater Manchester Council may be seen as having two types of rôle. There is the rôle of strategic planning for the County as a whole, and the provision of services which are county-wide in scope. In the latter connection Police, Fire and Public Transport spring directly to mind, but there are at least two others, one strictly practical and the other cultural.[6] The Consumer Services Department is responsible for ensuring that the various Acts of legislation relating to transactions in commerce and industry by traders are fulfilled.

Such duties as these have a long, historical antecedence: in Elizabethan Manchester the lord of the manor ensured, by the appointment through his Court Leet of special ale-testers and 'officers for wholesome bread', that the statutory regulations which fixed the weight for the penny loaf and the price at which ale might be sold—known as the assize of bread and ale—were enforced. There were even regulations in times of scarcity in regard to the hoarding of foodstuffs. Today, in addition to the

Trading Standards Office, which concerns itself with the prevention and detection of criminal offences against laws relating to trading, and the Scientific Services Division, which undertakes the scientific analysis of food and other goods, there is the Consumer Advice Centre, which provides pre-shopping advice on an extensive scale to the general public. The aim here is to assist the customer by means of a specially trained staff in the intricacies of shopping in an informal and friendly atmosphere. Two such Centres are already operating in Wigan and Trafford, and during the next few months the County Council plans to open similar Centres in the other Districts.

In the meantime, the Council's Recreation and Arts Committee has concerned itself with two spheres of service: to identify the deficiencies in recreational opportunities in the whole county and to take practical steps to stimulate the arts. In the former, the possibility of provision for centres for riding, ski-ing, sailing, canoeing and water ski-ing is being examined, while the building of a regional indoor sports centre is under consideration. Another important sphere currently under study by this Committee is the complex system of canals in the County, which had their origins in the eighteenth century.[7] Their scenic and recreational possibilities for the community offer most attractive prospects, however distant in time their realisation may be, while the canal towpaths present the most complete and direct network of local and long-distance footpaths in the County. But it is in the latter sphere of service that this Committee has already made a conspicuous contribution. Encouraged by the long-established cultural and artistic traditions of the region, the Greater Manchester Council has embarked upon the policy of directly associating itself with, and giving grants to, institutions such as the Hallé, the Royal Exchange Theatre and the Northern Dance Theatre, and to major regional museums and art galleries such as the Manchester Museum, the Whitworth Art Gallery and the North Western Museum of Science and Industry. The Council has also supported visits to the County by national companies such as the Royal Ballet, London Festival Ballet, Glyndebourne, the Welsh National Opera Company and the Prospect Theatre Company. This is wholly admirable and points the way to the criterion upon which the Greater Manchester Council should base all its policies, namely that 'only the best is good enough' for its citizens.

So far as the strategic planning of the County is concerned, a start has been made of putting into practice in its application to two related schemes the conserving and protecting of areas of the countryside and the restoration of major river valleys. Provision for conserving or protecting areas of the countryside has been in existence for nearly thirty years. In 1949 the National Parks and Access to the Countryside Act set up a National Parks Commission to designate 'those extensive tracts of country in England and Wales which, by reason of their natural beauty and the opportunities they afford for open-air recreation, should be preserved and enhanced.' These most laudable aims did not apply to the conservation of urban areas until 1968, when the Countryside Act was passed to enable local authorities to establish Country Parks for the purpose of making the neighbouring countryside easily accessible to town dwellers. In this respect the Greater Manchester Council has inherited five designated country parks, including Tandle Hill at Oldham, Etherow at Stockport and Haigh Hall at Wigan. It is expected that further areas within the County will soon be designated as country parks, one of which, Hollingworth Lake in the District of Rochdale, has been for some time under active consideration.[8]

Linked with this scheme for Country Parks is that of the restoration of the major river valleys in the county. For this purpose, as also with the country parks, some of which form the nodal points of river valley projects, the County Council and the District Councils have agreed to work together in this sphere on a 'Shared Responsibility' basis. Other interested bodies, such as the Regional Water Authority, have been invited to participate in the scheme, while those Civic Societies geographically associated with the river valleys have been invited to attend the Steering Committees as observers—an excellent move. As these various projects must be considered as a whole in that they form a strategic open space system devoted largely to recreational purposes for the whole of the Greater Manchester area, the County Council has wisely expressed its willingness to provide the major finance for the projects and for covering their subsequent management. This is to offset the parochial outlook as to 'who is obtaining the most benefit', with a view to apportioning costs. It has been rightly observed that such an attitude 'can only be counter-productive. It is necessary to keep clearly in mind the fact that the County is trying to create a strategic open space and recreational complex with a whole range of facilities available to all who wish to use them.' In like manner it is felt that for all such projects it is necessary to 'try to look at the County as a whole without undue regard to local authority boundaries, which may well be somewhat artificial in relation to a particular project.'[9] There are already six projects under active preparation in which both the County and the relevant District Authorities are involved. They are:

River Valleys and Country Parks	Authorities Involved
1 Croal-Irwell and Jumbles Country Park	G.M.C., Bolton, Bury, Salford
2 Medlock Valley & Country Park	G.M.C., Oldham, Tameside, Manchester
3 Tame Valley	G.M.C., Oldham, Tameside, Stockport
(It will be recalled that the Tame Valley Improvement Scheme was first mooted in 1964 and four years later became a principal objective of the Civic Trust for the North-West. It is now supported by the Greater Manchester Council.)	
4 Mersey Valley	G.M.C., Manchester, Trafford, Stockport
5 Bollin Project	G.M.C., Cheshire, Trafford, Manchester, Macclesfield
6 Hollingworth Lake Country Park	G.M.C., Rochdale

There are at least eight other schemes under consideration, including the Irk, Roche, Douglas, Goyt and Etherow Valleys, in which the Greater Manchester Council is associated with the geographically relevant District Councils.

It will already be evident that the County Structure Plan is not intended to be the monopoly of the Greater Manchester Council. By the very nature of its purpose, the Plan postulates a working partnership between the County Council and the District Councils. While the former is expected to deal with issues at the level of policy and general proposals, the latter are required to work out in detail their own local plans, which are to be designed

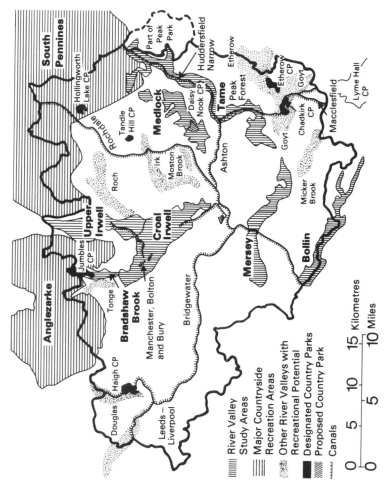

Projected river valleys and Country Parks

'to take things on from the structure plans'. They must pass through the same process of preparation as the structure plan, including consultation, publicity and public participation, but they do not require to be presented to the Secretary of State for his approval, although he has the power to direct that a particular local plan shall be submitted to him if he should so desire. As local plans will, in effect, translate the Structure Plan into definite and detailed local proposals, it is interesting at this point to ascertain what, in 1975, each Metropolitan District expected from the County Structure Plan.[10] The following is a brief summary as stated by each of the Districts in that year:

1. WIGAN looked for a general improvement in the quality of life in the County and especially in its more deprived parts. More specifically it desired the improvement of the economic structure and an increase in opportunities for employment; a widespread improvement of the visual aspects of the area and of the provision of recreational facilities and a safe and efficient communications network.

2. BOLTON Planning Department saw its own fundamental problem as 'a choice between encouraging the level of growth needed to meet the needs of our people, now and in the future, and to attract extra Government spending; alternatively enforcing a static situation which will prevent the urban area from spreading further and keep much of the present character of the town as it is.' While it is naturally the duty of the Council to make its decisions in the best interests of the Metropolitan Borough and all its people, it wisely called upon them to express their views and comments on this matter. It is difficult, however, to imagine Boltonians accepting 'a static situation'.

3. The Metropolitan Borough of **BURY** was similarly concerned about its proposed urban growth in relation to the preservation of its surrounding countryside. It also wished to ensure that 'development is sufficiently attractive and convenient to satisfy people's rising standards and expectations.' While welcoming the views of residents on its proposed local plans, the District Council and its officers do not intend to leave matters of this nature to be answered by the County alone, but are now actively presenting their own ideas through the medium of public exhibitions.

4. ROCHDALE, with its traditionally progressive outlook, had already set up Community Councils in the different areas of the District with the intention of enabling its citizens to make their views known on local plans which concern their neighbourhood. In particular, proposals were being put forward to industrialists to enlist their support for brightening up old industrial areas of factories and houses. The Borough Council's main objective seemed to be 'to bring about a change in the balance between the northern and southern parts of Greater Manchester especially in terms of housing, social facilities and derelict areas.' The Council considered that the County should support its endeavours in all these fields.

5. The **SALFORD** City Council, determined to maintain the impetus of its reforming zeal during the past decade, had set up a special 'task force' to review land in the District which can be developed for housing purposes. The Council was acutely conscious of the environmental and architectural aspects of this most important of all its local plans, and for this reason considered it essential that public meetings should be held to enable tentative local plans to be displayed and comments to be invited in the light of local knowledge.

6. The City of **MANCHESTER** had suggested to the County Council that they should work together on two local plans which have clear implications for the County as a whole. The first concerns the City Centre in all its present large-scale redevelopment, and the second the area surrounding Manchester Airport in which both the Councils are joint partners. It was anticipated that other plans of more local interest will soon be available for public scrutiny.

7. OLDHAM expected to benefit from the Structure Plan, in that it will concentrate upon the balance between town and countryside. The District Council was anxious to ensure that as much as possible of the Saddleworth area will be protected and used for farming and recreational purposes. Equally it looked to the Plan to ensure that land released for new housing, industry or community activities will take place in the most suitable areas. Conscious of the proximity of its neighbours, such as Royton, Shaw and, further afield, Rochdale and Ashton-under-Lyne, the Council wished to retain the small stretches of countryside which finely divide them. Oldham had a strong sense of the importance of physical environment, as may be evidenced from the decision of its Councillors to spend nearly £7 million on a new Civic Centre.[11]

8. Clearly **STOCKPORT** had no time for piecemeal development, which is why it welcomed the comprehensive nature of the County Structure Plan enabling it to assimilate the Borough's local plans and policies. For this purpose Stockport has its own Corporate Plan which aims at ensuring that each division of the new District will concern itself with one constructive end rather than individual goals. In all this, the highly developed community strategy of this forward-looking Borough is expected to play a vital rôle.

9. The **TRAFFORD** Council knew what it wanted from the County Structure Plan, namely that 'it pays full regard to all Trafford's needs, problems and opportunities.' Its needs are many: the famous industrial estate of Trafford Park is declining in the provision of employment and requires to be revitalised; there are many demands upon the surrounding countryside, which require to be investigated; large areas of housing lack landscaping, play-spaces and imaginative lay-outs; most serious of all are the problems of sewage and pollution. There are many opportunities here for fruitful co-operation between County and District.

10. TAMESIDE, regarding itself as one of 'the more deprived areas of Greater Manchester', naturally looks upon the County Structure Plan as potentially 'a most important document'. It expects its general proposals for new housing, new factories and offices, new road building and new or improved bus and rail services to benefit this new District in a variety of ways. Equally, Tameside's Director of Planning rightly regards its own proposed Local Plans as just as important and calls upon his fellow-citizens to express their views on them and on any other problems which they consider to be urgent. Tameside is clearly alive both to its opportunities and its responsibilities.

Just as the Greater Manchester Council must internally adapt its Structure Plan to meet the special needs of its Districts, so also must it externally take account of the wider regional issues contained in the *Strategic Plan for the North-West*. Commissioned by the Government in 1971 on behalf of the North-West Economic Planning Council and the local planning authorities, the Plan was devised by the North-West Joint Planning Team which worked in collaboration with senior officers of local and central government. The region covers the geographical counties of Lancashire and Cheshire and the High Peak area of Derbyshire, extending for ninety miles from Furness to Southern Cheshire and fifty miles from the Pennines to the West coast. It contains a population of $6\frac{3}{4}$ million, which is mainly concentrated in southern Lancashire and northern Cheshire, in the area described as the Mersey Belt. While ideally it may be said that the most important objective of the Strategic Plan is 'to make the North-West a pleasanter place to live in',[12] technically its chief purpose is to forge a link between matters of national concern (the province of central government) and those of local concern (the province of local government) in so far as decisions on work, investment, roads and other public facilities, and the use of land interact on each other and have a dual interest. This relationship between the national and local spheres has a particular, almost an ironical, meaning for the North-West. While the region is said to have a 'distinctly poor' environment and a 'general quality of life . . . often inferior to that of any other English region', the planning team's report acknowledges that its people and industry are paying more into the public purse than the region gets back in public spending. In recognising that 'the nation derived considerable benefit from the Industrial Revolution in terms of economic growth and international prestige, but at substantial and enduring cost to the region's environment', the team generously considers that 'it is not unreasonable, therefore, to claim some assistance from the national purse to ameliorate the harmful legacy of the Industrial Revolution.'[13]

The strategy of the Plan would appear to revolve around two central and related themes. The first is that of growth: how much growth of population, of jobs and of standards is desirable for the region? The team's answer is unequivocal: 'It is more important to secure improved living standards per head—by intervention directly where necessary—than to pursue some growth target in population or employment in the hope that, if it is achieved, it will result in better standards.' Clearly there is no desire here to pursue a chimera. The second theme naturally follows: 'The quality of life for the people already living in the North-West—and particularly in its towns and cities—is what matters most.' On this process of reasoning, the members of the team consider that 'the Strategic Plan is, therefore, much less concerned with future physical development than previous regional strategies and much more concerned with people, money and the policies which will be best for the North-West.' They are strengthened in their faith in the region both by the nature of its character and by the quality of those who live and work in it: 'The first asset of the region is its people. They belong to a highly-organised, complex and almost completely urban society with a long-shared experience of industrialisation. The North-West is used to technological change. The plan should give scope for inventiveness, adaptability to change and new outlets in trade and industry.' They recognise, also, another almost incalculable asset of the region in that 'the existing universities, institutes of technology, colleges of education and business schools must take their proper place in an accelerating industrial revolution.'

So, too, must the Manchester Polytechnic be encouraged to take its 'proper place in an accelerating industrial revolution', for it is eminently equipped to serve the Greater Manchester County in this sphere. Founded in 1970 on the amalgamation of the John Dalton College of Technology, the College of Commerce and the College of Art and Design, this young and virile institution is determined to stand in its own right and not as the poor relation of anybody. Already the largest of its kind in the country, it expects to have, within the capacity of the sector of the Manchester Education Precinct allotted to it, a student population of about 6,000 full-time and a similar number of part-time students. A characteristic outlook of Sir Alex Smith, Director of the Polytechnic, is his concern that part-time students should be looked upon as at least as important as full-time students, for it is through them and their connections with local industries that he wants to 'create and encourage an organic relationship with the region and a deep participation in its development'—what he describes as 'building bridges between education and productive industry'. The Director is clearly a man of vision and practical good sense, engaged in creating and giving permanence to a new institution, with new ideals in higher education, 'to the benefit and use of men'.

Much will naturally depend upon what happens to the national economy during this decade. One of the 'working assumptions' of the Planning Team's report is that there will be continuing economic growth in Great Britain to provide the additional funds needed and that, even if this were to prove false, it would not invalidate, in the team's view, the region's case for a larger share of whatever national resources are available. This prognosis has been questioned on the ground that 'in the present climate of uncertainty there may be greater doubts about what is or is not feasible in the future than the team is prepared to admit.'[15] More recently, a national organisation closely concerned with the proper use of environment and the countryside has suggested that 'we may soon cease to regard our growth performance as the primary indicator of our success.' In support of this opinion, its journal[16] quotes Professor Dahrendorf as declaring in his recent Reith lectures that 'the theme of belief in the unlimited possibilities of quantitative expansion is now spent', and that in its place is a new theme which is not an alternative to growth but something different—what Dahrendorf calls 'improvement'. This new indicator, the journal proceeds, 'is about quality and the recovery of cities for people rather than for cars and new slums' (again quoting Dahrendorf), and concludes: 'In an improving society (as opposed to an expanding one) change and development would be welcomed only if they were thought to be beneficial in terms of quality not quantity.'

Perhaps the members of the North-West Joint Planning Team were thinking along the same lines when they declared: 'Growth should not be seen as an end in itself—it is more important to ensure a good standard of life for the people of the region, however many or few they are.' Above all there hovers the crucial question: when will the present inflation and recession in trade end? Upon that much depends.

Envoy

'In which we serve'

Did the Local Government Act of 1972, in establishing the Greater Manchester County, merely create a superstructure designed to embrace some seventy local authorities which were well capable of managing their own affairs?

In a notable contribution to 'Manchester And Its Region' (a Survey prepared for the British Association on the occasion of its Annual Meeting held in the city in 1962), Mr T. W. Freeman set out to define what was then called 'the South-East Lancashire conurbation'. Conscious that 'in many ways it is easier to say what the conurbation is not, rather than what it is', of one thing he was certain. 'Greater Manchester it is not', he declared, and gave as his reasons: 'One of its main characteristics is the marked individuality of its numerous towns, such as Bolton, Bury, Rochdale, Oldham and Stockport, all of which have an industrial and commercial history of more than local significance ... whose relation to Manchester is tempered by their rugged individuality of form and spirit.' And again: 'In these towns there is a strong local sentiment against inclusion in any governmental body run from Manchester and a view that they are themselves centres which should absorb their neighbours.'[1] These are judgments which Mr Freeman had already pronounced in even stronger terms a few years earlier in a standard work on the national aspect of conurbations. For him the essential point was that 'on the northern side there are a number of major towns, Bolton, Bury, Rochdale, Oldham, each sufficiently strong to regard itself as in some ways a minor metropolis'; and he even went so far as to contend that for many residents these towns are 'scarcely parts of the conurbation at all but rather possible nuclei of separate subconurbations, such as greater Oldham ..., an enlarged Bolton, or an Ashton united with Stalybridge and possibly Dukinfield.'[2] Evidently Mr Freeman was well aware of the robust rivalry between these northern towns of South-East Lancashire, for he granted that 'if there is a greater Oldham, there may legitimately be a greater Rochdale.' There better had be, otherwise there would be ructions when their teams next met for a Central Lancashire Cricket League match at Dane Street! After all, Rochdale and Oldham are the two oldest clubs in the League, and Rochdale had its cricket club thirty years before Oldham.

There are two observations to make upon what Mr Freeman had to say about this 'congeries of industrial towns' and their relationship with Manchester. First, it is significant that eight of the ten Districts which make up the Greater Manchester County have been so designed, in accordance with the recommendations of the Maud Commission, that each constitutes an enlargement of the administrative area of the former county borough so as to make it Greater Rochdale, Greater Oldham, Greater Bolton and the rest. One has only to study the composition of each of these Districts, as set out in the table on pp. 240–41, to see this. The only exception among these eight Districts is, significantly enough, that of Manchester itself, which can hardly call itself Greater Manchester because it has taken unto itself the parish of Ringway! As for the remaining two Districts, Trafford and Tameside, they have also followed Mr Freeman's proposals in that the former is a fusion of three municipal boroughs with three urban districts and the latter that of five municipal boroughs with four urban districts. When one remembers, too, that each of these Districts has its own responsibility for eight important services to its own community of at least 200,000 citizens, and a responsibility for four equally important services shared with the County Council, one realises the wisdom of the recommendation of 'having units of population sufficiently large to provide a base for their effective organisation and high quality of service' in 'Districts all of which are populous and compact'.

The second observation relates to Mr Freeman's own conclusions. While emphasising the independent outlook and individual character of the towns of the South-East Lancashire conurbation, he yet acknowledges that 'Manchester has become a great commercial and service city, the heart of the conurbation, . . . a financial, cultural and entertainment centre of considerable note and possibly . . . the most metropolitan centre of England outside London.' Still defending 'the major local centres' in their 'great strength in trade as well as in industry', he readily agrees that 'the problems of re-housing . . . can only be solved by co-operative action between one authority and another', and goes on to broaden this concept to include 'such general problems as the attraction of new industry, new roads and water supply.' This would seem to imply the acceptance of a large authority vested with powers not only to 'deal with those housing problems that transcend the boundaries of the Districts', but also to undertake responsibility for transportation, comprehensive planning and major development for the whole area. This is the *raison d'être* for the concept of the two-tier metropolitan county, this is why the Greater Manchester County has come into being. 'In short,' as Mr Freeman concludes in 1962, 'the conurbation has happened: it is there on the ground', and 'it is worthy of consideration even if only because it is the home of nearly two-and-a-half million people.'[3] In the event it has proved to be rather more than that in population, but the domestic analogy still holds good.

It holds good because the emergence of the Greater Manchester County is in no sense an artificial creation, nor the irrational whim of a national government. It is rather the natural result of a long period of gestation covering many centuries, in which the historical evolution of a great and closely-knit community, which has known great triumphs and great suffering, may be clearly discerned. What is needed now is the recognition of certain truths. There is, for example, in the concept of the two-tier county, the suggestion that one authority is superior to all the others, that the County Council is the primary authority and the District Councils secondary to it. The Maud Commission was aware of this dangerous idea and spoke its mind on it in no uncertain terms: 'In a metropolitan area, we do not regard either the metropolitan authority or the district council as primary. Nor do we regard the relationship between metropolitan and district council as one between an upper and a lower tier. Both tiers in metropolitan areas are equally important; each will be responsible for the major functions appropriate to it.' To counteract any *folie de grandeur*, the Commission stated explicitly: 'Each metropolitan area will be governed by a combination of metropolitan authority and district councils. Success will depend on their collaboration and there should be a firm obligation on the metropolitan authority ... to consult the metropolitan districts on all matters that concern them.'[4] Fortunately, it seems that the relationship between the members and officials of the Greater Manchester Council and those of the District Councils is, to say the least, as good as that in the rest of the country because, it is claimed, 'the county has set up machinery for major policy decisions to be taken co-operatively' in that 'it has believed in full consultation with the Districts all along.'[5] And if this does not work, the Lancashire wit is always there among the crowd to cut the over-mighty down to size.

The problem of status, especially for the former all-purpose authorities (county boroughs), is a natural one which must have caused considerable strain among them and may still do so. At least one such authority has acknowledged the radical nature of the reform: 'The application of the Local Government Act (1972) brings to this country the greatest upheaval in local government seen this century and undoubtedly vitally affects every man, woman and child.'[6] The alternative to radical reform was expressed equally strongly by the Maud Commission: 'If we are not willing to face the pains involved, the prospect for local government is bleak.'[7] In this metropolitan reorganisation, there may well be a suspicion, if not a fear, among not only councillors and officials but even more so among ordinary citizens of these once independent boroughs, that the whole business simply means more rules, more regulations and more municipal red-tape; in effect, that more laws mean less liberty. In a revealing appraisal of the formative years of early medieval society, a distinguished Oxford historian has shown that 'liberty is a creation of law, and law is reason in action.' He demonstrates this great truth by relating it to the various gradations of medieval society:

'High and low alike sought liberty by insisting on enlarging the number of rules under which they lived: The most highly privileged communities were those with most laws. At the bottom of society was the serf, who could least appeal to law against the arbitrariness of his superiors. At the top was the nobleman, governed by an immensely complicated system of rules in his public life and taught in his private relationships to observe an equally complicated code of behaviour.'[8]

If, then, one is prepared to accept that the creation of a large metropolitan county does not promote an arbitrary or despotic authority, one has to ask what exactly is behind its promotion and whether indeed the whole is greater than the sum of its parts. In a challenging article, the County Treasurer of Greater Manchester has stated what he considers to be the function of local government in England vis-à-vis central government: 'In this country central government has chosen to use local government as the means of providing many of the major public services whose intent is to improve the conditions in which people live, work, and take their leisure.' He goes on to demonstrate that the kinds of problems involved here 'are found more acutely in the major conurbations where there is good reason for desired levels of expenditure to be above average', with the result that the central government's rate support grant 'has been weighted more towards the local authorities in and around the major population centres.'[9] In this situation it would appear that there is all the more reason why the County and District Councils of Greater Manchester should operate as partners in their own corporate interests. It is as if one were to separate all the parts of a watch and place them on a table. Materially the watch is there, but not until every part has been conjoined into its correct position will the watch function and, when it does, it produces a remarkable service called 'time', which arises out of the harmonising of the sum of the parts. One could enumerate many examples of this, from the House of Commons in daily session to the assembly of a parish council. This is probably what the Maud Commission was after when its members expressed their united conviction that 'local government is more than the sum of the particular services provided. It is an essential part of English democratic government.' And again, in the concluding paragraph of its great *Report*: 'A powerful system of local government can in some crucial ways enhance the quality of English national life.'[10]

In all this, why 'Greater Manchester'? One hardly likes to accept that it is a matter of *faute de mieux*, for that would be an attitude of faintheartedness, a quality entirely alien to the traditions of this great region. Two other titles had earlier been suggested: that of 'South-East Lancashire', which Mr Freeman rightly judged would be geographically incorrect; and that of 'SELNEC', geographically in order but, as a composite name, wholly out of order as being impersonal and merely a convenient label. Why, then, not 'Greater Manchester'? While, of the six new metropolitan counties created by the Local Government Act of 1972, it is the only one named after the metropolis of the region, there is a precedent for it in the creation of the Greater London County in 1963 when, for once, London got ahead of Manchester. By far the most cogent reason for taking the name of the metropolis itself is the natural one based upon the historical evolution of the region. Manchester and its neighbouring towns have grown up together over many centuries, and more especially during the past two centuries, when together they provided the setting for the world's first industrial development. At the height of it, German traders coined the name *Manchesterthum*, meaning not merely Manchester but all that its 'mighty region', in Disraeli's phrase, symbolised for men of commerce everywhere. It is in this sense that Greater Manchester *is* the whole county, whose name is honoured and respected wherever men of industry, commerce and culture meet in the market places of the world. It is very important, therefore, that the County Council should seek, in the duties allotted to it,

> 'not to impose a mechanical uniformity, but to bring about an organic unity, based upon the fullest utilisation of all the various resources that both nature and history have revealed to modern man. Such a culture must be nourished not only by a new vision of the whole, but a new vision of a self capable of understanding and co-operating with the whole.'[11]

In the Royal Navy a prayer is used regularly which contains the words, 'the Fleet in which we serve'. For those who have followed the fortunes of a small, early medieval town in company with its neighbours, which together in course of time became 'one community with common interests', the words of an eminent Professor of Harvard written on the occasion of the 250th anniversary of the founding of his College may have particular relevance:

> 'Our fathers built a little skiff and launched it in familiar and circumscribed waters and it served them well; but an unheeded current bore it slowly down toward the tide and the scent of the open sea. Their sons enlarged and strengthened it and ventured forth beyond the headlands in brief voyages of discovery. For us the skiff has been transformed into a mighty vessel . . . and its dependence is no longer on the changeful winds which blow upon it, but on a motive power which is within itself.'

This 'motive power which is within itself' lies at the heart of the Greater Manchester County, just as the engine, throbbing in the bowels of a ship, drives it forward steadily and surely on its course. *Bon Voyage!*

References

Chapter 1

1. I. A. Richmond, *Roman Britain*, The Pelican History of England, vol. 1 (1960), p. 35

2. N. J. Frangopulo, 'The Site of the Roman Fort', *Rich Inheritance—A Guide to the History of Manchester* (1963), pp. 169–70

3. F. H. Thompson, 'The Roman Fort at Castleshaw', *Transactions of the Lancashire and Cheshire Antiquarian Society*, vol. 77 (1967), pp. 1–18

4. G. D. B. Jones, 'The Romans in the North West', *Northern History*, vol. 3 (1968), p. 16

5. W. T. Watkin, *Roman Lancashire* (1883, reprinted 1969), p. 199

6. ibid. ch. 3, 'The Roman Roads of Lancashire'
   (a) for details of road from Manchester to Wigan, including branches of minor roads off it, see pp. 37–49
   (b) for details of road from Manchester to Chester, see pp. 49–50
   (c) for details of road from Manchester to Slack, see pp. 50–2
   (d) for details of road from Manchester to Ribchester, see pp. 52–5
   (e) for details of road from Manchester to Buxton, see pp. 55–6
   (f) for details of road from Manchester to Melandra (near Glossop), see p. 56
   (g) for details of road over Blackstone Edge (via Littleborough), see pp. 56–66
   For a later work which puts Watkin's pioneering study into perspective, consult I. D. Margary, *Roman Roads in Britain* (1957), vol. 2, pp. 91–103

7. Thompson, op. cit. p. 2

8. J. A. Petch, 'The Roman Occupation of Lancashire and Cheshire', *Transactions of the Lancashire and Cheshire Antiquarian Society*, vol. 69 (1959), p. 2

9. ibid. p. 6

10. ibid. p. 10

11. Watkin, op. cit. p. 218

12. F. H. Thompson, 'A History of Cheshire', *Roman Cheshire*, ed. J. J. Bagley, vol. 2 (1965), p. 46

13. Richmond, op. cit. p. 159

14. Thompson, op. cit. p. 76

15. G. D. B. Jones & Shelagh Grealey, *Roman Manchester* (1974), p. 29

16. Shelagh Grealey, 'Exploration 1540–1972', *Roman Manchester* (1974), pp. 11–21

17. J. D. Bu'lock, 'The Problems of Post-Roman Manchester', *Roman Manchester* (1974), p. 169

18. Sir John Denham, *Of Prudence*, l. 225

Chapter 2

1. W. H. Thomson, *History of Manchester to 1852* (1967), p. 38

2. G. H. Tupling, 'Lancashire Markets', *Transactions of the Lancashire and Cheshire Antiquarian Society*, vols. 68 & 69

3. J. Tait, *Mediaeval Manchester and the Beginnings of Lancashire* (1906), for translation of the Manchester Charter, pp. 114–19; for analysis of the clauses of the Charter, pp. 60–114

4. D. Defoe, *A Tour Through the Whole Island of Great Britain* (1721), vol. 2, p. 261

5. J. S. Millar, *Manchester—City Centre Map 1967* (1967), p. 3

6. ibid. p. 15

7. A. Briggs, *Victorian Cities* (1963), p. 116

8. B. Disraeli, *Coningsby* (1844), pp. 127 & 131

9. J. Ogden, *A Description of Manchester* (1783), p. 93

10. J. Aikin, *A Description of the Country from Thirty to Forty Miles round Manchester* (1795), p. 191

11. Ogden, op. cit. p. 93

12. Defoe, op. cit. vol. 2, p. 261

13. *The Court Leet Records of the Manor of Manchester* (1890), vol. 12 (1832–46), pp. 94–103

14. R. Cobden, *Incorporate Your Borough* (1837), p. 7

15. *Manchester Guardian*, 22 Oct. 1837

16. *Manchester Court Leet Records*, vol. xii, Introduction, p. xxii

Chapter 3

1. *Statutes at Large* (33 Henry VIII c.xv), vol. 2 (1509–1640), p. 187

2. A. P. Wadsworth & J. De Lacy Mann, *The Cotton Trade and Industrial Lancashire 1600–1780* (1931), p. 15

3. R. Hollingworth, *Mancuniensis* (c. 1650), p. 101

4. Wadsworth & De Lacy Mann, op. cit. p. 34

5. J. Booker, *History of the Ancient Chapel of Blackley* (1854), p. 208

6. D. C. Coleman, *The Domestic System in Industry* (1960), p. 3

7. Wadsworth & De Lacy Mann, op. cit. p. 25

8. ibid. p. 28

9. H. T. Crofton, 'Moston and White Moss', *Transactions of the Lancashire and Cheshire Antiquarian Society*, vol. xxv (1907), p. 44

10. Owen Ashmore, 'The Woollen Industry', *The Great Human Exploit*, ed. J. H. Smith (1973), p. 13

11. C. Aspin, *The Turners of Helmshore and Higher Mill* (1970), pp. 14–23

12. W. H. Chaloner, 'The Cotton Industry to 1820', *The Great Human Exploit*, ed. J. H. Smith (1973), p. 19

13. D. Bythell, *The Handloom Weavers* (1969), p. 48

14. J. Aikin, *A Description of the Country from Thirty to Forty Miles Round Manchester* (1795), pp. 230, 243, 299, 294

15. W. H. Chaloner (ed.), *The Autobiography of Samuel Bamford*, vol. i, *Early Days* (1967), pp. 111–13

16. S. Bamford, *Passages in the Life of a Radical* (1844), Chs. 30–39

17. D. Read, *Peterloo—The 'Massacre' and Its Background* (1958), pp. 22–4

18. S. Bamford, op. cit. p. 131

19. A. Prentice, *Historical Sketches and Personal Recollections of Manchester* (1851), p. 159

20. H. Horton, *Peterloo, 1819—A Portfolio of Contemporary Documents* (1969), plate No. 18, 'The Meeting at Peterloo'

21. C. Aspin, *Lancashire: The First Industrial Society* (1969), p. 48

22. J. Harland, *Ballads and Songs of Lancashire* (1865), p. 253

Chapter 4

1. L. Faucher, *Manchester in 1844: its present conditions and future prospects* (1844), p. 11

2. ibid. pp. 135–6

3. F. Engels, *The Condition of the Working Class in England*, tr. and ed. W. O. Henderson & W. H. Chaloner (1958), Editors' Introduction, p. xiv

4. E. P. Thompson, *The Making of the English Working Class* (1968), pp. 297–8

5. D. Bythell, *The Handloom Weavers* (1969), p. 130

6. Frances Collier, *The Family Economy of the Working Classes in the Cotton Industry 1784–1833* (1964), p. 6

7. J. P. Kay, *The Moral and Physical Condition of the Working Classes Employed in the Cotton Manufacture in Manchester* (1832), p. 4

8. *Manchester Guardian* (leading article), 4 March 1958

9. Faucher, op. cit. pp. 89–91

10. H. Butterfield, *The Origins of Modern Science 1300–1800* (1949), p. 187

11. B. Disraeli, *Coningsby* (1844), p. 127

12. W. H. Chaloner, 'The Making of Lancashire', *Manchester Evening News*, 14 Nov. 1969

13. J. Aikin, *A Description of the Country from Thirty to Forty Miles Round Manchester* (1795), p. 183

14. ibid. p. 184

15. J. Aston, *A Picture of Manchester* (1816), p. 21

16. J. Ogden, *A Description of Manchester* (1783), p. 76

17. G. H. Tupling, 'The Early Metal Trades and the Beginning of Engineering in Lancashire', *Transactions of the Lancashire and Cheshire Antiquarian Society*, vol. 61, pp. 1–34

18. Aikin, op. cit. pp. 176–7

19. A. E. Musson & Eric Robinson, *Science and Technology in the Industrial Revolution* (1969), pp. 427–8

20. Love & Barton, *Manchester As It Is* (1839), pp. 200–1

21. C. F. Carter (ed.), *Manchester and its Region* (1962), quoted by W. H. Chaloner, pp. 136–7

22. for a more detailed analysis of this important subject consult L. Wharfe, 'The Emergence of the Metropolis', *Rich Inheritance*, ed. N. J. Frangopulo (1963), pp. 107–9

23. B. F. Duckham, *The Transport Revolution 1750–1830* (Historical Association pamphlet, 1967), p. 2

24. W. Harrison, 'The Development of the Turnpike System in Lancashire and Cheshire', *Transactions of the Lancashire and Cheshire Antiquarian Society*, vol. 4 (1886), p. 83

25. *Public Notice* (1721), reproduced by Salford Museum and Art Gallery

26. Aston, op. cit. p. 230

27. Duckham, op. cit. p. 91

28. Faucher, op. cit. p. 93

29. ibid. p. 15

30. *The Guardian*, 26 April 1974

31. A. H. Body, *Canals and Waterways*, 'It Happened Round Greater Manchester' series, no. 1 (May 1975)

Chapter 5

1. M. Kennedy, *Portrait of Manchester* (1970), p. 91

2. Harvie, Martin & Scharf (ed.), *Industrialisation and Culture 1830–1914* (1970), pp. 41–2

3. L. Faucher, *Manchester in 1844* (1844), p. 21

4. ibid. pp. 21–2

5. M. Arnold, *Culture and Anarchy* (1869), pp. 9–13

6. City of Manchester Art Gallery, *Art Treasures Centenary*, Introduction, p. vii

7. ibid. p. ix

8. *Chamber's Journal of Popular Literature, Science and Arts*, 3rd Series, vol. 9 (Jan.–June 1858), pp. 251–4

9. B. Disraeli, *Coningsby* (1844), pp. 130–1

10. R. M. Hartwell, *The Industrial Revolution in England*, Historical Association pamphlet no. 58 (1965), p. 5

11. R. H. Tawney, *Social History and Literature* (1958), p. 28

12. R. Williams, *Culture and Society, 1780–1950* (1958), p. 16

13. M. Kennedy, *The Hallé Tradition* (1960), quoted on p. 5

14. Faucher, op. cit. p. 49

15. W. E. A. Axon, *Annals of Manchester* (1886), p. 222

16. J. F. Russell, 'Music and the Free Trade Hall', *Commemorative Brochure of the Re-opening of the Free Trade Hall* (1951), p. 29

17. Faucher, op. cit. p. 49

18. W. H. Shercliff, *Entertainments*, 'It Happened Round Manchester' series (1968), p. 29

19. Russell, op. cit. p. 29

20. Shercliff, op. cit. p. 31

21. J. N. Hampson, *History of the Besses O' Th' Barn Band* (1893), p. 3

22. J. F. Russell & J. H. Elliot, *The Brass Band Movement* (1936), p. 134

23. ibid. p. 61

24. *Manchester Guardian*, 1 Feb. 1858

25. Kennedy, op. cit. chs v & vii

26. personal communication with his son, Sir Leonard Behrens

27. Kennedy, op. cit. chs xxiii–xxv

28. M. Kennedy, *Barbirolli; Conductor Laureate* (1971), p. 172

29. M. Kennedy, *The Hallé Tradition* (1960), p. 386

30. *Hallé Concerts Society Seventy-Third Annual Report* (1971–2), p. 4

31. *The Lancashire County Cricket Club Centenary Brochure* (1964)

32. *Lancashire Cricket Annual* (1974), p. 101

33. *Daily Express*, 23 August 1966, quoted by G. Turner, *The North Country* (1967), p. 264

Chapter 6

1. J. Priestnall & W. E. Mitchell, *The Play of St George, The Knights and The Dragon* (1930)

2. W. H. Shercliff, *Entertainments*, 'It Happened Round Manchester' series, p. 18

3. *The Manchester Mercury*, 13 Nov. 1753

4. J. L. Hodgkinson & R. Pogson, *The Early Manchester Theatre*, p. 21

5. J. Aston, *A Picture of Manchester* (1816), p. 200

6. Hodgkinson & Pogson, op. cit. p. 107

7. W. Robertson, *Rochdale Past and Present* (1875), pp. 275–6

8. L. Faucher, *Manchester in 1844* (1844), p. 21

9. J. P. Kay, *Committee on Public Walks* (1833), p. 66

10. T. A. Lockett, *Three Lives*, 'It Happened Round Manchester' series (1968), p. 30

11. Alice Foley, *A Bolton Childhood* (1973), p. 66

12. H. B. Charlton, 'Manchester and the Drama', *The Soul of Manchester*, ed. W. H. Brindley (1929), p. 190

13. M. Kennedy, *Portrait of Manchester* (1970), p. 101

14. Charlton, op. cit. p. 190

15. W. H. Thomson, *History of Manchester to 1852* (1967), p. 353

16. R. Horsfield, 'The Portico Library, Manchester', *The Manchester Review*, vol. 12, no. 1 (Summer 1971), p. 15

17. P. M. Roget, *Thesaurus of English Words and Phrases*, Preface to the First Edition (New Edition 1936), p. viii

18. *Proceedings of the Manchester Borough Council*, 1 Sept. 1852

19. Municipal Information Bureau, *Manchester—World Famous Libraries* (1963)

20. 'A Pilot Study at the Commercial Library, Manchester Central Library', *Aslib Proceedings*, vol. 25, no. 7 (July 1973), p. 250

Chapter 7

1. R. Vaughan, *The Age of Great Cities* (1843)

2. A. Toynbee, *A Study of History*, vols. i–x (1954)

3. R. H. Tawney, *Religion and the Rise of Capitalism* (1926)

4. Vaughan, op. cit. p. 77

5. ibid. p. 141

6. W. Cooke Taylor, *Notes of a Tour in the Manufacturing Districts of Lancashire* (1842), pp. 276 & 10

7. C. L. Barnes, 'The Manchester Literary and Philosophical Society', *The Soul of Manchester*, ed. W. H. Brindley (1929), p. 145

8. J. Aston, *A Picture of Manchester* (1816), p. 174

9. *Memoirs and Proceedings of the Manchester Literary and Philosophical Society*, 2nd series, vol. 5

10. T. S. Ashton, *The Industrial Revolution 1760–1830* (1968), pp. 16–17

11. A. E. Musson & Eric Robinson, *Science and Technology in the Industrial Revolution* (1969), pp. 101–2

12. *The Times*, 5 August 1932

13. Aston, op. cit. p. 167

14. H. McLachlan, 'Cross Street Chapel in the Life of Manchester', *Memoirs and Proceedings of the Manchester Literary and Philosophical Society*, vol. xxxiv (1939–41), p. 31

15. Ashton, op. cit. p. 16

16. F. A. Bruton, *A Short History of Manchester and Salford* (1927), p. 235

17. T. Swindells, *Manchester Streets and Manchester Men* (1906), First series, vol. 1, p. 166

18. W. H. Thomson, *History of Manchester to 1852* (1967), p. 332

19. *University of Manchester Calendar* (1973–4), pp. 282–3

20. Royal Manchester Institution, *Council Minute Book* (1823–35), Introduction

21. ibid. p. 19

22. C. Stewart, *The Stones of Manchester* (1956), p. 32

23. W. G. Sutherland, *The Royal Manchester Institution* (1945), p. 12

24. Earl of Crawford and Balcarres, 'The Soul of Cities', *The Soul of Manchester*, ed. W. H. Brindley (1929), pp. 28–9

25. W. Brockbank, 'Manchester's Place in the History of Medicine', *Manchester And Its Region*, ed. C. F. Carter (1962), pp. 198–201

26. H. Brougham, *Practical Observations upon the Education of the People*,

addressed to the Working Classes and their Employers (1825), p. 27

27. Mabel Tylecote, *The Mechanics' Institutes of Lancashire and Yorkshire Before 1851* (1957), p. 37

28. ibid. p. 131

29. A. Prentice, *Historical Sketches and Personal Recollections of Manchester* (1851), p. 249

30. Tylecote, op. cit. p. 287 (quoted)

31. ibid. pp. 121–2

32. T. S. Ashton, *Economic and Social Investigations in Manchester 1833–1933* (1934), pp. 27–33

33. J. Wheeler, *Manchester—Its Political, Social & Commercial History* (1836), p. 416

34. I am indebted to Mr T. A. Long, a former member of the Athenaeum, for kindly placing his resources at my disposal

35. W. S. Churchill, *The Second World War*, vol. III (1950), pp. 98–9

36. Vaughan, op. cit. p. 3

37. published as a pamphlet in Manchester by Robert Robinson in 1836

38. G. N. Burkhardt, 'The University of Manchester', *Chemistry and Industry* (1949), p. 427

39. W. H. Chaloner, *The Movement for the Extension of Owens College Manchester 1863–73* (1973), p. 4

40. ibid. p. 7

41. Earl of Crawford and Balcarres, op. cit. p. 27

42. H. B. Charlton, *Portrait of a University, 1851–1951* (1951), p. 123

43. ibid. p. 17

44. W. T. Cowhig, *Textiles*, 'It Happened Round Greater Manchester' series (1976), p. 49

45. D. Read, *Peterloo—The 'Massacre' and its Background* (1958), p. 25

46. W. R. Ward, *Religion and Society in England 1790–1850* (1972), pp. 13–15

47. McLachlan, op. cit. p. 41

48. private correspondence with the Rev E. J. R. Cook, Minister of Cross Street Chapel

49. *Manchester Evening News*, 18 July 1974

Chapter 8

1. J. Ogden, *A Description of Manchester* (1783), p. 93

2. W. H. Chaloner, 'Manchester in the Latter Half of the Eighteenth Century', *Bulletin of the John Rylands Library*, vol. 42, p. 42

3. W. H. Chaloner, 'John Galloway (1804–1894), Engineer of Manchester and his Reminiscences', *Lancashire and Cheshire Antiquarian Society* (1954), p. 93

4. *Manchester Court Leet Records*, vol. 9, p. 252

5. J. Wheeler, *Manchester Chronicle*, 24 Mar. 1814

6. A. Briggs, *Victorian Cities* (1968), p. 96

7. a paper presented by Dr Oleesky in 1970 in the Old Medical School

8. H. B. Charlton, *Portrait of a University* (1951), p. 67

9. J. Aston, *A Picture of Manchester* (1816), p. 105

10. N. J. Laski, 'The History of Manchester Jewry', *Manchester Review* (Summer 1956), p. 373

11. B. Williams, *The Making of Manchester Jewry, 1740–1875* (1976)—'In this book the author traces the origins of what has become the largest and perhaps the most influential Jewish community in provincial England' (Manchester University Press)

12. *Manchester Guardian*, 30 Mar. 1936

13. A. Redford, *Manchester Merchants and Foreign Trade* (1956), vol. 2, p. 56

14. I am indebted to Mrs E. A. Guessarian for information on this subject

15. A. Valgimigli, *La Colonia Italiana di Manchester, 1794–1932*—this work may be consulted in the Local History Library, Manchester Central Library

16. N. K. Firby, 'Andrea Crestadoro 1808–1879', *The Manchester Review*, vol. 12, no. 1 (Summer 1971), p. 19

17. A. Crestadoro, *The Art of Making Catalogues of Libraries; or, a Method to Obtain in a Short Time a Most Perfect Complete and Satisfactory Printed Catalogue of the British Museum Library* (1856)

18. L. M. Hayes, 'Our Manchester Moors', *Reminiscences of Manchester from the Year 1840* (1905), pp. 204–17

19. Redford, op. cit. vol. 2, p. 68

20. *The Concise Oxford Dictionary* (4th edn, revised by E. McIntosh, 1951)

21. L. Faucher, *Manchester in 1844* (1844), p. 3

22. Laski, op. cit. p. 374

23. information kindly supplied by Mr H. Wagner, Secretary to the Council of Manchester and Salford Jews

24. University of Manchester, *Broomcroft Hall—Notes for residents* (1972), p. 1

25. E. J. B. Rose & Associates, *Colour and Citizenship—A Report on British Race Relations* (1969), pp. 20 & 25: for a full treatment of this read J. A. Tannahill, *European Voluntary Workers in Britain* (1958)

26. Ibid. p. 97

27. Community Relations Commission, *Facts and Figures about Commonwealth Immigrants* (1973), p. 2

28. *The Daily Telegraph*, 16 Sept. 1968

29. *West Indian Culture Week* (5–10 Aug. 1974), p. 3

30. I am indebted to Mr S. Kumar, formerly Senior Officer of the Manchester Council for Community Relations, for information and advice

31. *West Indian Culture Week*, p. 3

32. Community Relations Commission, op. cit. p. 11

33. I am indebted to Mr A. Cardus, who at present occupies this office

34. Community Relations Commission, op. cit. p. 12

35. *The Observer*, 11 Aug. 1974

36. Mr S. Kumar, op. cit.

Chapter 9

1. A. G. Parke, *The History of Ordsall Hall* (1963), p. 1

2. V. I. Tomlinson, *Salford in Pictures* (1974), pp. 14–15

3. W. Cooke Taylor, *Notes of a Tour in the Manufacturing Districts of Lancashire* (2nd edn, 1842, reprinted 1968)

4. Tomlinson, op. cit. pp. 22–3

5. *Official Guide: Salford* (1972), p. 33

6. *The County Borough of Wigan: Official Handbook* (1972)

7. ibid. p. 50

8. J. Tait, *Mediaeval Manchester and the Beginnings of Lancashire* (1904), pp. 199–200

9. N. J. Frangopulo, *The History of Queen Elizabeth's Grammar School*, Ashburne, Derbyshire, 1585–1935 (1939), pp. 91–2

10. J. J. Bagley, *A History of Lancashire With Maps and Pictures* (1956), p. 42

11. J. Aikin, *A Description of the Country from Thirty to Forty Miles Round Manchester* (1795), p. 264

12. W. T. Cowhig, *Textiles*, 'It Happened Round Greater Manchester' series (1976), p. 20

13. Aikin, op. cit. p. 263

14. Cooke Taylor, op. cit. p. 26

15. ibid. p. 45

16. W. E. Brown, *Bolton As It Was* (1972), p. 19

17. Aikin, op. cit. pp. 265–70

18. C. G. Hampson, *The Urban District of Tottington 1899–1974* (1974), pp. 6–9

19. *Bury Link*, Issue no. 4 (Sept. 1974), p. 3

20. *The County Borough of Bury Official Guide* (1974), p. 29

21. F. Collier, *The Family Economy of the Working Classes in the Cotton Industry, 1784–1833* (1964), p. 27

22. ibid. ch. 4

23. Cowhig, op. cit. pp. 36–8

24. Aikin, op. cit. pp. 268–9

25. R. P. Taylor, *Rochdale Retrospect* (1956), p. 91

26. ibid. p. 8

27. I. A. Richmond, 'Britons, Angles and Norse in the Roch Basin', *Transactions of the Rochdale Literary and Scientific Society* (1926), vol. 16, pp. 27–8

28. W. H. Brown, *The Rochdale Pioneers* (1944), p. 23

29. D. Ayerst, *Guardian—Biography of a Newspaper* (1971), pp. 415–16

30. N. Pevsner, *South Lancashire*, 'The Buildings of England' series (1969), p. 376

31. ibid. p. 356

32. A. A. Mumford, *Hugh Oldham 1452–1519* (1936), pp. 14–16

33. *Royal Commission on Secondary Education* (1895), vol. 7, p. 115

34. Aikin, op. cit. p. 237

35. ibid. p. 239

36. E. Baines, *The History of the County Palatine and Duchy of Lancaster* (1868), vol. 1, p. 458

37. *Official Handbook of Oldham* (1973), p. 21

38. *Oldham Centenary—A History of Local Government* (1949), p. 180

39. Cooke Taylor, op. cit. p. 182

40. Aikin, op. cit. p. 442

41. Tait, op. cit. p. 52

42. Aikin, op. cit. p. 445

43. O. Ashmore, *The Industrial Archaeology of Lancashire* (1969), p. 236

44. Aikin, op. cit. p. 445

45. J. C. Cox, *Three Centuries of Derbyshire Annals* (1890), vol. 2, p. 174

46. Aikin, op. cit. p. 446

47. J. H. Smith, 'Felt Hatting', *The Great Human Exploit* (1973), pp. 41–6

48. Aikin, op. cit. p. 208

49. Tait, op. cit. pp. 30 & 103

50. F. A. Bruton, *A Short History of Manchester and Salford* (1927), pp. 218–19

51. Aikin, op. cit. pp. 380–1

52. A. Sharratt & K. R. Farrar, 'Sanitation and Public Health in Nineteenth-century Manchester', *Memoirs and Proceedings of the Manchester Literary and Philosophical Society*, vol. 114 (1971–2), pp. 50–69

53. *Borough of Stretford Official Guide and Handbook* (1972)

54. A. Redford, *The History of Local Government in Manchester* (1939), vol. 1, p. 8

55. E. Gray, *Trafford Park Tramways 1897 to 1946* (1964)—gives a well-informed account of these enterprises in transport history
D. Gill, *Transport Treasures of Trafford Park* (1973)—mainly pictorial but very illuminating

56. Pevsner, op. cit. p. 404

57. Aikin, op. cit. p. 227

58. Civic Trust for the North West, *Use the Tame Valley*, p. 1

59. Civic Trust, *The Civic Society Movement*, p. 1

Chapter 10

1. Sir C. W. Macara, 'A Half Century of Manchester Life'—*The Manchester Guardian Civic Week Supplement* (2 Oct. 1926), p. 2

2. Sir Bosdin Leech, *Manchester City News* (May 1882)

3. Sir Bosdin Leech, *History of the Manchester Ship Canal* (1907), vol. 1, p. 82

4. W. H. Chaloner, 'The Birth of Modern Manchester', *Manchester and Its Region* (1962), p. 143 (quoted)

5. Leech, op. cit. vol. 1, p. 94

6. *Council Proceedings*, 6 Dec. 1882

7. Leech, op. cit. vol. 1, p. 103

8. A. Redford, *The History of Local Government in Manchester* (1940), vol. 2, p. 376

9. Manchester Ship Canal Company, *Resolution and Achievement* (1961), p. 24

10. Leech, op. cit. pp. 105–7

11. ibid. Preface, p. vii

12. W. H. Shercliff, *Entertainments*, 'It Happened Round Manchester' series (1968), p. 13

13. *Manchester City Council Minutes*, 31 Oct. 1928

14. Manchester Corporation Publicity Office, *Information* (1970), p. 17

15. Manchester Corporation Publicity Office, *Manchester International Airport* (1974), p. 15

16. W. G. S. Hyde (ed.), *Manchester Tramway Album* (1969), p. 60

17. ibid. p. 54

18. I am indebted to Mr Edward Gray, Headmaster, Walkden County Secondary School, for information on this subject

19. supplied by Mr K. M. Ledson, Assistant County Engineer (Transportation Planning), Greater Manchester Council

20. J. S. Millar, *Manchester—City Centre Map 1967* (1967), p. 27

21. L. P. Green, *Provincial Metropolis* (1959), pp. 97–122

22. I am indebted to Mr Edward Darby, formerly Public Relations Officer, Greater Manchester Transport Executive, for his advice and information

23. Millar, op. cit. pp. 35–6

24. SELNEC Passenger Transport Authority and Executive, *Public Transport Plan for the Future* (1973), Synopsis, p. 3

25. *The Guardian*, 29 Nov. 1972

Chapter 11

1. *The Guardian*, 27 July 1965

2. A. J. P. Taylor, 'The World's Cities, (1) Manchester', *Encounter* no. 42, Mar. 1957

3. C. Stewart, *The Stones of Manchester* (1956), p. 13

4. *The Building News and Engineering Journal* (1861), quoted by Stewart, op. cit. p. 13

5. G. Bradshaw, *Illustrated Guide to Manchester* (1857), quoted by Stewart, op. cit. p. 36

6. Stewart, op. cit. p. 68

7. *Manchester Police Regulation Act* (1844), Sections 65 & 66

8. Shena D. Simon, *A Century of City Government* (1938), p. 312

9. *Manchester Guardian*, 4 Oct. 1866

10. *Council Proceedings*, 2 June 1886, Medical Officer of Health's Report

11. R. Nicholas, 'Planning the City of the Future', *Manchester and Its Region*, ed. C. F. Carter (1962), p. 254

12. E. D. Simon and J. Inman, *The Rebuilding of Manchester* (1935), pp. 21–2

13. *Council Minutes*, 11 Oct. 1916 (Alderman Sir Edward Holt, Bt.)

14. W. H. Shercliff (ed.), *Wythenshawe—A History of the Townships of Northenden, Northen Etchells and Baguley*, vol. 1 to 1926, published for Northenden Civic Society by E. J. Morten (1974)

15. E. M. Hunt, 'Services and Occupations, 1850–1926', *Wythenshawe*, ed. Shercliff, op. cit. p. 316

16. Simon, op. cit. pp. 419–20

17. ibid. Preface, p. 10

18. ibid. pp. 201–9

19. ibid. p. 304

20. G. Turner, *The North Country* (1967), p. 69

21. Simon and Inman, op. cit. p. 124

22. I am indebted to Mr G. D. Godfrey, Assistant Director, Housing Aid and Research, Manchester Corporation, for advice and information

23. N. Pevsner, *South Lancashire* (1969), p. 53

24. *The Observer*, 13 Oct. 1974

25. *The Guardian*, 23 Nov. 1965

26. Mr J. S. Millar, County Planning Officer, private correspondence

27. I am indebted to Mr Brian Parnell, City Planning Officer for Manchester, for a copy of the draft report on *Urban Renewal*, prepared by his department

28. *The Guardian*, 8 Jan. 1975

29. J. S. Millar, *Manchester—City Centre Map 1967*, p. 1

30. ibid. pp. 3–7

31. ibid. pp. 39–40

32. I am indebted to the Headmaster and Mr Penry Williams, Senior History Master of the School, for advice and information

33. A. H. Body, *Canals and Waterways* (1975)—ch. 6 describes in log-book form the journey undertaken in 1967 and ch. 7 describes how the Cheshire Ring has been made navigable

34. *Civic Amenities Act 1967*, c. 69, s. 1

35. City Planning Office, *St Ann's Square Conservation Area* (1972)

36. Civic Trust for the North West, *Pamphlet* (1971), p. 3

37. Civic Trust, *Index of Conservation Areas 1967–1971*

38. Millar, op. cit. p. 39

39. *The Guardian*, 4 Jan. 1975

40. W. H. Chaloner, *The Movement for the Extension of Owens College Manchester 1863–73*, p. 20

41. ibid. pp. 20–1

42. *The Guardian*, 4 Jan. 1975

43. University of Manchester, *Report of Council to the Court of Governors, Part 1* (Nov. 1973), p. 29

44. H. Wilson and L. Womersley, *Manchester Education Precinct—The Final Report of the Planning Consultants* (1967), pp. 6–7

45. Millar, op. cit. p. 71

46. Wilson and Womersley, op. cit. p. 8

47. University of Manchester, op. cit. p. 3

48. *The Guardian*, 9 Oct. 1967

49. University of Manchester, op. cit. pp. 89–90

50. H. B. Charlton, *Portrait of a University* (1951), p. 97

51. C. M. Wood, N. Lee, J. A. Luker & P. J. W. Saunders, *The Geography of Pollution* (1974), pp. 1 & 11—this study of the subject, as applying to Greater Manchester, has been undertaken by the Pollution Research Unit, University of Manchester, and is of especial value

52. Proceedings of the Manchester Police Commissioners, 5 Sept. 1800

53. Simon, op. cit. pp. 202–3

54. Environmental Health Department, *Report on the Health of the City of Manchester* (1973), pp. 95–9

55. I am indebted to Mr J. E. Richards, Assistant Director (Pollution Control), Environmental Health Department of the City of Manchester, for valuable advice and information

56. Environmental Health Department, op. cit. Appendix

57. V. I. Tomlinson, *Salford in Pictures* (1973), p. 7

58. *The University of Salford Graduate Prospectus 1974–75*, pp. 11, 123–4

59. Greater Manchester Council, *Context*, December 1974, p. 8

60. Bolton and District Civic Trust, *The Buildings of Bolton* (1969), p. 1

61. Bolton Corporation, *A Book of Bolton* (1974), p. 37

62. *Bury Link, The public relations newspaper of the Metropolitan Borough of Bury* (Issue no. 2, April 1974)

63. Pevsner, op. cit. p. 374

64. ibid. p. 358

65. I am indebted to Mr R. Peroni for this informative personal tour of the Local Interest Centre

66. Greater Manchester Council, *Context*, December 1974, p. 8

67. ibid. loc. cit.

68. J. L. & B. Hammond, *The Age of the Chartists 1832–54* (1930), p. 364

Chapter 12

1. J. Swarbrick, *Greater Manchester: The Future Municipal Government of Large Cities* (Feb. 1914), pp. 12–15

2. Manchester and District Joint Town Planning Advisory Committee, *Report upon the Regional Scheme* (1926) with maps and text

3. *Manchester Evening Chronicle*, 25 Apr. 1935

4. General Register Office, *Census 1951—Report on Greater London and Five Other Conurbations* (1956)

5. D. Read, *Edwardian England*—Historical Association General Series, no. 79 (1972)

6. T. W. Freeman, *The Conurbations of Great Britain* (2nd revised ed. 1966), 'The Manchester Conurbation', pp. 126–55

   L. P. Green, *Provincial Metropolis—The Future of Local Government in South-East Lancashire* (1959)

7. P. Geddes, *Cities in Evolution* (1915), pp. 31–4

8. C. B. Fawcett, 'Distribution of the Urban Population in Great Britain, 1931', *Geographical Journal* (Feb. 1932)

9. *Royal Commission on Local Government in England 1966–1969* (1969), vol. 1, Report p. 76

10. ibid. pp. 219–33

11. White Paper: *Local Government in England* (H.M.S.O. Feb. 1971), pp. 6–7

12. ibid. p. 11

13. *Census 1971*

14. Greater Manchester Council, *Context* (Dec. 1974), p. 8

Chapter 13

1. *Greater Manchester, First Review of the Study Area* (1973), p. 11

2. J. Longland, 'Leisure Needs of the Community', *Roscoe Review* of the Department of Extra-Mural Studies, University of Manchester (1974), p. 4

3. A. de Tocqueville, 'Manchester', *Industrialisation and Culture 1830–1914*, ed. C. Harvie, G. Martin & A. Scharf (1970), p. 42

4. *Town and Country Planning Act 1971* (as amended by the Town and Country Planning Amendment Act 1972)

5. Department of the Environment and the Welsh Office, *Structure Plans and the Examination in Public* (1973), pp. 5–9

6. Greater Manchester Council, *Context*, Supplement (Dec. 1974), pp. 1–3

7. *The Guardian*, 5 Mar. 1975

8. Greater Manchester Council, *Context* (Dec. 1974), p. 6

9. Concurrent Functions Committee (Recreation), *Management of River Valleys and Country Parks*, p. 5

10. Greater Manchester Council, *Context* (Dec. 1974), with separate issue for each District

11. *The Guardian*, 4 June 1975

12. Greater Manchester Council, op. cit. p. 2

13. A Summary Report by the North West Joint Planning Team, *North West 2000* (1974), p. 9

14. Manchester Polytechnic, *Statements on Development, 1. Policy for Development* (1973)

15. *The Guardian*, 7 May 1974, p. 16

16. Civic Trust, *News*, Mar. 1975, p. 2

Envoy

1. T. W. Freeman, 'The Manchester Conurbation', *Manchester And Its Region*, ed. C. F. Carter (1962), pp. 47, 59

2. T. W. Freeman, *The Conurbations of Great Britain* (1959), pp. 146, 153

3. Freeman, op. cit. p. 60

4. *Royal Commission on Local Government in England 1966–1969*, vol. 1 (1969), Report, p. 8

5. *Manchester Evening News*, 24 Feb. 1975

6. *Rochdale Official Handbook* (*1974*), p. 37

7. *Royal Commission on Local Government in England 1966–1969*, op. cit. p. 146

8. R. W. Southern, *The Making of the Middle Ages* (1952), pp. 105–6

9. *The Guardian*, 2 June 1975

10. *Royal Commission on Local Government in England 1966–1969*, op. cit. pp. 146–7

11. F. Mumford, *The Transformation of Man* (1957), p. 138

Select Bibliography

This section is designed to encourage local historians to analyse and demonstrate the contribution of their own towns to the reality of the Metropolitan County. Of the seventy former local authorities now within the county, twenty-four, consisting of the former county and municipal boroughs, have been selected.

County of Lancaster

The Victoria County History: Lancashire (8 vols., 1906–12), vols. 4 & 5
   This famous History of the Counties of England was undertaken as a national historic survey: vol. 4 contains Manchester, Salford, Ashton-under-Lyne, Stretford and Wigan; vol. 5 contains Bolton, Bury, Oldham, Rochdale.
BAINES, E., *The History of the County Palatine and the Duchy of Lancaster* (5 vols., 1837), revised and enlarged edition by James Croston (1893)
COOKE TAYLOR, W., *Notes on a Tour in the Manufacturing Districts of Lancashire* (1842), with a new introduction by W. H. Chaloner in the Cass Library of Industrial Classics (1968)
HALLEY, R., *Lancashire—its Puritanism and Nonconformity* (1869)
EKWALL, E., *The Place-names of Lancashire* (1922)
CROSTON, J., *County Families of Lancashire and Cheshire* (1887)
WADSWORTH, A. P. AND DE LACY MANN, J., *The Cotton Trade and Industrial Lancashire, 1600–1780* (1931)
MILLWARD, R., *Lancashire—the History of the Landscape* (1955)
   Particularly useful for the study of an industrial landscape.
ASHMORE, O., *The Industrial Archaeology of Lancashire* (1969)
BAGLEY, J. J., *A History of Lancashire* (6th edition 1976)

Local Publishing Societies

Chetham Society (vol. 1 in 1844)
Historic Society of Lancashire and Cheshire (vol. 1 in 1849)
Record Society of Lancashire and Cheshire (vol. 1 in 1878)
Lancashire and Cheshire Antiquarian Society (vol. 1 in 1883)
Lancashire Parish Register Society (vol. 1 in 1898)
The printed volumes of these five Societies contain a wealth of information and interpretative articles, many of which bear directly upon the towns of the new County. Searches among them, with the aid of indexes, will amply reward the local historian.

Manchester and the Region

AIKIN, J., *A Description of the Country from Thirty to Forty Miles Round Manchester* (1795)

Reprinted by David & Charles in 1968, this very substantial work, with many attractive engravings and maps, was published at a particularly important stage of the Industrial Revolution. It contains most useful and detailed accounts of the historical, demographic, commercial and manufacturing features of the towns and chief villages of the region.

BUTTERWORTH, J., *A Complete History of the Cotton Trade including, also, that of the Silk, Calico-printing and Hat Manufactories: with remarks on their progress in Bolton, Bury, Stockport, Blackburn and Wigan, to which is added an account of the chief mart of these goods, the town of Manchester* (1823)

ASHWORTH, H., *Statistical illustrations of the past and present state of Lancashire, and more particularly of the Hundred of Salford* (1842)

To be found in the journal of the Manchester Statistical Society for that year.

FORDYCE, W., *History of the City of Manchester, Past and Present, and of the Borough of Salford, together with a brief sketch of the numerous populous towns . . . round this great metropolis* (1862)

TAIT, J., *Mediaeval Manchester and the Beginnings of Lancashire* (1904, reprinted 1972 by E. J. Morten)

This authoritative work provides a succinct survey of the early history of Manchester in its many aspects and of the formative years of the County of Lancaster.

GREEN, L. P., *Provincial Metropolis—The Future of Local Government in South East Lancashire* (1959)

This important study in metropolitan analysis merits close attention not only in regard to the metropolis itself but also to the towns of the region.

FREEMAN, T. W., *The Conurbations of Great Britain* (1959)

Attention is drawn to the section on 'The Manchester Conurbation', pp. 126–55.

CARTER, C. F. (ed.), *Manchester and its Region* (1962)

This valuable work, published at just the right time for its subject, contains nineteen chapters written by a team of distinguished contributors, each of whom is an authority on the topic presented. It is an exhilarating book.

GENERAL REGISTER OFFICE, *Census 1951—Report on Greater London and Five Other Conurbations* (1956)

Includes an important section on South-East Lancashire, pp. xliii–lx.

Royal Commission on Local Government in England 1966–1969 (1969), vol. I

The Report contains details and maps of the proposed SELNEC Metropolitan Area.

PEVSNER, N., *South Lancashire*, 'The Buildings of England' series (1969)

CLARK, D. M., *Greater Manchester Votes* (1973)

Described as 'a guide to the new metropolitan authorities'.

The Districts and their Towns

CITY OF MANCHESTER

For a fairly full and annotated bibliography of the beginnings and growth of Manchester, reference may be made to:

FRANGOPULO, N. J. (ed.), *Rich Inheritance: a guide to the history of Manchester* (1963, reprinted 1969 by EP Publishing Limited)
The bibliography will be found on pp. 295–305.

KENNEDY, M., *Portrait of Manchester* (1970)
Contains an important chapter entitled 'Greater Manchester', pp. 151–68.

MAKEPEACE, C., *Manchester As It Was*, 3 vols. (1972)
Pictorial scenes relating to Victorian Manchester.

CITY OF SALFORD

Salford

CROFTON, H. T., *Notes on Joseph Hill's Plan of Salford* (1740)

MANCHESTER STATISTICAL SOCIETY, *The Condition and Occupation of the People of Salford* (1889)

LEECH, H. J., *Salford, Past and Present: with incidents in its past history, an account of its present condition and pictorial illustrations* (1900)

SALFORD CORPORATION, *The Ancient and Royal Borough of Salford . . . History, Commerce and Industries* (1924)

SULLIVAN, J. J., *Salford—the Gateway to South-East Lancashire* (1924)

SALFORD CORPORATION, *City of Salford Historical Pageant* (1930)

HAMPSON, C. P., *Salford Through the Ages* (1930, reprinted 1973 by E. J. Morten)

ROBERTS, R., *The Classic Slum: Salford life in the first quarter of the century* (1971)

SMITH, A., *Salford As It Was* (1973)

TOMLINSON, V. I., *Salford in Pictures: an outline of the growth of an industrial town* (1974)

GORDON, C., *The Foundations of the University of Salford* (1975)

BERGIN, T. et al., *Salford—A City and Its Past* (1975)

Eccles

BOGG, W., *The Borough of Eccles* (1893)

SWINDELLS, T., *Chapters in the History of Eccles* (1914)

WALLACE, R., *Eccles Civic Services* (1948)

JOHNSTON, F. R., *Eccles from Hamlet to Borough* (1965)

Swinton and Pendlebury

HOLLAND, P., *Recollections of Old Swinton* (1914)

JOHNSTON, F. R. (ed.), *Eccles and Swinton: the past speaks for itself* (1957)

MULLINEUX, C. E., *Mast and Pannage: a history of Swinton to 1765* (1964)

SWINTON AND PENDLEBURY BOROUGH COUNCIL, *Official Guide to the Borough of Swinton and Pendlebury* (Commemorative edn. 1934–1974)

METROPOLITAN DISTRICT OF BOLTON

Bolton

WHITTLE, P. A., *Bolton-Le-Moors and the Townships in the Parish* (1855)

BRISCOE, J. D., *A Handbook of the History and Topography of Bolton* (1861)

CLEGG, J., *Annals of Bolton* (1888)

Samuel Crompton Centenary: official souvenir (June 1927)
Contains a life of Crompton and an account of Bolton's industrial and civic growth.

ASHWORTH, J., *This is Bolton . . .* (1947)

SAXELBY, C. H. (ed.), *Bolton Survey* (1953, republished 1971 by S.R. Publishers)
The book aims at providing 'valuable background information to the origin and development of the town'.

BOLTON CORPORATION, *A Book of Bolton* (1957)

BROWN, W. E., *Bolton As It Was* (1972)

Bolton Public Libraries, Local History Section, contains some of the source material on the history of Bolton, with particular reference to the development of education, compiled by I. R. Cowan. A pamphlet is available (1969).

Farnworth

BARTON, B. T., *History of Farnworth and Kearsley* (1887)

BOROUGH OF FARNWORTH, *Official Guide* (1956)

FARNWORTH BOROUGH COUNCIL, *Your Town and How it Grew* (1962)

METROPOLITAN DISTRICT OF BURY

Bury

BUTTERWORTH, J., *An Historical and Topographical Description of the Town and Parish of Bury in the County of Lancaster* (1829)

BARTON, B. T., *History of the Borough of Bury and Neighbourhood* (1874)

Bury Town Council and Radcliffe Urban District Council Official Handbook: Bury & Radcliffe as manufacturing and commercial centres (1900)

Bury Times Centenary Supplement (7 July 1955)
This gives a brief outline of the history of Bury, particularly since 1855.

GRAY, MARGARET, *The History of Bury, Lancashire, from 1660–1876* (1970)

Radcliffe

HAYHURST, T. H., *Radcliffe Historical Almanack 1891–6* (1896)

NICHOLLS, W., *History and Traditions of Radcliffe* (1920)

BOROUGH OF RADCLIFFE, *Charter Celebrations 21st September 1935*
An illustrated account of the history of the borough and the activities of the Corporation.

JACKSON, H., 'Lancashire Worthies', *Country Life* (10 May 1951)
    Recollections of the village of Radcliffe 50 years ago.
Radcliffe, Lancashire: the official guide (1954)

Prestwich

MIDDLETON, G., *The Annals of Prestwich* (1902)
NICHOLLS, W., *History and Traditions of Prestwich* (1905)
Prestwich, Lancashire: the official guide (1955)

METROPOLITAN DISTRICT OF OLDHAM

BUTTERWORTH, E., *Historical Sketches of Oldham: with an appendix containing
    the history of the town to the present time* (1856)
ANDREWS, S., *Annals of Oldham* (1887)
BATES, W., *The Handy Book of Oldham: comprising an historical review, notes of
    friendly societies and five routes in which every public building and place of interest
    is pointed* (1897)
MIDDLESTON, J., *Oldham, Past and Present* (1903)
    A concise history of Oldham progress.
BATESON, H., *Oldham History Papers*
    Bound newspaper cuttings from the Oldham Chronicle 1924–1931.
CLIFF, H., *The Romance of Oldham* (1931)
    An account of the cotton spinning industry in Oldham.
CLYNES, J., *When I remember . . .: reminiscences of life as a piecer in an Oldham
    cotton mill* (1940)
    Comparison of condition of working classes c. 1880 with that of c. 1940.
ATKINS, C. (ed.), *Oldham Industries* (1948)
BATESON, H., *A Centenary History of Oldham* (1949)
OLDHAM CORPORATION, *Oldham Centenary—A History of Local Government*
    (1949)
LICHFIELD, N., *The Oldham Study* (1973)
    Environmental planning and management; study commissioned by
    Department of Environment and undertaken in collaboration with
    Oldham County Borough Council.

METROPOLITAN DISTRICT OF ROCHDALE

Rochdale

BUTTERWORTH, J., *A Description and Directory of the Town of Rochdale in
    Lancashire* (1820)
ROBERTSON, W., *The Social and Political History of Rochdale* (1889)
MATTLEY, R. D., *Annals of Rochdale* (1899)
    A chronological view from the earliest times to the end of the year 1898.
FISHWICK, H. (ed.), *Rochdale Jubilee: a record of 50 years' municipal work 1856–
    1906* (1906)
ROBERTSON, W., *Rochdale and the History of its Progress* (1913)

HEYWOOD, T. T., *New Annals of Rochdale* (1931)
A short history since 1899 and a chronological view from the earliest times to the end of the year 1930.

WHITTAKER, J., *I, James Whittaker* (1934)
The autobiography of a man 'born and bred in the slums, living mainly in Rochdale'.

COLLINS, H. C., *Rochdale Roundabout* (1938)

TAYLOR REBE, P., *Rochdale Retrospect* (1956)
Published by the Corporation of Rochdale on the occasion of the Centenary of the Borough.

WADSWORTH, A. P., 'The Early Factory System in the Rochdale District', *Transactions of the Rochdale Literary and Scientific Society*, vol. xix (1935–37), pp. 136–56

WADSWORTH, A. P., 'The History of the Rochdale Woollen Trade', *Transactions of the Rochdale Literary and Scientific Society*, vol. xv (1923–25), pp. 90–110
These are excellent examples of the value for the local historian of the Transactions of this Society.

Heywood

BUTTERWORTH, E., *An historical description of the town of Heywood and vicinity* (1840)

HEYWOOD BOROUGH COUNCIL, *Heywood in Lancashire—The Official Industrial Handbook* (1952)

Middleton

CROFTON, H. T., *Scrapbook of Newspaper Cuttings relating to Middleton and Neighbourhood* (1889)

DEAN, J., *Historical Middleton* (1907)

HILTON, A. G., *The Promise of Life: a romance of Middleton* (1936)
'Shows the development of Middleton 1886–1936.'

METROPOLITAN DISTRICT OF STOCKPORT

BUTTERWORTH, J., *History and Description of the Towns and Parishes of Stockport, Ashton-under-Lyne, Mottram, Longdendale and Glossop* (1827)

UNWIN, G. et al., *Samuel Oldknow and the Arkwrights: the industrial revolution at Stockport and Marple* (1924)

STOCKPORT CORPORATION, *A Century of Local Government in Stockport (1835–1935)*

STOCKPORT CORPORATION, *Stockport: a report on planning and development* (1945)

ASTLE, W., *'Stockport Advertiser' Centenary History of Stockport* (1922, republished 1971 by S.R. Publishers)

CHRISTIE-MILLER, J., *The Development of Stockport 1922–73 and the History of the Stockport Advertiser 1822–1972* (1972)

WATERHOUSE, R., *Conservation and Change in Stockport* (1973)
A study of Stockport's past, present and possible future.
LEES, H., *A Picture of Stockport* (1971)
A collection of early photographs of the town, with text by W. J. Skillern.
ASHMORE, O., *The Industrial Archaeology of Stockport* (1975)

METROPOLITAN DISTRICT OF TAMESIDE

Ashton-under-Lyne

BUTTERWORTH, J., *History and Description of the Parish of Ashton-under-Lyne, with some remarks on the village of that name, also of the other villages therein* (1827)

BUTTERWORTH, E., *An Historical Account of the towns of Ashton-under-Lyne, Stalybridge and Dukinfield* (1842)

GLOVER, W., *History of Ashton-under-Lyne and the Surrounding District* (1884–5)

HASLAM MILLS, W., *Grey Pastures: sketches of life in a Lancashire town, Ashton-under-Lyne*

FOSTER, G. F. (ed.), *Ashton-under-Lyne: its story through the ages* (1947)

Borough of Ashton-under-Lyne: official handbook (1953 & 1956)

BOWMAN, W. M., *England in Ashton-under-Lyne: being the history of the whole ancient manor and parish* (1960)

HARROP, SYLVIA A. AND ROSE, E. A. (eds.), *Victorian Ashton*, Tameside Libraries and Arts Committee (1974)
With a very useful 'Reading Guide', pp. 112–16.

Dukinfield

BUTTERWORTH, J., *History and Description of the Town and Parish of Ashton-under-Lyne in the County of Lancaster and the Village of Dukinfield in the County of Chester* (1823, republished 1972 by E. J. Morten)

Congregationalism in Dukinfield 1805–1905 (1906)
Centenary memorial volume.

HICKEY, J. E., *History of the Old Chapel Sunday School, Dukinfield, 1800–1950* (1950)

The Borough of Dukinfield: official guide and industrial handbook (1964)
Dukinfield Public Library has published a list in pamphlet form of local history books and maps available for loan.

Hyde

MIDDLETON, T., *Annals of Hyde and District* (1899, republished 1973)

HYDE CORPORATION, *Official Guide to Hyde* (1920)

Mossley

HOLT, A., *The Story of Mossley, Ancient and Modern* (1926)

KENWORTHY, F., *The Industrial History of Mossley during the early 19th century* (1928)

ROSE, E. A., *The story of Mossley Methodism* (1969)

Stalybridge

HOARE, W. W., *On the Old English Manor of Staley in Cheshire* (1870)

HILL, S., *Bygone Stalybridge* (1907)

MARCH, J. W. (ed.), *Stalybridge, Cheshire, Centenary Souvenir 1857–1957* (1957)

METROPOLITAN DISTRICT OF TRAFFORD

Altrincham

INGHAM, A., *A History of Altrincham and Bowdon, with an account of the barony and house of Dunham* (1879)

LEECH, H. J., *Tales and sketches of Old Altrincham and Bowdon* (1880)

NICKSON, C., *Bygone Altrincham—Traditions and History* (1935, republished 1971 by E. J. Morten)

BUTLER, S. E., *Altrincham En Avant* (1937)

RODGERS, H. D., *Altrincham—A Town of the Manchester Conurbation* (1952)

Altrincham, Cheshire: official guide (1956)

Sale

Sale Borough Council: the official guide (1950)

SWAIN, N. V., *An Introduction to the History of Sale* (1964)

Stretford

Stretford Local Board: Official Handbooks for the years 1871–2 and 1879–8

Trafford Park Past and Present and Ship Canal Guide (1902)

BOSDIN LEECH, T., *Old Stretford: reminiscences of the past half-century* (1910)

STRETFORD CORPORATION, *The Borough of Stretford charter celebrations* (1935)
An historical account of Stretford, an account of municipal services, and a description of the new town hall.

STEVENS, T., *Some Notes on the Development of Trafford Park 1897–1947* (1947)

Stretford Borough Council: official handbook and guide (1954)

GRAY, E., *Trafford Park Tramways* (1964)

GILL, D., *Transport Treasures of Trafford Park* (1973)

METROPOLITAN DISTRICT OF WIGAN

Wigan

SINCLAIR, D., *The History of Wigan*, 2 vols. (1882)

FOLKARD, H. T., *Wigan: an historical sketch, with a note on its free public library* (1890)

FOLKARD, H. T., *Old Wigan: its history to beginning of the 18th century* (1899)

FOSTER, J. M., *The History of Wigan: being a short chronicle compiled from various authors and sources* (1899)

MEADOWS, T., *Wigan: official handbook* (1921)

HAWKES, A. J., *The Civil War in Wigan 1642–51* (1930)

MUIR, J. C. AND HAWKES, A. J., *'Ancient and Loyal': a series of illustrated historical sketches of the ancient and loyal borough of Wigan* (1930)

HAWKES, A. J., *Outline of the History of Wigan* (1935)

ORWELL, G., *The Road to Wigan Pier* (1939)
  A first-hand account of the life of the working class population of Wigan and elsewhere.

HALL, S. A., *Byways from Wigan* (1947)

FORTUNE, J. J., *Wigan 100 years Ago* (1950)
  Old-time glimpses of town and people.

Wigan Record Office, in the care of an Archivist, is at the Town Hall, Leigh.

Leigh

LEIGH CHRONICLE, *Diary of Local Events in the District of Leigh 1853–76* (1877)

ROSE, J., *Leigh in the 18th Century 1689–1813* (1882)

The Industries of Leigh and District (1885)

BURROW, E. J., *Leigh, Lancashire: the official guide* (1954)

LUNN, J., *Leigh: the historical past of a Lancashire borough* (1958)

Further Information

HISTORIES OF FORMER URBAN DISTRICT COUNCILS

In addition to the former county and municipal boroughs, there are situated in the Districts of the Greater Manchester County thirty-seven former urban district councils. Historically there is plenty of scope here, and three examples of what has recently been published in this sphere are given:

CLARKE, Heather, *Cheadle Through the Ages* (1973)
  Written by a local schoolmistress.

DORE, R. N., *A History of Hale, Cheshire (from Domesday to dormitory)* (1972)
  The author is a past President of the Lancashire and Cheshire Antiquarian Society and has long been regarded as the chief authority on the history of seventeenth-century Cheshire.

HAMPSON, C. G., *The Urban District of Tottington 1899–1974* (1974)
  Until his retirement, the author was chief chemist of a well-known paper works at Stoneclough near Bury, and still maintains an active interest in education, local history and music.

THE LOCAL HISTORY LIBRARY, CENTRAL LIBRARY, MANCHESTER

While each former county borough of the new County has, within its well-established public library, its own local history section and, in most of them, a local history librarian, it is well to remember that when the Local History Library in the Central Library, Manchester, was formed in the mid-1950s, the policy of those concerned with its establishment was that it should embrace not only Manchester itself but also the area some twenty-five miles around Manchester. During the past twenty years its resources and services, which may be freely consulted by any visitor to the Library, have expanded greatly. Thus a local historian concerning himself with any town or village of the Greater Manchester County would be well advised to supplement the resources of his own public library by investigating those of the Local History Library in Manchester. He will receive every help and guidance from the Librarian and his colleagues, and will find there a very extensive collection of printed books, periodicals and news-papers, many of them unique, a fine collection of maps and plans, and a veritable treasury of illustrations containing portraits, street scenes and pictures of buildings. One example may suffice to indicate the metropolitan value of the services of this Library: among its microfilms are copies of the parish registers of the diocese of Manchester, which sup-plement the printed volumes, also available, of the Lancashire Parish Register Society.

ARCHIVES COLLECTION

An Archives Service, with its own Archivist, is situated in each of the following towns: Bolton, Manchester, Salford, Stockport, Wigan and Ashton-under-Lyne. An Archivist is responsible for the work of accession-ing, sorting, calendaring and storing documents which may cover such varied types of record as those concerned with local administration, educational and charitable foundations, trade unions and professional bodies, business affairs, family and estate papers and ecclesiastical records. It is again well to remember that the Archives Collection in the Central Library, Manchester, contains, in addition to records specifically relating to the City of Manchester, various antiquarian collections such as the Farrer Papers (Dr William Farrer was co-editor for the Victoria History of the County of Lancashire), which cover the area of the Greater Manchester County within the County Palatine. There are also located here many other collections of considerable value to the local historian.

BIBLIOGRAPHY OF NORTH WEST ENGLAND

JOHNSON, R. H. AND WHARFE, L. (eds.), *A Geographical Bibliography of North West England* (1969)
Compiled by members of the Manchester Branch of the Geographical Association, this 'guide to the geographical literature on Northern England' includes, *inter alia*, sections on general reference works, the cul-tural environment, urban studies and rural settlement and the evolution of the rural landscape. Each of these contains references to the cities, towns and villages of the Greater Manchester County.

Index

Note: References to 'Greater Manchester' before Chapter 12 are not recorded in the index.

300

Maud, Sir John, 231
Medlock, River, 2, 47
Mellor, 161
Mersey, River, 158, 167, 170, 197
Mersey and Irwell Navigation
    Company, 47, 171, 173
Merseyside Metropolitan
    County, 238, 248
metropolitan, meaning of, 230,
    232, 238, 266, 267
Middleton, 27, 29, 30, 32
    publications on, 293
Milnrow, 29, 32
Moroccan community, 123
Mosley, Anthony, 24
Mosley, Sir Nicholas, 24
Mosley, Sir Oswald, 21
Mosley Street, Manchester, 44,
    46, 82, 92
Mossley, 32
    publications on, 294
Moston, Manchester, 26
Municipal Corporations Act, 20,
    103

Neild, William, 102
New Commonwealth immigra-
    tion, 126–33
North-East Cheshire, 232, 261
North-West Joint Planning
    Team, 261, 263
North-Western Museum of
    Science and Industry, 142,
    234
North-Western Regional Health
    Authority, 244, 249
North-West Water Authority,
    215, 244, 251, 255
Northwich, 233, 234

Octagon Theatre, Bolton, 80
Ogden, James, 17, 18, 42, 113

Oldham, 32, 44, 48, 49, 61, 66,
    75, 101, 108, 126, 130, 154–
    8, 171, 173, 197, 222, 229,
    231, 240, 259, 260, 264
Civic Centre, 260
College of Technology, 101
enfranchisement (1832), 19
historical, 155–8, 222, 223
immigrant children, 130
incorporation as a Borough
    (1849), 22
Local Interest Centre, 223
Lyceum, 99
Metropolitan Borough
    Council, 246, 259
Metropolitan District, com-
    position of, 240
Polish community, 126
Ukrainian community, 126
    publications on, 292
Oldham, Hugh, 154
Oldknow, Samuel, 159, 161
Old Trafford, 55, 67–9, 166, 183
'Orator' Hunt, 18, 61
Ordovices, 1
Owens, John, 106, 107, 109, 111,
    209
Owens College, 97, 108, 111, 115,
    206, 211

Partington, Manchester, gas-
    works at, 228
Paulhan, Louis, 178, 179, 181
Peak Forest Canal, 161
Peel, Sir Robert (elder), 38, 146
Peel, Robert, 94
Percival, Dr Thomas, 89, 90, 92,
    245
Peterloo, 18, 30–3
Pevsner, Nikolaus, 80, 154, 166,
    206, 222
Picc-Vic Tunnel, 188
Pomona Pleasure Gardens,
    Hulme, 63, 177

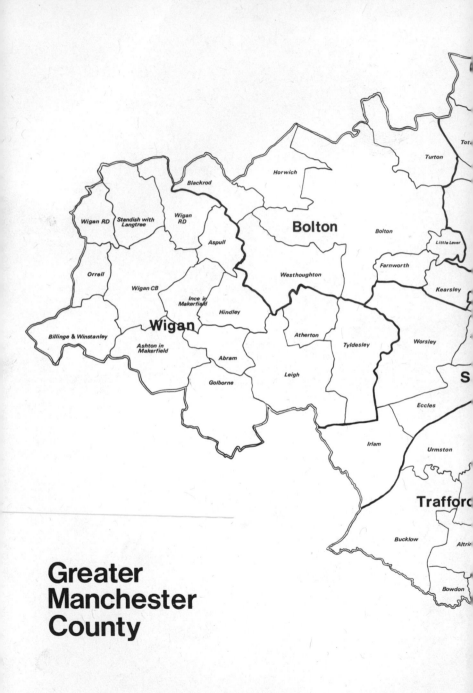

Greater
Manchester
County